D1502422

The Literary Vision of
LIAM O'FLAHERTY

The
Literary Vision of
LIAM
O'FLAHERTY

∽∽∽

John Zneimer

SYRACUSE UNIVERSITY PRESS

Contents

JOHN ZNEIMER is associate professor of English at Indiana University Northwest, Gary, Indiana. He received the B.A. degree from Ripon College, the M.A. from Columbia University, and the Ph.D. from the University of Wisconsin.

Preface

WHEN I first began reading the works of Liam O'Flaherty, it seemed so obvious that he was a writer with the same sort of awareness as Dostoevsky, Sartre, Camus, or the film-maker Ingmar Bergman that I was surprised to learn that this was not the common interpretation. Despite O'Flaherty's debt to Dostoevsky (which is always recognized), critics and commentators have tended to see him according to the Irish measure—as a naturalist, a realist, a social critic or historian, or a voice of things Irish, an acquaintance of Yeats, George Russell, and Sean O'Casey. And in this assessment O'Flaherty usually ends up somehow as an Irishman *manqué*.

I respect the opinion that it takes an Irishman to understand the Irish, and I know that what I set out to do here is undertaken at considerable risk—I also respect the barbed Irish wit. But granting that much about Irish literature is accessible only to Irishmen, much also is obscured by a characteristic Irish bias. My intention here is to show that if O'Flaherty were seen less as an Irishman and more as a man, many of the "problems" associated with his work would be illuminated or eliminated. In any case this is not intended to be a definitive study or the last word on O'Flaherty. Nor is this an effort to rescue him from relative obscurity, for I do not pretend to know what place he will ultimately be assigned in the history of Irish, English, or world literature. I do believe, however, that his place belongs as much in an existentialist tradition as it does in an Irish tradition, despite the appeal of his novels set in Ireland.

This study is based on all of O'Flaherty's published work with the exception of the Gaelic, and it attempts to see this work as an interrelated whole. The accuracy of the biographical details, most of which are drawn from O'Flaherty's own accounts, is not as important as how he conceives of himself as a character in the autobiographies. Some primary sources of the period are used to relate O'Flaherty to

Dublin's literary society, particularly the fourteen volumes of *The Irish Statesman* magazine published weekly by George Russell (A.E.) for six and one-half years from 1923 to 1930. Material from these sources, if it contains critical opinion, is used more to illustrate what was being said about O'Flaherty than for its inherent value as literary criticism. Most valuable to this study were the 143 unpublished letters from O'Flaherty to Edward Garnett which are part of the manuscript collection of the Academic Center Library of the University of Texas in Austin. I wish to express my gratitude to the Committee of the Academic Center Library for permission to read and quote from these letters.

Introduction

LIAM O'FLAHERTY should have a special contemporary appeal because he speaks in his novels about traditions that have failed in a world that is falling apart, about desperate men seeking meaning through violent acts. What is significant about the man and his work is related to modern consciousness and not to some specific Irish quality; yet some discussion of the Irish is necessary because O'Flaherty was affected by his sense of being Irish and the burdens this imposed, and his subsequent literary reputation has been almost solely in the hands of the Irish. If O'Flaherty is neglected now, it is in some measure due to Irish disappointment. If he is esteemed, it is often for the wrong reasons—reasons related to a kind of orthodoxy of expectations imposed upon Irish authors by Irish critics.

The Irish literary movement in the early decades of this century (or Celtic renaissance) and the literary criticism that derives from it are bound together by the Irish dream. Nothing is more important in the movement and nothing more difficult to define. The history of Anglo-Irish literature is a history of the expression of the dream. It inspired writers and patriots. It had its prophets, saints, and martyrs, its priests, its schisms, and its heretics. The Irish dream was real in the way that anything is real—in its effects. It drove men to great deeds and to poetry. It was a projection of all men's highest strivings and ideals—the image of beauty and love and hope. The dream was freedom, not only from English tyranny and landlord oppression but from all earthly limitations, not only from poverty but mortality. Kathleen ni Houlihan, the image of Holy Ireland, stood in the same spiritual relationship to Ireland as Henry Adams' Virgin stood to the Middle Ages, and where the rest of the Western world was in the power of the dynamo, its energies scattered and dissipated, Ireland was unified, an island of purpose in a sea of doubt. The dream bound Ireland together.

But because it was a dream—a shimmering in the hills or a feeling in the heart—no abstract analysis can say exactly what the dream was about. Perhaps the only point of agreement the Irish themselves could reach was that it was an Irish dream—the living spirit of the land and of the people. Men could die for it and poets express it, and the poetry was genuine as it expressed that shimmering in the hills or feeling in the heart that evaded analysis and abstract thought. The Irish argued about what it meant to be Irish, but what they sought was the purity of the dream. They searched for the purest Ireland in Sligo and the Connemara hills, among the peasants and in the old stories, even in the Gaelic language itself. They wanted to go back to the source of the dream, as if Ireland herself dreamed and they would wake her, gently, and take that dream fresh from her own lips.

But O'Flaherty came to the Irish literary scene during a period of change: when reality more and more was set against the dream; when Ireland's strife, poverty, political organization, agriculture, and manufacture became the reality and the dream seemed but a dream. The custodians of the dream—men like A.E. (George Russell), John Eglinton, and Monk Gibbon—did not talk as if they had lost the dream. But the more they railed against the realism and disillusion they saw reflected in literature, the more they indicated the urgency of their illusion—the passage of the Censorship Bill in 1928 was one evidence of the fading of the dream, and the decline of A.E.'s journal, *The Irish Statesman*, was another. In the last issue, April 12, 1930, as A.E. appraised himself as editor, he recognized the change: "He belongs to a movement which began at the latter end of the last century and which by now has almost spent its force." William Butler Yeats was prophetic when in "Nineteen Hundred and Nineteen" he wrote what might be the epitaph of the dream:

> Oh but we dreamed to mend
> Whatever mischief seemed
> To afflict mankind, but now
> That winds of winter blow
> Learn that we were crack-pated when we dreamed.

Try as he might, O'Flaherty could not dream the Irish dream or shape the essential spirit of his art to the expected orthodoxies. When being Irish was a national obligation, O'Flaherty was compelled even more by a personal obligation. Or rather, he could not choose to make his perception Irish when he was borne along by the stronger currents of a more general Western consciousness and Western literary tradition.

What O'Flaherty wrote is, of course, a part of the history of Irish
literature. But first of all it is a part of literature written by a man
sharing with men his own interpretation of what it means to be human.
That O'Flaherty is an Irishman helped shape that interpretation, for
no man exists in a vacuum, and Ireland supplied the materials through
which the interpretation could be made. It is the same with language.
A literary artist must write in a language, and the works and structure
of the language are his writing, but they do not determine it. His
writing is an example of the language, but he does not write to create
this example. So it is between the literary artist and his society. He
is an artist because he shapes something from the potential that exists
between himself and his world. His art is the shaping, and that shaping
is the main object of literary study. Because O'Flaherty is an Irishman,
his writing illustrates Irish literature, but the emphasis here will not be
on how he illustrates it, as if he were a typical example.

This study is not a biography or a critical biography, though it
makes use of many biographical elements. The main problem undertaken here is that of understanding O'Flaherty's work, not his life,
though each helps shape the other. Enough biography can be derived
from O'Flaherty's own accounts to show how he projected himself into
his work, and the emphasis here is on this projection. Enough information is available from his letters and from other biographical and
autobiographical materials of the period to show his relationship to
Dublin's literary society, but the stress here is on the informing spirit
of O'Flaherty's work, not on the details of his life.

Some of the earliest critics were aware of a special quality about
O'Flaherty. When William Troy assessed "The Position of Liam
O'Flaherty" for *Bookman* (March 1929), he spoke of the "easily
recognizable distinction" of O'Flaherty's work. And he was also aware
that O'Flaherty eluded the conventional labels of tradition and genre.
He believed that melodrama, "the elaboration of human motives on a
grand scale, against immense background, and the accompaniment of
enormous music," was the appropriate medium for O'Flaherty's genius
and for his theme—the conflict of nature and intellect. A sense of this
same quality struck Sean O'Faolain: "Always we feel that something
vast has entered into the imagination of the author, and we are impressed, and oppressed, by the weight of it." [1] O'Faolain explained this
as an Irish quality related to O'Flaherty's ideal Ireland. Troy saw this
as a universal quality, stemming from O'Flaherty's powerful apprehension of the relationship between man and nature. It is the "something
vast" that I am concerned with in this study and that I see at the basis
of O'Flaherty's unique artistic vision.

If Troy could see from his necessarily limited view that the single underlying theme of O'Flaherty's work is the conflict between nature and the intellect, a whole view makes this conclusion even more apparent. The autobiographies, travel book, and critical writings confirm directly what was revealed in the early novels and also make explicit the nature of that conflict. Dominant in O'Flaherty's work is his unceasing awareness of man's mortality and ultimate annihilation in a universe that has no meaning and offers no consolation. Success and failure, social good and social evil—all dwindle to insignificance in the light of this awareness. O'Flaherty's main concern is not for man in society and set against society's norms but for man cut off from society, for whom society offers no rationale.

When O'Flaherty considers himself and his role as an artist, he does not conceive of this role as social. For him the artist is beyond social good and evil. The measure of an artist is his ability to endure the vision of annihilation, to stand, in his phrase, "bolt upright against annihilation," and to represent that vision in his art. Thus in O'Flaherty's novels the consistent pattern is that of men being cut off from society and turned in upon themselves until they are brought to this vision. Then they reveal themselves most fully and significantly. His short stories are, characteristically, expressions of a kind of mystical vision of nature that arises from his most intense moments of awareness of mortality and chaos. The "something vast" that O'Faolain felt had entered into O'Flaherty's imagination is his overwhelming awareness, and it is this that causes in O'Flaherty's work what Troy called an "extension of action beyond the boundaries in which we are accustomed in normal social experience."

We shall see that O'Flaherty's thought and art are centered around what is best described as religious quest. His novels are spiritual battlegrounds whereon his characters, representing himself or facets of his own character, struggle to find meaning in a universe that intellect presents as devoid of meaning. More often than not the end is tragic. The short stories are records of mystical insights that have been won from the death and despair of the novels. They are moments of peace in which O'Flaherty views the world with eyes opened by a kind of spiritual rebirth. Religious quest and fleeting spiritual rebirth form the basic impulse behind his art. In his autobiography O'Flaherty tells of saying to an astonished beggar in front of Notre Dame Cathedral: "Has thou not heard that God is dead?" [2] In this announcement O'Flaherty gives the basic motif of his work. But his is not the optimism of John Dewey, who can make the discovery of the death of the deity a battlecry for more vigorous and meaningful human endeavor. Eternity looms, and the brooding imminence of death. Here is the tension from which many of the themes of his work are projected. We shall see in detail the nature of this tension, how it is made manifest in O'Flaherty's writings, and how it shapes his art.

In Dublin: Patterns of Change

LIAM O'FLAHERTY left Dublin in June, 1922, as he described himself in *Shame the Devil*, "a lean man with terrified, furtive eyes, wearing a shabby trench-coat, with a revolver strapped between his shoulder-blades" (p. 34). The Republican headquarters had just been captured by the Free State troops in Dublin, and O'Flaherty was among those disbanded Republicans who stood watching the final action of the few still holding out. While he stood there he overheard an old woman talking: "Did ye hear that bloody murderer, Liam O'Flaherty, is killed, thanks be to God?" And he heard himself referred to as "the man that tried to sell Dublin to the Bolsheviks," and as the one "who locked the unemployed up in the Rotunda and shot them unless they spat on the holy crucifix." With that he nudged his comrade and said that he was going. "There's nothing more to be done." He had no profession. He had abandoned hope in the coming of the revolution. At that time he felt dead. He was twenty-six.

In the early part of 1924 O'Flaherty returned. In that span from June, 1922, to the first months in 1924 he had done well. His first novel, *Thy Neighbour's Wife* had been published. His second, *The Black Soul*, was completed and nearing publication. His sketches were being published. His talent had been recognized by none other than Edward Garnett, an intimate with the literary great of England and America, whose friends or discoveries included Joseph Conrad, W. H. Hudson, Ford Madox Ford, John Galsworthy, Stephen Crane, and D. H. Lawrence. O'Flaherty had made himself into a writer entirely apart from the established tradition of the Irish literary revival and had made his mark not just in little Ireland but in the world of literature.

Dublin had changed too. The Civil War was over and the country had settled down to the business of making a nation out of the shambles of rebellion and war. The writers set themselves to the job of deciding their roles and the role of literature in the new nation. James

Stephens wrote an article for *Century* (October, 1922) in which he discussed "The Outlook for Literature with Special Reference to Ireland." In this article he saw that Ireland was no longer alone, but had entered the world when she had achieved freedom, and that Irish literature could no longer grow from the old root but had to start again, this time in the stream of European thought. "Irish literature will become a part of world literature," he predicted. But because Ireland was new, and because she was a "center of essential energy," she was particularly well-suited to undertake the "art technic experiments" of Western culture. Stephens saw that literature was changing too, and new techniques were being tried to depict the new view of man given by modern psychology. The writer had to adapt to the new antirationalism and relativism that made truth only "that to which we are sympathetically attracted" and life into "bundles of proceeding and digested actions" which made thinking "look like nothing at all." "By the side of an action no thought is valid." The artist had to deal with "endless successions of deeds that are passions" which he must translate "out of the whirl of movement into the quietude of words and paint and speculations," and this translation could be effected "only by a passion that is the equal of itself." Because the writer had to become so personally involved in this translation, he would be essentially "engaged in his own portrait." By undergoing a double evolution, internal and external, he thought, Ireland could (and must "or we are done for," he said) accept this challenge. The external evolution was a shift to European thought away from that which was Irish-centered. The internal was a shift to the Irish language, which he thought was enough of the past to anchor the new literature firmly. Literature in the Irish language was essential because Irish literature in English could be "only a timid and ineffectual imitation of the English mode."

The next year Padraic Colum surveyed "The Promise of Irish Letters" in the *Nation* and saw that Irish literature would have to change to adapt to the new conditions. He predicted that literature would not die because of the Free State but that a new tradition would emerge to replace the tradition of Kathleen ni Houlihan which had lapsed. He thought that poetry and drama in Ireland had already had their day in the old tradition and that the new tradition would be expressed in prose forms—the novel and short story—which came to the Irish as something new, not having had their Irish expression. "It seems to me that there will be a new movement in Irish literature—a beginning all over again." Like Stephens he saw great promise in the Gaelic language which he thought the Free State would work to pre-

serve, and he predicted a modern literature in Gaelic which could be
Ireland's new expression. He noted that though the founders of the
old literary revival—A.E. and Yeats—were still present and still active,
the new writers would produce work in another plane.

When O'Flaherty arrived in Dublin, A.E. and Yeats were the leaders
of Ireland's literary society, and the society functions at which they
presided were regular weekly "at homes" at Yeats's or James Stephens'
apartments where the well-known and the lesser-known gathered to
reflect on Ireland's literary future. Sean O'Casey described these social
events and an A.E. "at home" in his autobiography:

> Curious gatherings these of Dublin! Yeats's, and its very elect
> assembly; A.E.'s with its rather less select gathering of literature
> and timid politics; and Stephens', with a few select, but many more
> of the lesser known, more homely, more honest-to-God, more
> happy than the other two conclaves. Sean strolled . . . thinking of
> how astonished he had been the first night he had gone to an A.E.
> *At Home.* When the room filled, desultory chat ended, and each
> settled himself for ordeal or treat. A.E. was climbing into his
> throne. This was a chair placed on a platform, and those present
> sat in a humble semi-circle around this royal seat. A.E. climbed
> heavily, hoisting himself into it, the rotund belly and big backside
> eclipsing the throne for the rest of the evening. He ceremoniously
> lighted his pipe, while he waited for someone to start the talk
> rolling along like ole man river. It seemed plain to Sean that A.E.
> used the talk and the comments as a vocal rehearsal for what he
> would say in his Journal [*The Irish Statesman*] during the coming
> week. When he spoke . . . he became the policeman on point-
> duty directing the way through the avenues and lanes of this life,
> and those of the life to come.[1]

The conversations at those meetings must have been directed toward
the same subjects that Stephens and Colum discussed as they pondered
the future of Irish literature, with always the question of what new
direction literature would take. The letters and columns of *The Irish
Statesman* give a sample of the currents that were stirring. Sean
O'Casey was interested in the laboring classes, in their social condition
and cultural life. In an article of December 22, 1923, entitled "Life
and Literature," he stressed that some unity must be established between the workers and literature, that literature was not the exclusive
property of the leisure class. On February 2, 1924, Lennox Robinson
protested in "Back to the Provinces" that "the novel about Dublin has

been done to death," with *Ulysses* in mind and a spate of novels that must have followed it exploring every detail of Dublin geography. He facetiously proposed that the University give a degree in Irish Social History from the Parnell Split to the Treaty for those who had mastered all the details of Dublin's geography and politics. He proposed that the writers turn back to the life of the country towns which had been neglected. "Back to the provinces, must be our cry, back to the country town, to the small shop, the big licensed grocery business, the country doctor, the country priest, the schoolmaster." On February 9, 1924, "Querist" (whom O'Casey, in his autobiography, identified as A.E.) asked the question "Is Literature in a Blind Alley?" He thought that Shakespeare had led literature into a blind alley by becoming absorbed in character for its own sake. He proposed, instead, that to escape from Freudian materialism the artist should seek to discover the transcendental element in human life in a literature "where humanity is depicted acted on by spiritual influences, or by its interblending with the life of nature." The artist should "conceive life as part of a divine procession in which the personal dwindles, but the immortal may be exalted by a profound consciousness of cosmic purpose."

So the talk must have gone. O'Casey continued in *Inishfallen* that A.E. was a pompous windbag and a bore, full of high-sounding and meaningless words, prattling about the rural life, "but never once having had a sickle, a scythe, a fork, or a hoe in his hand" or having "touched with his stout, pudgy finger the udder of a cow," full of talk about mysticism and "internal light," hiding, not as Lady Gregory once said, "a mystical light in a turnip," but "a turnip in a mystical light" (pp. 289–90).

O'Flaherty did not enter this society with his hat in his hand, but neither did he storm in laying about him left and right. He felt that he was superior to the bickering, felt that he had descended from London to a lesser world, but at the same time he was eager for Irish acceptance and praise. His letters of that period to Edward Garnett give an account of his experience in that society.[2] On March 10, 1924, he tells of attending one of A.E.'s Sunday evening "at homes." About twenty people connected with art and literature were gathered there, among them James Stephens, Professor Edmund Curtis ("a writer of ten guinea reviews for the American Press)," American journalists, "an Indian hereditary saint travelling in Ireland," and "young poets and women of an indiscriminate type who just seemed to be connected with the men, like all Irish women seem to be in public, unless they are very pretty like the professor's wife."

O'Flaherty considered himself somewhat above the whole situation. James Stephens was "a nice enough fellow, but rather proud of himself." The literary situation did not look promising: "There is absolutely nothing doing from a remunerative point of view in the literary field." He looked at the group and decided "they are a pack of scoundrels anyway" and that "the country is not worth anything" because the people do not read. In a subsequent letter (March 21, 1924), referring to this or a similar gathering, O'Flaherty reflected that the literary people were just as boring in Ireland as in England: "I went to their club one night and I got disgusted with them. . . . One comes home bored and tired and enraged with that manuscript that has not grown a single line since the day before. . . . One says getting into bed 'What a stupid chap Moore has become and his wife has got pimples all over her forehead.'" He told Garnett that although he got on well enough with these people by keeping his mouth shut and agreeing on every point, somehow he was more interested in London than Ireland.

Both of those last positions were to change. O'Flaherty was not one to keep his mouth shut for long, and soon he spoke out in full-scale participation in Irish literary affairs. It is obvious that he was casting about for the role he intended to play in this society, and he soon found it. Regardless of his personal opinion of A.E., O'Flaherty looked on him as someone of consequence whose advocacy would be valuable; and it appears that O'Flaherty deliberately set out to win A.E.'s favor to advance his own career and serve his own ends. Less than a month after he reported that first "at home," O'Flaherty was able to announce to Garnett that he had not only gained A.E.'s favor but that also he was in the process of making himself independent of that favor: "I have won A.E. over to my side, but when he finds out what a scoundrel I have been he will dump me I believe. In another month however I will have formed a powerful clique of my own and I am going to lick the bunch of them" (April 3, 1924).

O'Flaherty had been anxiously awaiting publication of *The Black Soul,* the delay of which was driving him to a frenzy: "I have the population of Dublin in a white heat of excitement about it and if it is delayed much longer the damn thing will fizzle out and they will say 'Oh that chap O'Flaherty is a bore.'" The book came out shortly after that, and A.E. reviewed it in *The Irish Statesman* for May 3, 1924. It must have appeared to A.E. that O'Flaherty had written *The Black Soul* to his specifications; it was full of spiritual influences and the interblending with the life of nature. He gave it a good review, calling it "great and promising." It recalled to him "the ancient sympathy between the spirit of man and the spirit of nature asserted in Irish legend."

Although he was not generally pleased with the English reviews of *The Black Soul,* O'Flaherty took satisfaction from A.E.'s because, as he wrote Garnett, A.E. was "the only man in Ireland whom everybody regards as the greatest man in Ireland" (May 2, 1924). At that time O'Flaherty felt that his position in the Irish literary world was established: "I pat myself on the back. I licked all these swine into a cocked hat. When I came here nobody would speak to me. Everybody hated me. I wound them all round my fingers. I got A.E. to give me a thundering review. I got all the old women to praise me. Now that I have fooled them I am telling these damned intellectuals what I think of them in choice scurrilous language. I have gathered a group of faithful followers about me and am starting a monthly paper called 'To-morrow.' " He appeared to have found his role. The paper was to give voice to the nonconformists and radicals opposed to the existing literary order, but O'Flaherty had aims at least as personal as idealistic. He added a note to Garnett about the paper: "Of course I use it merely as a platform for myself" (May 16, 1924).

The first issue of *To-Morrow* appeared in August, 1924, with a masthead stating that the contributors included W. B. Yeats, Lennox Robinson, and Joseph Campbell, no doubt for the prestige effect of these established names. Although Yeats was associated with the old order to which this publication was to be an antidote, he had a good reason to lend his name and contribution. His poem "Leda and the Swan" had been refused publication in *The Irish Statesman* because of its revolutionary implications which A.E. thought might be misunderstood.[3] It was published in *To-Morrow* no doubt with even more enthusiasm because it had been refused by the staid *Irish Statesman.* In addition to "Leda and the Swan" (which, in perspective, justified the publication even if nothing else appeared) there was also enough writing by and about O'Flaherty to confirm his statement about its being his own platform, and in addition there was a story by Margaret Barrington, the pretty wife of Professor Curtis whom O'Flaherty had noticed at A.E.'s. By this time she had become O'Flaherty's lover and later was to become his wife. O'Flaherty's short story "The Red Petticoat" appeared there, along with a review of *The Black Soul* by L. K. Emery, who gave it the highest praise for its "primitive passions" and "immense dramatic structure." He thought that *The Black Soul* should silence "all pallid peasant novelists," who wrote mostly "tittle-tattle and futility" in an effort to turn an Abbey Theater play into a novel.

The editorial policy of *To-Morrow* was dedicated to art "based on the immortality of the soul." The editors, H. Stuart, a young poet, and Cecil Salkeld, an artist, stated that they were Roman Catholics, but the "Renaissance variety" who applauded "antedeluvian strength" and "the lust of the goat" as the handiwork of God. For them all bad writers were atheists, regardless of their religion. They condemned the art of modern Europe, which lacked belief in immortality, because where belief is lost "art turns from creation to photography." They condemned also, though with sympathy—no doubt with James Joyce in mind—"those who would escape from banal mechanism through technical investigation and experiment." New form, they thought, did not come from experiment but from a new subject "which must come from the restored soul."

On August 16, 1924, *The Irish Statesman* reviewed *To-Morrow* with a condescending pat on the head. Y.O., the reviewer, noted that a Dublin printer had refused to print it because of its materials, but he thought it "delightfully solemn and young." He sympathized with the young writers' efforts to be provocative but thought that they would have to liven up the magazine to achieve the reaction they sought. He did not reckon with the forces of the Church.

To-Morrow lasted for just two issues—August and September, 1924. O'Flaherty later commented on the reasons for its quick demise. The Jesuits, he said, though they lacked any legal authority, had so much power that "no group of free-thinking citizens dare band together for the purpose of producing a periodical that is manifestly non-Christian or purely intellectual." On those rare occasions when such an endeavor was made "these periodicals have come to a sudden end." [4] The first issue of *To-Morrow* contained a story by Lennox Robinson, "The Madonna of Slieve Dun," which was probably the immediate cause of this end. The story was about a young girl in the west of Ireland who dreamed that she had been chosen to give birth to Christ. The parish priest had preached that the people of her town were so wicked that they would not accept Christ if he were born again, but she believed that Christ was so good that the priest certainly was wrong. On Christmas eve while she was walking in the hills she was accosted by a tramp and fainted. In her faint the tramp raped her, and she returned home unaware of all that had happened. That night she had her marvelous dream, and the next day she felt possessed of great holiness. In the evening she told her mother that she was going to be the mother of Christ. According to Yeats, who took this instance as an example of Catholic narrowness, the Irish religious press attacked Robinson for this story, and a Catholic Ecclesiastic and an Ecclesiastic of the Church of Ireland both resigned from the Committee of the Carnegie Library because it would not censure him.[5] O'Flaherty wrote about this same problem to Garnett on January 20, 1925, telling him about the "terrific battle raging at the present time about *Catholic literature* and *immoral literature*." According to O'Flaherty, Lennox Robinson had been "hounded off the Carnegie Trust by the combined churches—Jesuits and C. of Ireland."

Although *To-Morrow* ceased publication, O'Flaherty and his friends did not cease issuing manifestoes through letters to *The Irish Statesman.* In what appears to have been a planned campaign, he and Austin Clarke and F. R. Higgins shot off a salvo at the whole literary establishment. In a review of a biography of Mahatma Gandhi by Romain Rolland, A.E. admired Gandhi and contrasted the Indian passive resistance policy with Irish violence (October 4, 1924). Two weeks later O'Flaherty sprang to the attack in an article entitled "National Energy." Sarcastically he admired the enthusiasm of the review, but thought that enthusiasm misdirected. He considered the whole policy of passive resistance to be ghostly, associated with philosophy and death and not with the creative vitality of a living people: "The human race has not advanced from savagery to culture on the feeble crutches of philosophy." He likened Ireland to England in Shakespeare's time: "His race was emerging, with bloodshot eyes, lean, hungry, virile, savage, from the savagery of feudalism into the struggle for Europe." He thought Ireland should be proud of its gunshots and not abjure force, which was the opposite of sluggishness. "Ours is the wild tumult of the unchained storm, the tumult of the army on the march, clashing its cymbals, rioting with excess of energy."

The next week, in "Art and Energy," F. R. Higgins and Austin Clarke joined in resounding support of O'Flaherty's position: "It is realized that a new movement in Irish Letters must take cognisance of the primal emotions of our time. Passionate events have changed the mind. Who is there to achieve the happy subjecting of those writers, who now seem to us, as giants before the flood? This generation remains unashamed of its modern unrest." They advocated "vehemence" and "even excessive energy" in prose and in verse, "the anvil rather than the little teacups of Japan." They thought that there was a danger in "preciousness," that "misers of words grow mean in spirit." At the end of their letter A.E. added a comment, gently reproaching the young poets for the violence of their opinions and noting that they themselves were more akin to the old than the new. He thought that they were attracted to O'Flaherty because he was a novelty to them, as people are attracted to their opposites. And A.E. defended the careful use of words, refusing to equate careful use with meanness of spirit. But he suggested that they develop their ideas further in the next issue. This they did, stressing the argument that "sheer technique" had led to the view that verse should be "sparse, ascetic." They, on the contrary, believed that the native Irish tradition was "rich and wild, colorful, lavish."

O'Flaherty got in his own word a few months later in a review of T. F. Powys' *Mr. Tasker's Gods* for *The Irish Statesman* of March 7, 1925. O'Flaherty had known Powys in England and thought that he was a genius. He then gave his own criterion for a novel: "In order to be a work of genius, a novel must offer something more than a perfect style, the imprint of a cultured mind, and that gentleness of soul which makes everyone love Mr. Powys. It must be a relentless picture of life, as lashing in its cruelty as the whip of Christ when there are moneychangers to be beaten from the Temple, as remorseless as the questions of a jealous lover. It must have the power to invoke great beauty or great horror in the same breath as it calls forth laughter from the lips." O'Flaherty thought Powys' novel passed this test. He got the impression that the novel was the product of great personal intensity, "that every scene" was "wrung out of Mr. Powys' very soul amid terrific agony."

Except that they preferred loud noises to soft, gunshots to passive resistance, the violence of the storm to studied serenity in literature, it is not clear just what O'Flaherty and his group were rebelling against. But they were determined to establish a place of their own in Dublin's literary world, out of the shadow of Yeats and A.E.; when *To-Morrow* failed, they turned in a new direction to give themselves mutual support for their own literary ventures.

Soon after he arrived in Dublin O'Flaherty met Sean O'Casey, whose play *Juno and the Paycock* was running at the Abbey Theater. "He is a friend of mine," O'Flaherty wrote Garnett (March 10, 1924), and he described a visit he had with O'Casey: "I found him dressed in a suit of dungarees sweeping out a hall where workmen gamble at night. That is his occupation. Fine chap. He is about forty and a nervous wreck like myself. He said he locks himself in at night and then feels happy and very often is afraid to stretch his legs in bed lest he might suffocate. He is also losing his eyesight. . . . He is an artist, unlike the other bastard writers I met here." O'Flaherty thought the play "a fine piece of realistic work," but he thought O'Casey spoiled it with tragedy. O'Casey appeared to O'Flaherty as someone worth knowing, someone who shared his own artistic convictions; and when the line between the new and the old writers seemed to be drawn, O'Flaherty thought that O'Casey should fall in with him. "O'Casey, Salkeld, and myself are trying to start a small club," O'Flaherty wrote Garnett, "to protect us against the old fogies, like Yeats and A.E. and the rest" (July, 1925). Shortly after, however, O'Flaherty said without particular comment that O'Casey had dropped out of the club. O'Flaherty thought it was more important that they "keep out Yeats, Senator Gogarty, etc. who want to have their finger in every pie and make a mess of it" (September 6, 1925).

In his autobiography O'Casey is much more specific about his relations with this literary clique. The club was directed against Yeats, according to O'Casey, and consisted of a group of younger writers who "disliked his booming opinions on literature and insubstantial things without any local habitation or name." F. R. Higgins, Liam O'Flaherty, Brinsley Macnamara, and Cecil Salkeld were the leaders of this radical club, O'Casey says, and its purpose was "to nourish the thoughts and ambitions of the young writers, in opposition to the elderly and wild speculation of Yeats and the adulatory group that trailed longingly after him." Their purpose in approaching O'Casey was to enlist his "newer influence" to put Yeats "in his improper place." [6] O'Casey, looking back, was sure that he had been taken in. O'Flaherty brought Edward Garnett to visit O'Casey at his tenement, and O'Casey was persuaded to tell them about the new play he was writing. He goes on, in *Inishfallen*, to describe that interview and his impressions of O'Flaherty:

> Garnett said he was delighted with the description given of the play, The Plough and the Stars, and O'Flaherty bravely simulated the happiness of his companion. On the strength of this praise, O'Flaherty built a hope that Sean would do anything he wished; and so for long, and continuously, he argued against the influence of Yeats on literary thought in Ireland and elsewhere, saying Yeats was too damned arrogant, too assured of the superiority of his own work over that of all the others. Sean, however, had no bubbling desire to be O'Flaherty's gillie, so he countered the arguments used, for he saw clear enough that O'Flaherty, in the way of arrogance and sense of being a superior being, was worse than Yeats without the elder man's grace and goodwill.

All of O'Casey's reminiscences of Dublin literary life were embittered by what followed, when *The Plough and the Stars* was produced. The riot that this play stirred is famous. After a successful opening night, what happened the second night was for O'Casey completely unexpected. He tells in *Inishfallen* of arriving at the theater to find everything in turmoil, the cause apparently voiced by the hysterical women who, amidst the general frenzy and uproar "kept squealing that Irish girls were noted for their modesty, and that Ireland's name was holy; that the Republican flag had never seen the inside of a public house; that the slander of the Irish race would mean the end of the Abbey Theatre" (pp. 231–39). In Horace Reynold's account in *The American Spectator* (December, 1934), Yeats is the hero, striding out magnificently to address the audience with the famous line, "You have disgraced yourselves again." But what embittered O'Casey more than the riot were the letters to *The Irish Statesman* that followed the play, for it appeared that the young Radicals had chosen this occasion to strike at Yeats and also at O'Casey for refusing to join them.

On February 20, 1926, O'Flaherty sent a letter to *The Irish Statesman* commenting on the riot and the play. His attack centered on Yeats: "Mr. Yeats had positively no right to strut forward and cry with joy that the people of this country had 'been cut to the bone.'" O'Flaherty said that he too had been cut to the bone by the play because he thought O'Casey did not do Pearse and Connolly and all the patriots of the Easter Rebellion justice. He himself, though not a Nationalist in the political sense, still looked on Easter 1916 as the most glorious gesture in the history of the country and did not want to see its dignity lessened in any way. Though O'Flaherty called *The Plough and the Stars* "a bad play," he wanted it known that his principal objection was not to O'Casey but Yeats, and he was sorry to see O'Casey defended publicly "by a man who rose to fame on the shoulders of those who stirred this country to fervent enthusiasm for ideals in the last generation." He called Yeats a "pompous fool" and thought the really contemptible thing in life was "the strutting of pompous people who spit at the justified anger of enthusiasts." Higgins and Clarke aimed their attack at the play itself. Clarke called the play a "crude exploitation of our poorer people in an Anglo-Irish tradition that is now moribund," and he identified himself as one of "several writers of the New Irish School" that shared this belief. The following week Higgins attacked the artistry of the play, calling it "gushly over-portrayed" and lacking "the sincerity of an artist." He thought it was more a review than a play and defective in its artistry: "The play should have driven the audience to demolish the slum and not the theater."

For a while, O'Casey said in his autobiography, he was bewildered by this attack, until he came to realize that it was aimed at Yeats and not prompted by "fear for Ireland's honour, the integrity of art, or the dignity of Irishmen." Yeats was the target, "and if it obliquely hurt and bothered Sean, all the better." Though O'Casey understood the attack he could not forgive it, and one of the vows he made as he took his departure from Ireland was that "he would never be in contact with any controversial literary Dublin clique." As he looked again at the situation he was leaving, he remembered his experience with one of those cliques that "had tried to entangle him into an effort to undermine the literary influence and authority of Yeats." So cut was he by the attack on him of those "fame-fleas," as he called them, that he was sure Yeats's little poem "To a Poet, Who Would Have Me Praise Certain Bad Poets," which contained the line "But was there ever a dog that praised his fleas?" was aimed at them. (This poem had been published in *The Green Helmet* [1910], many years before, however.)

If O'Casey was embittered by the enmity of the younger writers which he believed was due to his refusing to join their club, Yeats was apparently unaffected or indifferent. If anything, he took a rather benevolent interest in the storm of energy these young writers were trying to generate. His poem, "The New Faces," written at about this period might have had the new writers in mind:

> Let the new faces play what tricks they will
> In the old rooms; night can outbalance day,
> Our shadows rove the garden gravel still,
> The living seem more shadowy than they.

But his article telling of "The Need for Audacity of Thought" was in defense of just the sort of boldness these same young writers had attempted in *To-Morrow*. The problem that existed for Europe and for Ireland "in an acute form" was the lack of a body of religious thought "capable of withstanding the onset of modern life." The solution had to lie in the "audacity of speculation and creation" that these writers were attempting, which would "consider anew the foundations of existence" (p. 118). And he was liberal with praise for O'Flaherty's novels, continually recommending them to Mrs. Shakespeare. In a letter dated

March 13, 1927, quoted by Jeffares, he suggested that she read *The Informer* and *Mr. Gilhooley* which were "great novels and too full of abounding life to be terrible despite their subjects." He imagined that part of the desire for censorship in Ireland was to keep them out, which suggests the impact he thought they possessed. He contrasted O'Flaherty favorably with George Moore: "He joyously *imagines* when Moore *constructs*, and yet is more real than Moore." [7] Yeats had nothing to fear from these young writers. His fame was established. If he was among the last romantics, and if the high horse which Homer had once ridden was riderless, still, with mixed dread and hope he could see in the darkening flood, in the Galilean turbulence, a second coming in which the cycle of civilization would be renewed. The raging of these young men must have seemed to him a fulfillment of the pattern into which he saw Western culture falling.

O'Flaherty never had a published word of praise for Yeats, never mentions him at all except in his letters to Garnett, and then only in the most terse way: "I have avoided all the Yeat's and the Stephen's [*sic*] etc. They are no good at all" (April 3, 1924). O'Casey's explanation of this enmity appears to be correct. He attributed it to a "mean and reprehensible envy of the poet's literary standing." [8] Whether or not the envy was mean and reprehensible, it appears that some sort of resentment of Yeats's overshadowing stature prompted O'Flaherty to set himself against him. Kelleher's reflections on the period would seem to show the young writers had some justification, since they recognized that Yeats's fame would continue to shade out their own.[9] This would be especially onerous because the direction their writing would take could not follow in the tradition which he had brought to a culmination.

From O'Casey's autobiography it is easy to understand his disaffection with Ireland and the Dublin literary scene. He had been hurt by the reception given to *The Plough and the Stars* and especially by the betrayal of the young writers he might have considered his friends. He thought that A.E. was full of foolish windy talk which had no relationship to the real state of affairs in Ireland. O'Casey had ceased to respect the opinions of Dublin's literary leaders. Most of all, he was disappointed with Ireland herself, where the dream of revolution had given way to middle class stodginess. The terrible beauty had been born in Russia, and not in Ireland, he said. The reality was there before him, "Cancerous streets that were incensed into resigned woe by the rotting houses, a desperate and dying humanity, garbage and shit in the roadway: where all the worst diseases were the only nobility present."

And O'Casey wondered why the poor people there could not rise up and "tear the guts out of those who kept them as they were." In contrast he saw the "trifling group of the drawing-room" who "would never deliver Ireland from what was coming—they thought of themselves too much" (pp. 220, 376).

From the beginning O'Flaherty had set himself against the established order in Dublin, but it is difficult to tell if it was because of some deep-seated difference in taste and artistic philosophy or because of a rebellious personality that instinctively set itself against whatever power existed. There is no reason to believe that he had any well-developed theories about art or Ireland before he came to Dublin. He had submitted himself to Edward Garnett when he began *The Black Soul* and followed his recommendations diligently. His first letters to Garnett indicate that he felt Dublin or Irish literature had no claim on him. "I go around and get all sorts of copy here but I never hear anything of what is happening in the civilised world—which is of course across the channel," he wrote Garnett (April 3, 1924) a few months after arriving in Dublin. And if he had any theories it was the one he expressed in a letter of May 2, 1924: "One writes as one sees or else one is a mountebank. You yourself were principly [*sic*] the cause of my becoming a puritan in art, instead of becoming an artist who is subtle enough to accept what THE BEST PEOPLE think proper and artistically refined in his own age. I will write in the future for the satisfaction of my own soul since that to me is the most important thing in the world or in the next either."

Although his letters indicate that almost from the beginning he was interested in joining with those young writers who felt oppressed by the established order, it was not until after the publication of *The Black Soul* and its reception in Dublin that he began to express any theories about literature, and those theories were primarily a restatement of the response to *The Black Soul* by the Dublin reviewers who favored it. When O'Flaherty came to Dublin, he could not have been sure of what he was as an artist in relation to that society. He had written *The Black Soul* out of his own being, away from Ireland, with the shaping guided by a man who was not only not Irish, but dedicated to art for its own sake without concern for its social values. The reviews of *The Black Soul* let him see himself in a role. A.E. had recognized its "elemental" quality and its affinity with the great forces of nature. In the *To-morrow* review L. K. Emery noted its "primal grandeur," and thought O'Flaherty had rid himself of the malaise of the century by not being afraid of passion or instinct. He could see in *The Black Soul* a new vista for Irish literature, a movement away from analysis and formalism to "the comprehension of the surviving instincts of our primordial life." When O'Flaherty wrote his inflammatory letter on "National Energy" in *The Irish Statesman,* his description of the national character was almost exactly what had been described of his own work. And when Higgins and Clarke supported his position, recommending a new movement in Irish letters that recognized the "primal emotions" that required "vehemence" and "excessive energy" and that stressed the "objective, the elemental, the primary colour . . . in the hard sun," they in effect were echoing these same reviews. O'Flaherty had projected himself into Irish letters as a distinctive force (which A.E. recognized as having the appeal of novelty to those who had joined him) and he played his new role to the hilt.

In a letter of September 25, 1924, the view of himself and of Irish literature that began with *The Black Soul* reviews found its way back to Garnett. O'Flaherty judged the existing culture as dead but forecast that another age of primitivism was coming and that the new uncultured phase of the movement would require spokesmen with a sting in their tongues. He foresaw a revolutionary wave in the offing, which, if it passed through his generation, would leave him with an audience of one hundred intelligentsia who appreciated his "art, so called" but would not appreciate his "impetus" because it was foreign to them. (He did not explain what that "impetus" was, but that impetus is one of the primary concerns of this study and will be developed at length in the analysis of his literary works.)

O'Flaherty had come to Ireland feeling that his place was more in world literature than Irish literature, but as he found his Irish niche he began to identify himself more and more with Ireland. On June 20, 1925, he wrote a letter, *"A View of Irish Culture,"* to *The Irish Statesman* criticizing it as "not Irish, not national, and not representative." He thought Irish culture could not develop because it was "submerged beneath a rotting mound of British traditions." The only hope lay with the younger generation, which was "tired of bravado and politicians and mountebanks" and it was up to the younger generation to decide Ireland's future: "The younger generation alone can decide whether in twenty years time we will still be a nation of bigoted and intolerant people or whether we are going to build up a civilisation distinctly our own, a civilisation and culture that will make us a force in Europe." It was from this position that the attack on Yeats and O'Casey was launched, and it would appear that in two years' time he had evolved from his detached position into a full-scale Irishman, ready to take up the cudgel against anyone who would blight the fair name of Ireland. But it is apparent that the rebel existed before the Irishman and that the attack on Yeats was the end result of a pattern which found O'Flaherty taking up and playing a role that had been created for him by the response to *The Black Soul*. The primary concern of O'Flaherty and his friends was to assert themselves, to make themselves heard, and to do that they chose any position and any opportunity that offered that possibility.

While all the controversy raged and O'Flaherty was engaged in clubs and cliques, attacks and manifestoes, making whatever storm he could in Dublin's literary society, he was also engaged in the business of being a writer. He was working on *The Informer*, which was published in 1925. The public activity which eventually found him in the role of an Irish patriot defending the dignity of Ireland was in no way reflected in this novel. If anything, the opposite was true, at least in the estimation of S.L.M., who reviewed *The Informer* for *The Irish Statesman* on October 10, 1925. He saw reflected in *The Informer* the events of the past ten years which had "torn the top off civilisation" and exposed the characters of the slums (that disturbing layer) beneath. He linked O'Flaherty with O'Casey as realists and warned that O'Flaherty should not let his "fever of realism" reduce him into the monstrous. In this review S.L.M. followed generally the judgment of A.E., who had reviewed O'Casey's *Shadow of a Gunman* in *The Irish Statesman* the year before (June 7, 1924). Calling it "A Drama of Disillusionment," A.E. saw in the play evidence that something new was happening in literature. He accepted the novelty stoically but without enthusiasm: "Now that strange and terrible things have come to us, they show them to us."

This was to be the pattern of Irish literary criticism in the years following the advent of the Free State when O'Casey, O'Flaherty, and Joyce all came to be joined together as representing the new movement in Irish literature which the Irish critics called the "new realism." But the description implied in this term was based not as much on a literary as a nationalistic judgment, for the "realism" which they saw was not a literary technique but a picture of Ireland in the literature as that picture compared to the "ideal" picture. The tradition of Irish criticism after the Free State—a tradition including A.E., Monk Gibbon, Hugh Law, Ernest Boyd, Padraic Colum, and Sean O'Faolain—tended to look at the Ireland in Irish literature and to judge the literature on the basis of the Ireland represented there. The self-conscious

Messianism which Herbert Howarth showed as an important trait of the Irish literary movement [10] tended to ask the question, How is Ireland faring in relation to her ideals now that the Free State has been established? The criticism looked to Irish literature for the answer and judged the literature on the basis of its relation to the ideals.

A.E. was the accepted leader of Dublin literary society, the custodian of Irish ideals which he promulgated in his influential journal *The Irish Statesman.* Monk Gibbon credited A.E., John Eglinton, and Yeats with making these ideals into the spirit of Irish literature.[11] When the Free State was established, A.E.'s view that the future of Irish literature was bound up with the future of the Irish nation became an accepted standard. A.E.'s Ireland was a land of the spirit, a nation that would grow as her soul grew. He saw the role of literature to be the fostering of that growth. In his review of Hugh Law's study of Anglo-Irish literature in *The Irish Statesman* (January 22, 1927), he saw the literary critic's task as that of interpreting and describing those elements in Irish culture which were "the craftsmen of the national soul," and in another place he viewed the writer's task as creating "the Ireland in the heart, in the province of the national literature." [12]

In his *Anglo-Irish Essays* (1917) John Eglinton set down the credo of those literary ideals: "Happily there is in Ireland something older than race distinctions, older than the Catholic Church, older than archeology, older even than the gods—Mother Nature herself, in whose presence the poet can forget the squalid animosities of race and creed. The future of Irish literature is mainly an affair between the poet and this kindly mother, as she manifests herself to the solitary thinker on the hills and plains of Ireland." Twenty years later Gibbon looked back with nostalgia to those better times before Ireland had been drawn into the whirlpool of the world by all the advances in communications which had created a community of European thought. And he recalled how Eglinton had imagined that Ireland, because she was quiet and apart, could become the refuge of the poetic spirit put to flight by European strife. The debates that Yeats and Eglinton held were typical of those days, he thought, as they discussed whether the soul or the body of nature should be the poet's concern; and he recalled A.E.'s mediating by showing that the body of nature was the manifestation of soul. He contrasted that hope with present-day disillusionment, where instead of Synge there was Joyce, "the man with the muck-rake, exploring the hidden inhibitions of the soul." Gibbon thought it was symbolic of the times that Yeats had become an intellectual rather than the dreamer, and something had been lost. Art had become obsessed with psychology, inhibitions, the subconscious, and all the other paraphernalia of modern materialistic thought, and it had lost its true perspective. For poetry, he believed, was the "lonely adventures of the spirit," and the proper business of art was the soul "which has so often been the supreme preoccupation of the artist." He hoped for a prophet shy and inarticulate, then somewhere in Ireland, who would come forward with the needed note of conviction.[13]

Hugh Law shared with Gibbon the belief that the new realists, as they came to be known, were not the prophets that Ireland needed. His study of Anglo-Irish literature ended on a doubtful note. Looking at Joyce's *Ulysses*, O'Flaherty's *Informer* and George Moore's *Lake*, he was not sure that "the ever growing determination to dwell on the sordid side of life" was a sign of progress.[14] A.E., continually optimistic, saw the new realism as another manifestation of Irish genius, "really the same passionate intensity of mind directed to other ends." He thought O'Casey, Joyce, and O'Flaherty were winning for Ireland the repute of a realism "more intimate, intense, and daring than any other realism in contemporary literature." But it was not easy for him to adjust to the change that these writers brought about just when the conception of the Irish genius as "imaginative, poetic, and mystical" had been established, and he speculated that the latter stage would not have been possible without the former. His phrase "passionate intensity" is significant of his attitude. Consciously or subconsciously there must have existed the echo from Yeats's "The Second Coming" where "the worst/ Are full of passionate intensity," and he did not share with Yeats the myth that some violent upheaval was a prelude to the birth of a new spirit. He predicted a swing away from that realism to a literature of the intellect "enriching the Irish mind." In his preface to Hugh Law's study he put this same stress on the intellectual as the new outlet for Irish genius, predicting that the passion of the Irish must be dissipated unless "so intense an intellectual life was created" in Ireland that the exiles could have "the needles of their being . . . held turned to it as to a spiritual or cultural home," so that Ireland would become what Mecca was to Islam and Jerusalem to Jewry (p. xvi).

In 1926 O'Flaherty published *Mr. Gilhooley,* and O'Casey had produced *The Plough and the Stars,* both taking their materials from the everyday substance of Dublin life, and it must have seemed that a new direction was confirmed. "What has happened in the national being," asked Y.O., a regular contributor and reviewer in *The Irish Statesman* (June 4, 1927), "that a quarter of a century should have brought about such a change? . . . From the most idealistic literature in Europe we have reacted so that with Joyce, O'Flaherty and O'Casey, the notabilities of the moment, we have explored the slums of our cities, the slums of the soul." He thought some law of reaction had to be operating to cause Anglo-Irish literature, which twenty-five years before had been "romantic, idealistic, or mystic," to become the realism that had evolved. And he toyed with the notion that some law of heredity existed which evoked from each writer the opposite of himself. Following this line he saw that Joyce was the antithesis of Yeats, O'Casey of Synge, and O'Flaherty of Standish O'Grady. About the latter, he thought O'Grady would certainly disown the child his Cuchulain Saga (by the law of reaction) made inevitable. Yet "if *Cuchulain* had not been so noble *The Informer* would not have been so ignoble." Perhaps, he said, those illegitimate children, born of reaction instead of tradition, might yet be regarded with pride after the shock had worn away.

Realism and *disillusionment* were the two words that entered into almost every appraisal of Ireland's literary temperament by the Irish writers and critics on the scene in the middle twenties. Only a few saw the movement that they described as being something broader than an Irish phenomenon. From the days of John Eglinton's poetic oasis theory of Ireland the tendency was deeply ingrained to consider Ireland somehow separate, with a separate destiny. But R. M. Fox, considering "Realism in Irish Drama" in an article for *The Irish Statesman* (June 23, 1928), put that realism in another perspective. A drama of disillusion, he noted, had appeared in modern Europe and was not just Irish. The new realism sprang from this: "It is this growing self-consciousness combined with the modern spirit of disillusion which gives the keynote to the new realism." He cited *The Informer* and *Mr. Gilhooley* as examples of this realism and called O'Flaherty "another modernist writing with a ruthless pen, exploring the deeps and refusing to be put off with platitudes." Fox was not satisfied with this approach to literature and warned that the realist who blew out the light in man by extinguishing his higher nature was not nearer but further from giving a true view of mankind.

Francis Hackett turned his attention to the critics in an article entitled "A Note in Criticism in *The Irish Statesman* (August 20, 1927). Criticism, he said, was molded by the Victorian influence, and the critic came to literature looking for hope or feeling or some kind of moral uplift. The critic wanted literature to make him feel good. It was that attitude which predominated in Irish criticism, Hackett said, and thus "the critic today in Ireland shudders at realism." He pointed to the writings of Joyce and O'Flaherty to illustrate how the critic would be repelled by the brutality or sordid realism without making the esthetic judgment which was his real obligation. He urged Irish criticism to "stop wallowing in British Moralism."

Whether they approved or disapproved, for the right or for the wrong reasons, the Irish critics of that period agreed that something had changed in literature. And the evidence for that change was somehow involved with the triumvirate of Joyce, O'Casey, and O'Flaherty, whose names immediately came to mind in any discussion of the new direction of Irish literature. A new terminology developed to describe that change, first *realism* and then, to explain that realism, *disillusion*, until the words were fitted together into an inevitable pattern: romanticism and idealism gave way to disillusion and realism.

Nor was that description limited to just the immediate period. When Ernest Boyd discussed "Joyce and the New Irish Writers" in an article in *Current History* (December, 1934), he saw that the new Irish writers had one point in common—they were all "disillusioned realists of the Black and Tan period." And the result, he said, was that much that was "sordid and ugly and cruel," much that was "brutal and brutalizing in Irish life" had at last found expression in a literature which, whether by accident or design had heretofore concentrated . . . on the more smiling aspects of existence." Similarly, Sean O'Faolain, in his description of the Irish character, judged that romance died completely when the revolutionary period of 1916–22 ended in Civil War, and that "most Irish literature since 1922 has been of an uncompromising scepticism, one might even say, ferocity." [15] Even Professor Kelleher, whose studies of Irish literature are noteworthy for their freedom from Irish bias, followed essentially the same line when he said in his article "Irish Literature Today," that A.E. and Yeats did not lead the new generation because the difference between "their poetic fantasy and the younger men's prose realism was too wide for that."

The critical assumption that the representation of Ireland was the most significant criterion for Irish literature caused the connection between Joyce, O'Casey, and O'Flaherty and separated them from the supposedly more idealistic Yeats and Synge. Yet today, apart from Ireland, Joyce is usually thought of in terms of his symbolism and stream of consciousness technique, a bold explorer of the limits of human expression. If he is associated with Yeats, it is not as an antithesis but as a fellow symbolist, both sharing the assumption that words alone are certain good. O'Casey is not contrasted with Synge, but both are noted for their skill in reproducing (or perhaps creating) the color-ful idiom of native speech, the differences in locale being of far less significance than the similarities of technique. And each produced plays which, because of their so-called realism, outraged Irish nationalism. If O'Flaherty is thought of at all, it is more for his stories of animals and nature or for his reputation (unfounded) for knowledge of the inside workings of Irish revolutionary organizations. Yet at the time those names were connected, the similarity that seemed most obvious was that they all set their works in Dublin with characters from the lower ranges of Dublin society.

For whatever their artistic intentions, Joyce, O'Casey, and O'Flaherty necessarily used in their writings materials with which they were familiar. Joyce and O'Casey were native Dubliners. O'Flaherty had been in and out of Dublin as a student and as a writer since his eighteenth year. All were poor, Joyce and O'Casey knowing the intimate poverty of family life and O'Flaherty the poverty of the streets and the public houses. Lower-class society was the atmosphere they breathed. More often than not their own financial security was measured by the amount of money they had in their pockets. Theirs was not a life of drawing rooms and business ventures and the delicate moral refinements of upper-class society. They used the materials they knew to express their artistic aims, and the materials were not in any necessary way their commentary upon Irish life. Yet when Y.O. reviewed *The Assassin* for *The Irish Statesman* (June 16, 1928), he saw the same thing that S.L.M. had seen in *The Informer*. The char-acters in *The Assassin* were not part of the familiar Irish picture, but monstrosities "that a great national upheaval has brought up . . . from the abyss, and they are like blind, infuriated animals." He could see *The Assassin* only in terms of its representation of Ireland: "His Assassin is a madman who lusts after intense sensations and only at odd moments do these intensities of feeling beget affinities with any group in national thinking."

This has been a characteristic of Irish criticism, to look at Irish literature almost exclusively in terms of its specific Irish qualities, to judge it on the basis of how it expresses the national soul as if that were its primary function as literature. Estella Taylor's brief survey of some of the tendencies of the modern Irish writers only supports what everyone who has read around in modern Irish literature already knows—that the Irish critics look upon their literature as something they alone can really understand. But her conclusion regarding the Irish mind and character is worth restating. She notes that the Irish

critics were looking for the Celtic element in the works of their con-
temporaries and judging those works on the basis of Irish authenticity.
"The critic scrutinized the Irish mind and character for the purpose of
establishing criteria by which he subsequently estimated the worth of
all who purported to make a literary representation of the Irish." [16]
This cut two ways. The non-Irish writer could not write about the
Irish because he could not understand the national soul, and the
Irish writer was judged on the basis of how his representation of the
national soul coincided with the ideal.

These tendencies are reflected particularly well in Joyce criticism.
Padraic Colum, considering "*Ulysses* and Its Epoch" in *The Saturday
Review of Literature* (January 27, 1934), tended to discount the
Homeric structure and attendant symbolism of *Ulysses* in favor of its
realism, singling out the Cyclops episode as such a true rendering of
certain qualities of Dublin speech that only a native could appreciate it.
When that article was written, at least, he considered the realism Joyce's
forte. In the same way Ernest Boyd disagreed with the critics who
said that with *Ulysses* Ireland made her reentry into European literature. He stressed in "James Joyce and the New Irish Writers," that
Irish critics were more impressed by the simple realism of *Ulysses* than
by any of its complexities of symbolism or technique. For both Colum
and Boyd the important thing about *Ulysses* was the picture it gave
of Ireland. *Ulysses* was realistic, they thought, because it depicted
lower-class society in everyday life. It is only a step from that position
to Monk Gibbon's, that *Ulysses* was "muck-raking," and another
short step to explain this as disillusionment, that the writer was
deliberately presenting the sordid picture because he wanted to contrast
it to the ideal.

The mistake is to look at the materials of art and interpret them and
not the art, which is the selection and arrangement of the materials.
When the Irish critics saw in Joyce, O'Casey, and O'Flaherty a
representation of Ireland that differed from the ideal, they took that
representation as a deliberate drawing of the national soul. Since that
drawing showed Ireland as it was, they assumed that this was done by
disillusioned writers who wanted to show Ireland to herself divested
of all her dreams. But Joyce, O'Casey, and O'Flaherty were under no
obligation to write about Ireland in relation to her national dream.
They could or could not express disillusionment as they chose, each
according to his own artistic aims. The common disillusionment that
the critics saw was not in the art but in the eyes of the critics.

By the end of the 1920's disillusionment was general in Ireland's literary climate, an attitude far-removed from Padraic Colum's hopeful "beginning all over again" predicted in 1923. In 1926 Colum looked once more and saw that what he had forecast as the beginning was actually the end: "In the space between the downfall of Parnell and the rise of the Irish Volunteers the intellectuals had the whole stage in Ireland—I mean the intellectuals in the best sense of that abused word. They formed a coterie that was homogeneous, in which everybody knew everybody's oddity. . . . They are still in Dublin, most of them, but the coterie has broken up; ideas have been de-limited and have taken on a practical tinge because of the demands of the new State." [17]

Sean O'Casey thought that all hope for Ireland died when the dream of the Republic was abandoned in favor of the Free State supported by a combination of Catholic Church and middle-class business interests. Tired of literary cliques and disputations, he left Ireland in 1926, fleeing the "holy water that would soon be raining down for forty days and forty nights," realizing that it was getting very dark in Ireland and that "there was no making love to Kathleen, daughter of Houlihan now, untidy termagant, brawling out her prayers." [18] The Censorship Bill, latent in the atmosphere O'Casey fled in 1926, was passed in 1928 despite the objections of men like A.E., Yeats, and Colum—the intellectuals who once "had the whole stage in Ireland." Writing about "Ireland After Yeats" in 1953, O'Faolain corroborated O'Casey's judgment that Ireland's troubles lay in the alliance formed between the Catholic Church and middle-class business interests: "It was a holy alliance between the Church, the new businessmen, and the politicians, all three nationalistic-isolationist for, respectively, moral reasons, commercial reasons, and politico-patriotic reasons. The intellectuals became a depressed group." [19]

In 1927 O'Flaherty expressed his own disenchantment with Ireland, giving up any hopes for creating in Ireland "a civilisation and culture that will make us a force in Europe." In his last letter or contribution of any kind to *The Irish Statesman* he called the situation hopeless. On December 17, 1927, he answered the charges of an unknown Una M.C. Dix, who accused him of writing in English because he had betrayed himself for money. A.E. had noted after the Dix letter that writers had no choice, that books in Gaelic would have no reading audience, but O'Flaherty came to his own defense. He said that he had written in Irish and had won a gold medal for his Irish composition when he was sixteen, but that when he began to write professionally he was no longer interested in the Irish language because he wanted to put across his ideas to the Irish people in the only language possible, because the Irish people did not understand Irish. But a few years later he "became less interested in the regeneration of the Irish people intellectually, having come to the conclusion that his people were too hopelessly sunk in intellectual barbarism to be capable of being saved by a single man." At that time he had written a play in Gaelic which played to a packed theater. But he was not paid for his work, and he vowed after that not to write in Irish or at least not to publish what he had written in Irish. But he reaffirmed his dedication to art: "I don't write for money. If I wanted to write for money I could be a rich man now. I am a good craftsman and I am cunning enough to understand the various follies of mankind and womankind." He said that if he ever got so hard up that he would lose his self-respect, he would "start a religious paper in the Irish language and make a fortune on it." That was not the case yet, however, and he would persist in his own way: "I write to please myself and two friends—my wife and Mr. Edward Garnett." In a postcript he noted that Padraic Colum and those like him who advocated the Irish language were humbugs because they were not in Ireland. "If he is interested in Irish why doesn't he stay in Ireland, learn the language, and write in it?"

In the December 31, 1927, issue, a P. J. McDonnell attacked O'Flaherty for attacking Una Dix. McDonnell was bitterly personal: "O'Flaherty . . . shows his contempt for everybody in Ireland, and for everything Irish, unless it be of the O'Flaherty brand. . . . Every conquered country has the misfortune to produce creatures of the O'Flaherty type—a swarm of toadies, flunkeys, and gombeen men." He accused O'Flaherty of making his money in England by defaming the Irish, because only the English would pay to read about the Irish in the terms that O'Flaherty had described them. Although McDonnell's attack represented a typical hyper-patriotic attitude toward O'Flaherty's work, the basis for this view was the same as that of the critics who stressed O'Flaherty's realism. Both saw his work almost exclusively as a representation of Ireland. O'Faolain's "Don Quixote O'Flaherty," an ingenious apology for O'Flaherty's violence, was based on this same view. O'Faolain thought that O'Flaherty had set out "in the most self-conscious and deliberate way to attack with violence the things that hurt the inarticulated dream of his romantic soul," and that his dark view of Ireland resulted because his ideal Ireland was "too lovely to be described except in terms of her shadows." The question is not whether O'Flaherty's view of Ireland should be attacked, de-fended, or apologized for, but whether his work should be judged or explained on the basis of how Ireland seems to be represented therein.

The next chapters will show that O'Flaherty's art is essentially personal, not social, and that he differentiated between himself as a man who could be involved in Irish affairs and himself as an artist necessarily aloof from social commitment. Although his art was constructed from Irish materials, this did not mean that his aim was to construct a picture of Ireland or the Irish. Rather, he saw his role as being "to listen and reproduce their passions: because all passion is beautiful." [20] In this he followed the direction that Stephens had forecast in his 1923 "Outlook for Literature." Stephens had seen that for the writer to express the "anti-rationalism" and "relativism" current in the age he must concern himself with the "successions of deeds that are passions" which he must translate "into the quietude of words" by means of "a passion that is the equal of itself." Stephens thought the writer's deep personal involvement in this translation would make him essentially "engaged in his own portrait." O'Flaherty showed a similar turn of mind when he praised the intensity of Powys' novel which gave him the impression that every scene was "wrung out of Mr. Powys' very soul amid terrific agony." And when Y.O. reviewed *Mr. Gilhooley* in *The Irish Statesman* (November 27, 1926)—looking this time at the qualities of a particular work instead of at O'Flaherty's general place in the Irish literary revival—more than the realism he saw the intense personal quality which he called a "pure identification of the writer with his subject." He praised the "vivid emotional powers" with which the "blind gropings of the individual" were realized: "It is the identification of the self with the thing seen to acquire understanding." This is the view of O'Flaherty's work that is lost by those who see his art solely in terms of his representation of Ireland, and this is the view that the subsequent chapters will explore.

∽ II ∽

The Man and the Artist

O'Flaherty said that one of the purposes of *Shame the Devil*, should he be considered worthy of a biography, was to rob "grave-robbers of their beastly loot" (p. 284). This study in no way intends to thwart that purpose nor to deny that O'Flaherty is worth a biography. But certain facts of his life are important in that they are woven as a recurring pattern into his work. More important, as O'Flaherty got himself or aspects of himself involved as characters in his works, he created for himself an artistic problem—a problem of detachment—that had a great bearing on the direction of his development as a novelist. We shall see that the man and the problems presented directly in the autobiographies *Two Years* (1930) and *Shame the Devil* (1934) are closely related to the men and problems in O'Flaherty's fiction.

Although O'Flaherty has written two autobiographical studies, one of which was to forestall future biographies, the facts of his life are far from clear. Donagh MacDonagh, in his Afterword to *The Informer*, comments that should O'Flaherty ever have an Ellmann or a Hone "to explain him to the world, his biographer will have no easy task, since the available facts are as shifting and evasive as the fog that swirls through the scenes of his only film" (p. 186). The capsule biographies written for dust jackets and anthologies are derived primarily from O'Flaherty's own account of himself at the beginning of *Shame the Devil*, where he describes his early education, his breaking from the Church, his joining the Irish Guard in World War I, his three years of tramping around the world, his revolutionary activities in 1922, and his flight from Ireland. All accounts agree fundamentally on these points. But the confusion about his later years is shown typically in the differing accounts given by *Twentieth-Century Authors* in the 1942 edition and the First Supplement (1955).

In *Shame the Devil* O'Flaherty gives an account of his early years.

26

He was born in the Aran Islands in 1896, one of several children in a poor family. His earliest memories were those of the stories his mother told him of giants and fairies, and he recalled how she would "mime the comic adventure of our neighbours, until our hungry little bellies were sick with laughter" (p. 18), like the delightful mother in his short story "The Red Petticoat." His own imagination grew and told him that God had "blessed him with a holy mind." But at the age of nine, the "angel of revolt" entered into him, and his tales became more fierce, until one day he told his mother a tale of how a local laborer had murdered his wife in a potato garden. He described the incident so convincingly and with such lurid detail (the wife's body was so fat "that the murderer had to dance on it in order to make it fit into the furrow" where he was burying it) that his mother dashed out in alarm to warn the neighbors. When she learned the truth, she made him beg God's aid in curing him of his "morbid leprosy" (p. 19). And from that day, O'Flaherty said, he hid his dream and became a dual personality.

His new silence was taken as being spiritually motivated and interpreted as being a vocation for the priesthood, which O'Flaherty said that even at that time he despised. But his zeal for scholarship was recognized, and when he was thirteen a priest from the Holy Ghost Order came to visit O'Flaherty's schoolmaster. The schoolmaster called O'Flaherty to his attention, and after a few talks, O'Flaherty became a postulant for his order, understanding mostly that through this he could get his education practically free. O'Flaherty left his home for the scholasticate of the Holy Ghost Order at Rockwell in Tipperary to be trained as a missionary to the African negroes. When after four years it was time for him to take his soutane, he refused, having not the slightest inclination to go to Africa or become a priest. He went home, despite the anger of the director, who accused him of pretending a vocation in order to get a free education. The next year O'Flaherty went to a college in Dublin belonging to the Order at Blackrock. He stayed there a year and then entered the Dublin diocesan seminary at Clonliffe. But he had no desire to become a priest, staying only so as not to disappoint his mother. When the time came again for him to wear the soutane, he rebelled once more, this time completely. He disliked everything about the whole business. "I danced on my soutane, kicked my silk hat to pieces, spat on my religious books, made a fig at the whole rigmarole of Christianity, and left that crazy den of superstitious ignorance" (p. 21). For a short time after he attended lectures at University College, Dublin, where he had won a scholarship, and then he joined the Irish Guards and went to war. This section of his life is closely paralleled by the experiences of Peter O'Toole in the short story "Child of God" who had similar experiences with religious education.

When O'Flaherty joined the Guards and began his basic training at Caterham barracks, he thought he had been condemned to hell. Always a rebel against authority, as he described himself, he found it difficult to adjust to the authoritarian crudities. But gradually "the vinegar turned into wine" (p. 237), and he began to feel himself a part of that well-disciplined troop and to see the fine humanity beneath the rough exteriors. Always a worshipper of the mind to the neglect of the body, he now began to worship the body. After his training O'Flaherty was sent to France and, as a replacement in the lines, underwent those special horrors of mud and rats, death and blood that marked the long trench warfare of World War I. At Langemarck in September, 1917, while guiding a transport officer to the front lines, he was caught in a shell bombardment and seriously shocked and wounded. For a long while he was unable to speak. After being shifted about from hospital to hospital, he was finally discharged from King George V hospital in Dublin for *melancholia acuta* (p. 83). *The Return of the Brute*, a novel about trench warfare in World War I, is O'Flaherty's only published use of these experiences in his fiction.

O'Flaherty's story picks up at the point he describes in *Two Years*,[1] when in August, 1918, he left home again. This time he went to London, and after working as a laborer in a brewery, a porter in a hotel, a clerk in an office, disgruntled by the whole meaningless debilitating commercial world, he went to sea as a trimmer in the stokehold. He jumped ship in Rio de Janeiro and lived as a beach hobo when his money ran out. After an excursion inland, he returned to the city and shipped out for Liverpool, with every intention of seeing the revolution in Ireland which began when the Republic was declared. Close at hand, with no evidence that anything really wonderful was happening, O'Flaherty lost interest and signed on a ship bound for the Mediterranean. At Smyrna he found himself involved in a mysterious transaction concerned with contraband arms. This provided the money for a Gargantuan debauch, at the end of which he had delirium tremens (which he shared with many of the crew). When the ship left Smyrna, it sailed through a dangerous storm, and, after a stop at Gibraltar, sailed on to Montreal.

In Canada O'Flaherty left the ship and set out once more as a hobo. His travels took him across the country working for his keep as a farm laborer, a factory worker in a condensed-milk plant, and a rail-road worker. His travels took him to Toronto, and from there he decided to leave the confusion of the cities in favor of the "wild forests and tremendous plains." He joined a lumber gang en route to Northern Ontario. On this job he met John Joseph Peterson, an extraordinary man from whom O'Flaherty said he gained his "interest in human psychology" or rather, his "insight into it" (p. 251). He also learned from Peterson about the I.W.W. and hobo jungles. Leaving the lumber camp under some pressure because of their I.W.W. propagandizing, they took a job at a nickel mine, then moved on to Port Arthur. At this point O'Flaherty began to tire of the primitive life and parted company with Peterson.

He saved some money on another lumber job and, when his bank-roll was set, took off for the United States and Boston to see his brother and sisters whom he had not seen in many years. His brother introduced him to a group of Irish and Irish-American social revolutionaries and to a quickened intellectual life which he had not experienced for some time. He learned about socialism and, in the process, capitalism and the machinery of modern production. His brother prodded him into trying to write, but his efforts were without conviction and unsuccessful. He took various jobs as Western Union messenger, printer's assistant, factory hand in a pastry factory, construction navvy. He persuaded his brother to learn about society, and they left Boston for New Haven, Connecticut, where they obtained work in a tire factory. Bored with this, O'Flaherty set out for New York City. He worked as a house porter in the Knickerbocker Hotel, and later as a waiter. He learned about Greenwich Village. He worked on a lobster boat, in a commissariat, in a Du Pont explosives factory. And finally, disenchanted with wandering and social revolution and feeling the seed for more meaningful expression growing within him, he took a ship which wound a devious way through Rio, Buenos Aires, Antwerp, and Hamburg back to Cardiff. A strange depression had set in for him, and when he arrived home he was "like a ghoul, speechless, gloomy, a companion of the rough winds and of the breakers." There, like Fergus O'Connor of *The Black Soul*, who had returned broken in spirit and health from similar wanderings, "a godless hermit, I began my communion with the cliffs, the birds, the wild animals, and the sea of my native land" (p. 351). In *Shame the Devil* O'Flaherty states that these wanderings occupied three years (to 1921) from which he returned to Aran an "ill man, without money, disillusioned" (p. 21). He stayed on the island some months and then plunged into the revolutionary movement in Dublin. In the early part of 1922 he and a small army of unemployed men seized the Rotunda and raised a red flag. Driven out after four days, he fled the country.

Here the career of Liam O'Flaherty the writer begins. He went to London to live with Miss Casey and her mother who kept a small shop. They had invited him because of his association with the Irish Revolution and articles he had written for revolutionary newspapers, and when he arrived, the daughter urged him to become a writer. His first writings were unsuccessful, "trashy," as O'Flaherty describes them; and infuriated by a snippy rejection, he resolved not to write in this vein again. To console himself he began to think about Aran, the waves, nature, and the simple life of the people. It seemed then to him that "a dam had burst somewhere in his soul" (p. 38). Words began to pour out in profusion as he wrote *Thy Neighbour's Wife*. And though this profusion dried up and he finished the novel with great difficulty, it was accepted by Jonathan Cape through the mediation of Edward Garnett, who saw in it the work of a promising young writer. Later O'Flaherty met Garnett, the most important association in O'Flaherty's life.

This was in February, 1923. His manuscript had been accepted just when O'Flaherty had been about to give up his literary career. A whole new world now seemed to open. In his flush of excitement he asked Miss Casey to marry him. But when O'Flaherty met Edward Garnett his notions of life and art took a different turn: "Like a father he took me under his protection, handling me with the delicacy with which one handles a high-strung young colt. . . . It was the first time I had come in close contact with a cultured English gentleman. The calmness of his judgment, the subtlety of his intellect, and the extraordinary nobility of his character were a glorious revelation to me. . . . Artistic beauty being the only thing of real importance in life to him, I became a fervent disciple in that religion" (p. 44).

On Garnett's advice O'Flaherty left his London garret (and the influence of Miss Casey) and moved to the country to begin his work on *The Black Soul*, which he submitted to Garnett page by page for approval. From this time until 1926 O'Flaherty's letters to Garnett give a close account of his life, for he wrote almost 140 letters in that period pouring out everything to his "dearest friend." In the country O'Flaherty met Mrs. Morris at Quaker Farm. Mrs. Morris was attractive and twenty-three, with a two-year-old daughter. She had no intentions of marrying again, but in August, 1923, O'Flaherty announced to Garnett that they were going to live together.

O'Flaherty wrote Garnett in May, 1923, that Mrs. Morris was the model for Little Mary in the "Summer" section of *The Black Soul*.

When *The Black Soul* was finished, toward the beginning of 1924, O'Flaherty returned to Dublin, hoping now to storm the literary heights in that land from which he had fled two years before. As a promising young author, with *Thy Neighbour's Wife* and several sketches in print, he was introduced into George Russell's literary circle. For him his most important introduction there was to Professor Curtis' wife "who made violent eyes" at him during the meeting (March 10, 1924). Although he could write to Garnett that "she does not enthuse me, at least not very much" (March 21, 1924), in their subsequent meetings O'Flaherty must have become more and more impressed, because shortly after he arrived in Dublin he announced to Garnett (March 21, 1924) that he was breaking off with Mrs. Morris ("she damn near killed me"). Not long after, he and Mrs. Curtis (who wrote under the name of Margaret Barrington) began living together while she attempted to get a divorce. Despite Professor Curtis' attempts at reconciliation and despite the opposition of the Roman Catholic Church, she obtained the divorce and eventually O'Flaherty married her.[2]

These were the years of O'Flaherty's most furious literary activity. Immediately after *The Black Soul* was published O'Flaherty began work on *The Informer*, and after this, *Firebrand*, which was published in 1927 as *Mr. Gilhooley*. And all the time he was writing the novels he was pouring out a profusion of sketches and short stories—ten in three weeks, he told Garnett (July 10, 1925)—articles, reviews, and letters to the editor in *The Irish Statesman*. *Darkness*, his only play, was published in 1926. At the same time he was involved in a Radical club (with men like Cecil Salkeld, Austin Clarke, F. R. Higgins) to oppose the "old fogies" like Yeats and Senator Gogarty "who want to have their finger in every pie and make a mess of it" (September 6, 1925).

A letter to Garnett dated January 24, 1926, states that Topsy (Margaret, his wife) is pregnant. It also indicated that O'Flaherty has had an argument with Garnett about the short stories in the collection, *The Tent*. O'Flaherty is desperate for money because "The Informer has been a failure." Now his interest in " 'pure art' and such trivial matters is not very great." He asks Garnett not to resign his position as O'Flaherty's "literary uncle" because he still writes as if Garnett will read every word, and even if Garnett never reads another word of his he still feels tender toward Garnett because he believes Garnett cares for him apart from his work. But apparently this marks a major break in the Garnett–O'Flaherty friendship and correspondence, because the next letter to Garnett was dated February 29, 1932, from England.

Except for the records of publication of his books and stories not much is available about O'Flaherty's personal life from 1927 to 1932. His last letter to *The Irish Statesman,* dated December 17, 1927, states that he has just about given up hope for Ireland. *The Assassin* was published in 1928, *The House of Gold* in 1929 (this is the *Ramon Mor* story discussed in a letter of July 31, 1925, to Garnett). In 1929 he also had published a short-story collection, *The Mountain Tavern.* In 1930 appeared *The Return of the Brute, A Tourist's Guide to Ireland,* and the autobiography, *Two Years.* At the beginning of *I Went to Russia* O'Flaherty states that he is writing this book because the publishers believe it is in fashion, just as he had refrained from writing an autobiography until "forced by hunger" to do so.[3] He left on the trip to Russia on April 23, 1930, and the book was published in 1931.

The February 29, 1932, letter to Garnett is a pathetic plea for Garnett to resume their friendship. When Garnett answers, O'Flaherty on March 3, 1932, tells about himself. He is separated from his wife and a divorce appears likely. He is not "enthusiastic about that" because it might put him "in danger of remarriage." Now he is doing what he believes best for his work, "to live without women." And he attempts to bring Garnett up to date on his career: "I have been through a lot during the last few years; so to speak, deliberately undergone a rather stupid cycle of experience to arrive at a clearer consciousness of what I want to do. Now, it's coats off; and to do it." He is writing *Skerrett,* and is in fine spirits because he is "alone and in debt." O'Flaherty is pleased to hear from Garnett again because he has had little intellectual relationship since they last saw each other. But this is the last letter in the Garnett collection.

Shame the Devil brings the O'Flaherty story up to 1934. He is without money and depressed. Apparently he is divorced from his wife because he rejects the idea of remarrying, but he still needs money to send to his wife and daughter. After *The Puritan* in 1931 and *Skerrett* in 1932 O'Flaherty's books become more widely spaced. *The Martyr* followed in 1933, but *Hollywood Cemetery* did not appear until 1935. (This last book about Hollywood motion picture making was derived from O'Flaherty's Hollywood experiences with *The Informer,* which won an Academy Award in 1935.) Nine years then intervened between

Famine (1937) and *Land* (1946). And *Insurrection* (1950) was his last novel.

Although the young O'Flaherty lived an adventurous life and endowed many of his literary characters with backgrounds similar to his own, the external facts are of little importance except as they indicate which characters share with O'Flaherty some common experiences. Of much more importance are his inner life and adventures, where he wages a battle within himself to find his role and his goal. It must have been this sort of thing that he referred to in his last letter to Garnett, where he tells of deliberately undergoing "a rather stupid cycle of experiences to arrive at a clearer consciousness of what I want to do." This clearer consciousness involved seeing himself clearly in his role as a writer, especially as this related to two causes which seemed to lay claim to his attention and dedication—communism and Ireland.

For Liam O'Flaherty the question of the place of the artist in modern society was of vital importance, not because he was a theorist about literature but because it involved his role in the ultimate scheme of things. In this concern O'Flaherty certainly is not unique. For the modern artist this is the overwhelming question. It is not a technical question involving just social strata. Nor is it merely a defense, as in Shelley's *Defence of Poetry*, proclaiming the poet's right to speak out in a voice worthy of respect. It is not metaphysical, even, for this may presuppose that there is some rational order to which the artist may relate. And it can be called religious only in the sense that it involves all of man in his total commitment to whatever is capable of absorbing his whole being.

It is a truism that the modern writer feels himself alone and apart. This is considered one of the necessary conditions for being a writer. The writer must reject the ordinary standards of society, the ordinary goals and gods. As Leslie Fiedler says, the artist must say No! in thunder. "The vision of the truly contemporary writer is one of a world not only absurd but chaotic and fragmentary . . . in which we share chiefly a sense of our loneliness: our alienation from whatever things finally are." "Demonic, terrible, and negative, this is the Modern Muse." [4] But though this may be the precondition of modern art, and a condition that the modern artist may at times, in reflection, confirm, it is not the condition for which he necessarily strives or yearns.

Indeed the opposite. The art is the struggle, probably unsuccessful, to get back. The art is the balance which the artist achieves to allow him to endure his terrible aloneness. All these forces push and pull as O'Flaherty continually attempts to define his role. As a contemporary artist or, rather, as a man with a certain spiritual and intellectual bent, he found himself apart. This was the problem. Ideally it should not be so. Like Fergus O'Connor in *The Black Soul*, "His intellect hungered after the meaning of things. He wanted to find something tremendous and binding, whose meaning he would be afraid to question, something that he could accept blindly like Catholics accepted the Pope." [5] And one part of O'Flaherty is always seeking such a commitment and security—in the cause of Ireland, or communism, or a combination of the two.

He would like, like Stephen Spender's workers, to be "One cog in a golden and singing hive." "No more are they haunted by the individual grief/ Nor the crocodile tears of European genius." This is the appeal of communism. It is a vital, sweeping movement, alive and powerful. It is the expression of the machine age O'Flaherty learns to respect and admire in America. But most of all, it offers a means of expression and fulfillment of one of his deepest intellectual convictions, stated in *Two Years*, that man's divine destiny is his "struggle towards the perfection of his species to a state of godliness" (pp. 216–17), and it is in this struggle that good men are always engaged, revolting against all confining norms, customs, limitations of any sort, in society or in themselves. The goal is perfection in all ways—social institutions, philosophies, and concepts of beauty. At times, at moments of exhilaration such as he experienced with the Breton fishermen in *Shame the Devil*, he believed that communism could be the instrument of that struggle for perfection. He sees that "the strongest driving force of our times is the driving force of the revolutionary proletariat" (p. 197). The writer must ally himself with this: "Let the rich wine of revolt stir our blood to the final conflict that shall usher in the vision of man fresh conflicts about which he has not yet dreamt. Let it usher in the stars and the banners that are to be planted on the stars; the race for colonies on Mars and Jupiter, who were gods but yesterday, but which are today fresh territories to be trodden by human feet" (p. 197). In this spirit O'Flaherty declares that a writer must be first of all a citizen and rejects the theory that one should leave the business of living to one's valet. The writer must participate, and either "be expelled, crucified, or burnt in boiling oil; or else met with banners and trumpets at the outskirts of the cities which he visits." The writer is either "an isolated voice singing in a garret, or a prophet to whom all hands are raised in homage" (p. 196). It would be as a participant in this movement that a writer could have his triumph, for it would establish a new aristocracy of men like the Breton fishermen, about which poets could sing epics without being panderers. So he bids all writers to "carry the wild rose of insurrection" and "sing us a wild song of revolt" (pp. 210–11).

His experiences in America with the power of the machine age and his socialist studies with his brother in Boston described in *Two Years* convinced O'Flaherty that it was necessary for any artist working in the twentieth century to study closely all social movements that would make men aware that the machine god had arrived; otherwise they would be just copyists of the past. The artists who shrink from the dirt, noise, and coarseness of the new age, who dislike the new caste of proletarian aristocrats that the machine age has brought into being, are "laggards, fallen behind in the march, whereas the artist must always be in the vanguard" (p. 299).

So, as he argues with the Jewish girl in the Paris restaurant in *Shame the Devil*, he tells her how he learned about Marx and as a result understands the construction of modern society, history, and life itself. He says that it is more necessary for a creative writer to know political economy than for a painter to have eyesight. A writer must not be indifferent to social movements of his time or he cannot write anything of value. And since the main social movement of the time is Marxism, which is the power and the explanation of our era, the present-day writer must be a Marxist and a worshipper of the machine (p. 32). From this it would seem that O'Flaherty was not really alone and apart at all, that he had submerged himself in a total commitment to a cause. This is not No! but Yes! in thunder, except that O'Flaherty protests too strongly and sometimes lets the sound of his own words run away with his ideas. The passion of his commitment here is mainly an indication of the strength of his desire for commitment, belonging, and purpose.

His army experience recounted in *Shame the Devil* affected him that way too. When he first joined the Irish Guards and went through his training at Caterham it seemed that he had been condemned to hell. He was horrified at having his individuality submerged into that of coarse and common humanity. But gradually, as he learned the grandeurs and miseries of the military life, he began to feel the bond that their oath of valor and discipline had created. "A rebel from my childhood, I was forced to accept authority, and so I found that it was a relief and an ennoblement to click my heels and salute instead of being a debasement and an insult to my pride." Always the artist, he dramatized his role and equated himself with Socrates and Sophocles, Tolstoy and Cervantes—each of whom had fought and "kept their rendezvous with death and were respited," and who "shine out most brightly as apostles of peace and human brotherhood in their writings" (pp. 237–39).

This same intense longing to attach himself to a cause, a grand movement that demanded his total commitment, excited him about Irish nationalism. When O'Flaherty began his literary career in 1923–24, the Irish community of art nourished only the embers of the movement that had stirred Yeats, Lady Gregory, George Moore, George Russell, and the revolutionaries like Pearse and Connolly to build a grand new Ireland on the basis of a heroic past. The Treaty and Civil War had blackened the Celtic twilight and obscured the heroic past with a horrific present. Only the violence that Yeats had decried in Maude Gonne and the revolutionary movement remained. After the Easter Uprising of 1916, Yeats announced that a terrible beauty had been born. The younger writers tried to make this terrible beauty of violence the new basis for Irish literature, and it was into this movement that O'Flaherty projected himself. In *Two Years* he saw Ireland as a reincarnation of Elizabethan England: "Violent, disorderly, inefficient, intemperate, and full of the poetry of life" (p. 68). When a Russian girl that he met in Greenwich Village admired and pitied the Irish, O'Flaherty bristled. There was nothing to be pitied, since the Irish were "one of the few races to-day that are growing, and at the beginning of their creative careers" (p. 324). His letter in *The Irish Statesman* criticizing passive resistance also compared Ireland to the England of Shakespeare's time, "on the march . . . and rioting with excess of energy." This is the same kind of wild song of revolt that drew him to communism, the same security of belonging that he found in the army, a movement that he can dramatize, that may let him be one of the fighters in the creative vanguard achieving man's divine destiny and at the same time saving him personally from the cold terrors of aloneness.

This is only one side of O'Flaherty. If there were no other he would not have been a writer. It illustrates well his passionate desire to belong. But there was another side also, and these forces warred within him on a battle line so clearly drawn that he could construct dialogues between one side of his character and another, the duality he became aware of at nine, when he told the violent tale that so alarmed his mother: "The one wept with my mother and felt ashamed of his secret mind. The other exulted in this mind and began to dream of greatness" (p. 19).

As much as O'Flaherty wanted to dramatize the great movement of communism or the creative stirrings within his own nation that could catch him up in their sweep, he was early aware that his role was one of isolation—rejecting and rejected. His earliest creative experiences showed him the dreadful burden that his secret mind placed upon him. After the months of the "brutal life" on shipboard that had made his mind almost incapable of individual thought, in *Two Years* he recalls a moment of decision. The loss of his individuality means for him being swallowed up by his environment, secure, perhaps, but "bestially secure, like a pompous pig" which will "belch with satisfaction at its swinish state." For this is the state of one who rejects man's divine destiny for security and acceptance of existing things. This acceptance cuts man off from beauty "which can only be attained by suffering and fearless disregard for all limits to the gropings of the mind" (p. 216). Urged by his mind to be *good*—that is to be what he must in man's struggle for godliness—he sees no means for him but with words: "My mind had but a tongue to pour forth words that lacked subtlety, words written on the air by my body's vapours, dying at their birth and striking with the feebleness of a moth's wings against the inhospitable ears of their hearers" (p. 217).

In a scene that O'Flaherty recalls with great vividness, he stands all night contemplating his destiny. It is not an easy choice, for he sees that choosing the life of the mind means the rejection of a normal life and normal human pleasures and satisfactions. "Should I hold with what remained of the spiritual fetishes of my people," he asks himself, "or cut adrift completely and stand all my life alone?" "What horror! What loneliness!" Yet to win "the empire of the mind" with its "unfathomable" beauties, this is what he must do. He must become "an outcast hermit, who makes a god of thought and eschews all contact with the material empire of this earth, denies its gods, spits on its honours, and turns his cold, loveless eyes from his mother, wife, child, friend, compatriot" (p. 219).

O'Flaherty does not make the choice here, though he feels comforted, probably because the problem has been defined. He tells how he plunges again into a life of frenzied action as hobo and woodsman and farmhand and factory hand. In Boston he learns from his brother about socialism, and in more jobs he becomes an agitator, preaching socialism, fired promptly in each case when his activities are learned.

But his self-awareness grows and the irrepressible mania stirs within him.

His lack of success and his lack of interest in ordinary causes and ordinary careers turn O'Flaherty in upon himself. He begins to see himself. He is aware of an "inner madness" growing within him, forcing him to retire within the walls of his mind, to abandon the world in which he was a helpless straw blown in the wind. "Ignorant, without belief," without the will to use his intellect for his own personal gain or power, he sees he must remain a wreck unless he accepts the role that nature had destined him for. Shrinking from the world's magnificent tumult, he takes refuge in the world of his imagination. "Hidden there from observation" he can "mime the outer strength" he lacked "with wordy subtlety" (pp. 349–50). Like Stephen Dedalus, who said, "I go to encounter for the millionth time the reality of experience and to forge in the smithy of my soul the uncreated conscience of my race," O'Flaherty chooses his role and chooses his exile, his native rock, his Aran: "A godless hermit, I began my communion with the cliffs, the birds, the wild animals, and the sea of my native land."

O'Flaherty had made his choice, adopting with Joyce the motto of Lucifer, *Non serviam.* Blessed and cursed with the madness of prophecy, "the greatest sin in the eyes of the herd," he had chosen, as he said in *Shame the Devil,* to "stand beyond good and evil," to become a man "without the right to love or hate" (p. 184). That book, written to tell the truth about himself, is essentially a self-study of the consequences of that choice. For when O'Flaherty made the choice described at the end of *Two Years,* he was not yet a writer, nor was he fully aware of the torments that "most strange of all forms of insanity, the mania of genius" (p. 192), would impose upon him.

It is one of his concerns to understand and recognize this duality of nature—the claims of the world and the claims of art that pull at him so violently. On three occasions in *Shame the Devil* this split gives rise to hallucinatory dialogues between O'Flaherty's contending personae. In the first, his conscience appears to him and upbraids him for his neglect of his family responsibilities as he plunges all his money on a horse race. But O'Flaherty the artist sees his conscience as a paltry fellow, an aspect of himself he is ashamed of. As an artist, marriage means nothing to him except possibly as material for use in his work. And at that moment the artist is more concerned about the beauty of a weasel he remembers seeing in Aran the year before. This conscience, this human part of himself which desires to love and be loved, is a

weakness in his nature. O'Flaherty the artist recalls observing O'Flaherty the man during a nervous breakdown, when the artist sees that
"when a man is bolt upright against annihilation he stands so far apart
from other beings that he can get no assistance from them" (p. 76).
The man calls hysterically for help and even tries to make the artist
afraid of God, but the artist is detached and faintly amused, for he is
able to study in that part of himself the shabbiness of human nature.

The hallucination disappears only to reappear in a reversed role
as O'Flaherty the man recalls his duties to his own wife and child as
he observes a man bid his family farewell in a railroad station. Now
it is O'Flaherty the artist who is the hallucination, and the artist chides
the man for his sentimental concerns. The artist uses the man, is master
of the man who would be just a timid common fellow without him.
And when the man protests and talks about the blessings of love, the
holiest thing in life, the artist says that the holiest thing in life is only
holy when it is food for the imagination. The artist would cut off the
man's feet to write a phrase and annihilate him for the sake of creating
something perfect. When the man says that even if he is merely the
artist's mask, he should not lose self-respect through disorderly conduct, the artist argues that it is only through disorderly conduct that
he can keep his self-respect, for this keeps the herd back, keeps him
an outcast from society whose rewards and flatteries could ruin him.
The artist must be an "angel of discontent," scorning public applause
and luxuries, "as ruthless with himself as an ancient hermit scourging
himself with a spiked thong." "That way alone is the way to perfection
for a creative writer" (p. 103). The artist must live alone within the
fortress of the man's body to carry on his war against self-deceit and
intellectual cowardice. When the man groans in despair at the thought
of this burden and asks when it will cease, the artist answers only
when the body is a carcass stiff in death and unresponsive to the fire
of lust and the beauties of nature. But then the artist bids the man
rise up and look at a group of children singing in a nearby carriage, to
look at them with the artist's eyes, who is "triumphant in the knowledge" that his love has "looked upon the face of God and therefore
must eschew all human bondage." And the man looks and feels purified and exalted. "All is holy," the train seems to say (p. 105).

As the artist cannot tolerate the responsibilities of family or the
ties of love or the demands of conventional social respectability, so he
cannot tolerate any other refuge that the man might attempt to take.
In *Shame the Devil*, when the man is thrilled by the nobility of the
Breton fishermen and the nobility that the cause of communism and

world revolution takes on in their persons and begins to see himself
marching triumphantly in that cause, the artist returns again. That, he
says, is a form of idealism that would be absolutely ruinous to his
work. "If a writer makes himself the idol of the mob by voicing the
ambitions of the mob, then he is reduced to the common level of the
mob's intelligence" (p. 216). The man at that time is full of love for
his fellow men and has no wish to rise above them, but the artist accuses him of cowardice, of being prepared to attach himself to anything when danger threatens. Now the man, who had just before convinced himself that he had been rehabilitated by his strong humanitarian feelings, falls into an even deeper pit of despair. But the artist
assures him that he has now escaped but does not realize it. The pit
is not the torture of mind the man suffers—"a continual vacillation
between one enthusiasm and another, a rapid passage from despair to
exaltation and from exaltation to despair." The pit is indifference born
of satisfied passions and self-satisfaction. Now the artist bids the man
renew his acquaintance with the earth, the sea, and the air, which are
man's "substance and his sustenance." "In that lies your chance of
regaining peace" (pp. 216–17).

The very nature of genius causes this duality. In his fable, *The
Ecstasy of Angus*,[6] O'Flaherty tells how this spirit came into the world.
In some far-off, golden day Angus, the god of love, son of youth,
through his beauty had inspired all nature to procreation, and thus was
the land of Banba peopled until the crowded land offered no more
room for generation. Discord begins, and famine and desolation. In
anguish for his people Angus goes to Mananaan, ancient god of the
encircling sea, to ask for aid, that the margins of the sea be rolled
back and his land be allowed to grow. He is repulsed with violent
storms and is driven, exhausted, to seek shelter.

When he awakens from a restful sleep, he sees a woman of extraordinary beauty, the fairy princess, Fand. Although pledged to
chastity lest he lose his youth and corruption be loosed upon the
world, he yields to her extraordinary beauty and magic temptations
in a perfect ecstasy of lust and love. Possessing his seed, Fand, now
to be the mother of a host of kings, leaves Angus exhausted and asleep.
When he awakens, all his beauty and youth have vanished. He sees
a great tree which has grown miraculously in the night, and a gloomy
spirit nearby. This gloomy spirit, with "evil and terrifying" eyes, is
yet fascinating; for his eyes, like those of a snake, hold "the glorious
melancholy of incurable happiness, the lust of conquest and the pride
of genius" (p. 39). The spirit identifies himself as the Genius of Un-

rest, and the tree as the Tree of Knowledge. He is neither god nor human but part of universal space, a realm unknown as yet to gods and humans. He tells Angus what has happened and what will be. All the gods are dead by Angus' act, and Fand will conceive a godless son, of the earth's substance and Angus' image. His seed, through the Tree of Knowledge and spirit of Genius, shall conquer the universe: "I shall enter unto him at birth and impregnate his mind with my quality, which shall give him no peace, until the cycle of his life has been completed and he hands on his task to his successors" (p. 41).

But Angus, not to be reconciled for the loss of his youth, curses the child to be born that he be forever under the spell of the maddening lust that has caused Angus' downfall. He curses the land of Banba that continual war shall desecrate its beauty and the people of Banba, unless they rise and slay his son. As Angus dies, the cry of a new-born babe comes from the tree: "Hail! Genius is born" (p. 43).

It was this very sort of thing that O'Flaherty felt was taking place within himself. Genius is the quality of being possessed, being driven, being used by a more than human force. It is what Yeats expresses when in "Byzantium" he says: "I hail the superhuman;/ I call it death-in-life and life-in-death." When thus possessed, by his "creative mania," as O'Flaherty calls it, then all mere human values cease to have a meaning: "All that man is,/ All mere complexities,/ The fury and the mire of human veins."

O'Flaherty recalls in *Shame the Devil* how, "drunk with creative enthusiasm" while writing *The Puritan*, he went to visit the grave of his mother. And recalling it, it was another person who stood there: "He smiled and looked about him, looting the scene with fierce, avaricious eyes, impervious to remorse, gloating over the majesty of the human intellect that can transcend the tragedy of death and turn it into ecstasy" (p. 16). But as O'Flaherty recalls the scene, the creative fire is dead within him, and he feels all the pain as he sees his mother's narrow grave, sparsely covered with sea-bleached grass, being a part of the common ruin, even as the land itself is being devoured by the sea, mocking all man's endeavors.

For O'Flaherty, genius is above all mere complexities. It is concerned with a different realm, "the cold majesty of Beauty," and to attain that, all mere human pleasures and aspirations must be forsaken. The writer must look at life, he said in *Shame the Devil*, "with the calmness born of understanding instead of wasting his frenzy in the destruction of icons and in teaching false philosophies to fools" (p. 154). After his argument about Marxism with the Jewish girl in Paris, he thinks himself a fool. He is really indifferent about Communists and Fascists. Their objectives are meaningless to him as a poet "who is only concerned with catching the wraith of beauty and bringing her to a life of flesh and blood with words; beautiful singing words" (p. 34). As much as he is impressed by the creative vitality of the Russian people in his visit there, as confident he is that this vitality must overwhelm decadent Europe, and as much as he would like to ally himself with such a movement, he can generate no sustained enthusiasm. His is the role of the onlooker on the human drama, to cheer or hiss the characters as they play well or badly. When he "soars in sunlit splendour," as he says in *Shame the Devil,* the petty loves of geese and ganders are no concern of his: "Why should I care if a ruler's head wore a royal crown or Lenin's cloth cap? My business being to watch and to sing without impartiality of man's thoughts and movements" (p. 145).

So O'Flaherty vacillates between exhilaration and despair, from detachment to enthusiasm, between the artist and the man. It is the man who is the Communist, the soldier, he Irishman, the man who craves belonging, human sympathy. For when the creative fire is out, O'Flaherty says, then he wallows in the pit between two heights. Then he can take sides, because in his weakness it is necessary to take sides and have a patron. "But when the little sorceress fans the flames within my navel and I am on the height, human controversy about right and wrong is like the anarchic screeching of the wind above the overwhelming sea. Then all is holy" (p. 208).

That, then, is the mood, the aspect of things that O'Flaherty sees when his creativity is upon him. It is not exactly clear. It is something that he continually attempts to define. It is the overt subject of *Two Years, Shame the Devil, The Ecstasy of Angus,* and *The Black Soul,* and it is the problem on which *I Went to Russia* founders. For even a commissioned book like this, in which O'Flaherty sets out to tell of what he sees in new revolutionary Russia, eventually turns into a discussion of his artistic obligation. This is more than the usual contemporary concern for the place of the artist in society. O'Flaherty's concern is beyond this. Although he may talk about the artist in society, the place he should take, and though he may rail at the critics who do not appreciate his books and scorn the tasteless middle classes who demand mediocrity, all this is conventional. It is what almost every writer says.

O'Flaherty's concern is for himself and for his gift, for the pressing burden of an obligation. He has been set apart from other men. As an artist he is a seer, a demon, a druid. He sees himself in the lofty roles of Faust or Satan or Prometheus, who will not yield—lofty, arrogant, possessing great power and because of it threatened with great ruin. Even this is the conventional romantic role, and O'Flaherty's experience goes beyond this. He is aware of his detachment, and he casts himself as the superhuman observer, beyond good and evil, like Joyce's God, paring his fingernails. But that is not the complete answer. For there is always the struggle. He cannot reach a conclusion and build a theory, he says in *I Went to Russia:* "In art, ambitious theories are always a sign of impotence and laziness and mediocrity" (p. 229). He has no patience with theory or technique. But he cannot reject this world and build a new world from his imagination. Each new creative attempt means a renewal of the whole struggle, the struggle with himself and his soul which yields his special kind of vision.

Almost all of his work is a record of these struggles. Art, he goes on to say, is not based on any preconceived dogma, "it springs out of life and is brought to life by a vision in the mind of the artist, which in itself, comes into the mind from a wild fever in the bowels and is inexplicable." Yet in O'Flaherty it is in a way, explicable—at least in terms of certain forces, circumstances, and equilibriums that cause and result in creativity. For his detachment and arrogance which separate him from the world in a special way do not bring him back to it in the form of creative impulse. They are just a part of the circumstances. Essentially his art springs from despair, and despair from intellect. It is intellect that sets him apart from his fellows, that lets him reason out man's destiny, that sees in itself enormous power if harnessed for the social good. But it is intellect also that sees the futility of all human endeavor.

O'Flaherty's reveries are full of his thoughts of death and annihilation. In *Shame the Devil* he describes an experience at the Paris races, where he suddenly sees the whole spectacle in the grand perspective of time: "Ten million years and they were tiny bladders floating in a warm pool, whence they climbed the cliff unto the shape of monstrous elephants and whales and megalomaniac men begetting gods in their fantastic brains. Ten million years and all pass once more into a savage wilderness of prowling stars" (p. 85). God, he says, is an invented state of perfection for which man strives, "which we have deliberately invented in order to protect ourselves against the discovery that annihilation is inevitable" (p. 88). Shakespeare's powerful rhyme may outlive the monuments of princes, but it cannot outlive death "which clutches all things in its jaws, even the earth itself and the proud sun with all its fire" (p. 90). He tells in *Two Years* how his despairing unbelief "pictures the universe as a foolish galaxy of toy balloons strung by an idiot in space" (p. 49).

Against this view of annihilation given by the intellect the artist must set himself. This is his ultimate challenge. When he considers Joseph Conrad's work, it is in this view that O'Flaherty finds Conrad lacking, for Conrad had *accepted*, had acquiesced in certain bounds not to be surpassed. He had not gone to the brink; he had not faced the challenge. Even Shelley falls short, because he "believed in his heart in the romantic God, and his revolt was the outraged horror of the sinner, not of the fearless, cold-eyed adventurer who curls his lips at all that has been and peers over the brink of chaos in search of truth." [7] This is what O'Flaherty the artist meant about being "bolt upright against annihilation" when the artist "stands so far from other beings that he can get no assistance from them." This is the moment of truth. The intellect of the artist functions to separate him, absolutely. This is his black soul that rejects everthing, that sees everything under the aspect of eternity and all human endeavor as futility. The artist must know all in order to reject all. And when all is rejected, and there appears to be nothing, and death seems the only choice, then life comes, and vision, and creativity. Then all is holy.

Such an experience as this O'Flaherty recounts in *Shame the Devil* when that which was dead within him reawakens, and the story "The Caress" springs into his consciousness: "Now it was no effort to write it. It rushed out of its own accord. The words danced to my piping. The rhythm flowed without interruption, finding its own balance without needing my direction. And as soon as I began to write it, my youth returned. . . . But it had nothing to do with truth, if truth lies hidden in the social shibboleths about which I had been raving. Now they were nothing more than the cries of pain of a pregnant woman, 'sound and fury, signifying nothing'" (p. 242). It was despair that brought him to this; and at the moment that despair seemed absolute, life asserted itself, the life within him burst out from the confining shackles of reason, burst out to meet, to join with, and fuse with the life around him—the unthinking life of nature that does not ask a meaning. He scoffs at Truth as a "slippery whore" whose face changes at every second he tries "to read it" with his mind. "Lay off," he tells his mind. Truth "will have none of your black-fingered groping." "She's only heated by the lance of beauty, straight from the loins of life." The final stage of creation is acceptance. The artist is "a vessel into which life pours sweet wine or vinegar, from a hand that is indifferently careless." "Wine or vinegar," O'Flaherty says, "I must accept and drink it to the dregs" (p. 234–35).

This is the final, total, complete acceptance, not of the intellect, not of the cowardly man yearning for obliteration of self in any cause, but of the artist. It is an acceptance which is not possible before complete rejection. The artist must continually put himself through these agonies to achieve creation. Or rather, by his very nature as an artist he is put through these agonies. He is used. It is his gift. It is the source of all his misery and all his joy. The artist is like Job, afflicted, driven to curse his lot; yet always in the face of death, life wells up. But he cannot accept the easy consolations of orthodox beliefs. His mind drives him to quest, forces him to reject, until finally, when all seems lost, when the question is overwhelming and no answer seems possible, a voice comes out of the whirlwind, mysteriously. Nature is presented in all its mystery and glory. Then Job knows that he has uttered what he did not understand, "things too wonderful for me, which I know not." "I have heard of thee by the hearing of the ear: but now mine eye seeth thee." It is this kind of acceptance—the acceptance of absurdity—that the artist must achieve; what his eye sees after this acceptance is his artistic vision.

Thus O'Flaherty can say in *Shame the Devil* that "the greatest virtue of genius is permanent dissatisfaction," and that "they who effect a harmony between their reason and their actions lose the power to create beauty" (p. 205). The cycles of exaltation and despair are essential to creation. Personal harmony and satisfaction are the pitfalls of the artist, who has chosen to perfect the work and not the life. Wanting happiness as a man, the artist must yet seek despair. O'Flaherty says in *Two Years* that though he thinks the harlot is a mean, filthy, and odious being, he as an artist is still attracted to her as he is to other objectionable human types because they "arouse that remorse of conscience which is the necessary prelude to a bout of creative energy" (p. 121). This is how the artist must be ruthless with himself, flogging himself like the ancient hermits. Always he seeks the ultimate negation, the Hard No, as Fiedler says, "and having endured a vision of the meaninglessness of existence . . . chooses to render the absurdity he perceives, chooses to know it and to make it known . . ." to attain "the most terrible and improbable of all human creations, beauty itself." [8]

With this view of art and the artist, it is not surprising that O'Flaherty writes almost nothing about artistic technique. If anything, he is suspicious of technique. "In order to be a work of genius, a novel must offer something more than perfect style," he says in his review of Powys' *Mr. Tasker's Gods* in *The Irish Statesman* (March 7, 1925). In his first attempts to learn the art of writing he tells in *Two Years* of reading and rereading De Maupassant's works and attempting unsuccessfully to write in that style (p. 313). He concluded that the art of writing was incomprehensible. Art for O'Flaherty is essentially whatever is created by genius in an inspired moment. It is not an exercise of technique but a spontaneous overflow of powerful passions. Art is the vision that results from a special form of spiritual exercise. Art is a struggle not only with technique but with spirit.

When O'Flaherty can most clearly see himself and his role, he can see that as an artist he must observe and not participate in any movement, regardless of how noble, that aims for the betterment of mankind. It is not an easy role for him to take. He desperately wanted to throw himself into a cause to relieve himself of the terrible loneliness and anguish that he saw in his role as an artist. At times he tried to make himself believe that through communism or Ireland or the two somehow combined he could find a life that would let him be both a man and an artist, in a new revitalized world where the artist's role would be to sing and celebrate mankind's highest endeavors. But the concern is always personal. If there is no place in the world where O'Flaherty the man and O'Flaherty the artist can be reconciled, he will have the world remade. It is a hope that he can cling to—anything to save him from facing, alone, the terror of his own existence. But this is really an evasion. As he says in *Shame the Devil,* "when the fire is out, when I wallow in the mire of the pit between two heights . . . then it is necessary to take sides and have a patron" (p. 208). When the fire is out, O'Flaherty the man struggles desperately for a spiritual home, which he continually sees, because he wants so much to see, just beyond the horizon in communism or a revitalized Ireland.

When O'Flaherty first declared himself a Communist, it was more from the impulse of the situation than any deep intellectual conviction. Although at the time he had read some of the works of Marx, Engels, Connolly, Bebel, and various other writers, except to force him to the conclusion that God, as his mother had known him, was dead, they had not affected his attitude toward life. But when the straight-laced Scotswoman that he was forced to work with in London at the beginning of *Two Years* called him a Bolshevik, this aroused his interest. Previously, the term had not had much meaning, but now he began to realize how dead was the one culture and how much he did not want to become a part of it. Perhaps bolshevism offered the promise of the new god. At least it offered a banner under which to revolt. In some vague idealistic way he identified the Communists with "the dynamic force that was going to bring a new beauty into the consciousness of man, a new poetry, a new consciousness of the universe," but mostly he identified them with "discontent and rebellion" (p. 72). And this initially was the appeal.

In *Two Years* he tells of his experience in a condensed-milk factory where he first was affected by "the god of machinery" (p. 236). He was impressed by the power of the factory, and in that power beauty. For the machine seemed to him to offer man a chance to subjugate the earth, and it was the machine, not Karl Marx, that was the father of social revolution. With the machine, where a town springs up about the factory, "a real revolution in human conduct is brought about." But though he found no real objection to the factory and the life about it, on the first pretext he left. "I also, like Karl Marx, am too lazy to work," he said (pp. 241–42).

Impressed as he was with the new god of the machine, especially as this was related to the real meaning of the Communist social revolution, he did not become evangelical about his new convictions until he met John Joseph Peterson, "a new sort of saint, preaching the cult of a new god, without the repulsive sanctimoniousness of the old Christian saints, balancing the delicate idealism of belief in a higher form of human society with a coarse and sensual materialism" (p. 254). Peterson, who after a hectic childhood had become a social revolutionary, was a member of the Industrial Workers of the World and preached continually to O'Flaherty about "the most beautiful thing in his life, the conversion of man to a belief in the machine age" (p. 259). Impressed as much by the man, who exhibited the wild power and beauty that O'Flaherty always admired, as by the creed, which espoused the liberation of the working classes from wage slavery, O'Flaherty, too, became an agitator.

When Peterson and O'Flaherty parted company, O'Flaherty gained a new perspective on the social movement through his brother in Boston. Up to this time it had been the wild spirit of revolt and the power of the machine that had most engaged him. Through his brother and the more orderly medium of the James Connolly Club he now learned the philosophical background of socialism; but though he admired the intelligence of the Boston socialists and learned from them about economics and capitalism, their movement lacked the revolutionary cast—the wild upheaval by which he thought life would be reinvigorated. O'Flaherty was not interested in an orderly reconstruction of the existing system, and though for a while he continued to preach socialism and get fired from a succession of jobs because of this, his enthusiasm soon waned.

It was through a Russian girl he met in Greenwich Village that he thought he discovered the true spirit of the revolution he was seeking, not in socialism but in the energy of the Russian people that was the driving spirit behind bolshevism. Though the girl was anti-Bolshevik, it made no difference. The new movement was the upheaval of a people, he says in *Two Years*, the unleashing of great creative power which only Dostoevsky had understood (who died before it came to pass) and prophesied (p. 334). But O'Flaherty was not constituted to be a propagandist in the world revolution that then seemed imminent. Tired of his aimless wandering and aware of an alien spirit within him that kept him aloof from social movements, he returned to Ireland. Although he played a prominent part in an uprising of the unemployed who seized the Rotunda in Dublin in the early part of 1922 and hoisted a red flag, this was the end of his career as a social agitator. This last action seemed to O'Flaherty, in *Shame the Devil*, to split him irrevocably from the majority of Irish people and make him "a public menace to faith, morals, and property, a Communist, an atheist, a scoundrel of the worst type, a man whom thousands would burn at the stake if they had the courage" (p. 22). But in effect this drove him into that artistic side of his nature which held aloof from participation, and to London, into the influence of Edward Garnett.

In all of O'Flaherty's letters to Garnett from 1923 until 1932 there is not one mention of communism, socialism, or other concerns about the organization of society. Garnett directed himself to O'Flaherty the artist. In *Shame the Devil* O'Flaherty recalls rushing to his typewriter to write a tirade against social injustice only to hear in his mind Garnett's voice reminding him that "To the artist, everything that exists justifies itself by the fact of its existence" (p. 230). For O'Flaherty this precluded all humanitarian concerns. Yet, according to H. E. Bates, Garnett was not unaware of social movements but felt, rather, that they imperiled the artist, not only in distracting from his art but in undermining the very basis of culture. For Garnett art was aristocratic, and he feared mass culture: "I think that this is a beastly system—the Industrial—that my sympathies are with the workers. At the same time the workers destroy beauty and grace and dignity as thoroughly as does the commercial class. They want to breed irrespective of the result of breeding. There's a great cheat in all socialism." [9] Obviously Garnett and O'Flaherty shared little intellectual ground regarding the machine age and the role of the workers. Their overriding dedication to art was their common ground, and when in a letter to Garnett (November 9, 1923) O'Flaherty vows "no rhetoric, no philosophy, no bias" in his writing, it is a pledge to purge himself of those vestiges of the agitator that might remain and prove detrimental to his art.

Never committed without reservation to the Communist cause, regardless of occasional flights of rhetorical rant, already in 1926 O'Flaherty could see that communism was alien to the Irish. In an article in the *Irish Statesman*, "Fascism or Communism" (May 8, 1926), O'Flaherty sees these movements as essentially alike in depriving man of freedom and personal liberty. And though he feels that great men like Parnell were more akin to the Communists, Ireland was not suited to either fascism or communism. Rather, the Irish had a kind of independence like the ancient Greeks. But O'Flaherty's chief objection to fascism and communism was not on ideological grounds. It was the fact that "these doctrines, which attracted the best types and the best brains in the countries of their origin, attract all the numbskulls, cranks, hooligans, sentimentalists and scoundrels" in foreign countries.

Nevertheless, in 1930 O'Flaherty set out on a trip to Russia to see for himself. His motives were not idealistic. In his opening pages of *I Went to Russia* he announces he is writing the book "for the sole purpose of making some money," such books about bolshevism then being in fashion. And he disclaims all political beliefs: "Bolshevism means no more to me than Lord Beaverbrook's Empire Crusade or the Roman Catholic Religion" (p. 10). Despite his cynicism he is not unimpressed by what is happening in the new Russia. From the time he sets foot on board the Russian ship he is struck with the vitality and religious fervor of the Russian Communists. They seem to him like an "avalanche prowling down, irresistibly upon Europe, sweeping before them all the decadent rubble into which our civilization and power has subsided" (p. 39). The movement is not an idea, but a force, a religion. The captain of the ship is a fanatic. O'Flaherty is awed by the force and yet feels cut off: "I again felt that no matter how much I wanted to become a Bolshevik, no matter how much I admired their ideas, their youth, their virility, I must remain outside; or even if brought in, baptised in their faith, grafted on their society, I must still remain suspect and in reality an alien, because a different religion and culture had become part of my being" (p. 47).

The more he is exposed to Russians the more he is struck by the religiosity of the movement, the saints and symbols, the utter commitment. He sees the immensity of the country as the cause. As a scene the country has the "grandeur of immensity" which affects the mind with "mystical ideas and ambitious philosophies, about the world and its own relation to the universe" (p. 117). This is the force that has been unleashed and that he sees at its purest in bustling Moscow where great gangs of workers rebuild the city with energy and joy, while at the corners of the buildings little red flags fluttered, "mystical symbols, signifying that all work, both the building of houses and the night-long conferences in the Communist Party headquarters, was for the glory of the new god" (p. 249).

Although his reason for the trip to Russia was to make money, O'Flaherty was also aware that he had made the trip to find a new purpose in life, something to which he could attach himself, "a community as vital and as worthy of great poetry as Elizabethan England" (p. 51). Despite the obvious defects, which O'Flaherty did not over-look—defects mostly in people—this community did seem worthy, yet he could not help feeling alien and hostile. Part of this was due to that side of himself, allied to his creativity, that must always be an onlooker: "To me they are all equally beautiful, the kind women, the red-nosed generals, the idealists, the enslavers, the Quakers, and the brooding fanatics with visions of world conquest and of human equality to be imposed by violence." Because of his "almost insane incapacity" for believing in the "topical religions" of mankind, he must always play the part of the "onlooker in the stalls" (p. 208). Nowhere was he more aware of the distance between his conception of the artist and the Communists' than at the Bureau of Revolutionary Literature, where he was astounded to see literature being mass-produced on a regular schedule along strict Communist lines. The bureau seemed foolish and unrealistic because for him writers were "by nature anarchists, jealous of governance" (p. 210).

Pulled one way by his being a Western European fully involved in and shaped by this culture, which though dying contained all his values, another by his artistic nature which made all activity material for his art and precluded commitment, and still another by his passionate desire to throw himself into a movement that would give his life direction and purpose, O'Flaherty plunged into the life of the people to make some order out of his chaos. At the end he concluded that there really was nothing new. He had partaken of every form of life in Moscow and concluded that underneath "the ludicrous evangelistic Communism on the surface" existed the "same greedy, ambitious, admirable human nature" (p. 281). Only the names of things were changed. People would be people; and regardless of the new ordering, human vices and virtues for him would remain the same. Yet when he returned to Western Europe "without a future, without sane ambition" he became deeply depressed: "I felt indeed lost, an outcast from both camps, too old and degenerate to belong to the Bolshevist religion, too intelligent to worship the degraded wreck of what once was European civilisation" (p. 298).

With this melancholy, deepened by the feeling that he had betrayed a noble cause in writing as he had done about Russia, O'Flaherty began the spiritual quest recorded in *Shame the Devil*. For as he looked back upon his Russian experiences and book he considered it "the greatest folly" of his life that his behavior there had been so flippant and his book a "criminal mockery" of that workshop "where the civilisation of the future is being hammered out by the gigantic labour of heroic millions" (p. 135). But by some malicious quirk he did not understand, what he wrote was "flippant and without sincerity," displeasing those he wished to please and amusing those he had hoped to irritate. And it had failed in its personal spiritual purpose: "Instead of helping me to restate the purpose of my life and to get fresh vigour from that restatement, it hastened the tempo of my disillusionment" (p. 151).

If his early interest in communism was as a gesture of defiance to separate himself from a society he found repugnant, by the time of *Shame the Devil* the problem of communism was woven tightly into his spiritual fabric. In this record of spiritual crisis communism stands for man's highest principles and aspirations. It is the dream of divine perfection. It stands for struggle and humanity and human sympathy. It is the cause to which O'Flaherty can ally himself without reservation because within it are contained all of man's highest goals. Embodied in fine men like the Breton fishermen, communism is perfection itself: "Here is truth, then, and virtue and God and certainty; to be at one with men like Pierre, who are going to be the aristocrats of the future. Men who worship machines and shall be masters of machines and shall use them for the welfare of mankind. . . . here is the restoration of true aristocracy, about which a poet may sing an epic without being a panderer" (p. 210). This kind of communism is not only perfection, but a spiritual home for both O'Flaherty the man and O'Flaherty the artist, where the man can feel an unquestioning sense of belonging and the artist can participate in the celebration of the common life of mankind. For O'Flaherty communism meant "to care." It meant selfless participation. It was not an abstract theory to be discussed but a demand for action—a demand for absolute commitment, without reservation, to a cause. And mainly, it was personal. What he sought through communism was not an objective reordering of society but a subjective reordering of his own soul.

Joseph Wood Krutch in *The Modern Temper* projected on a general scale what O'Flaherty felt on a personal. What wracked O'Flaherty as a personal spiritual poverty—an intense longing for belief, for purpose, for identification with a force greater than himself—Krutch saw as a characteristic of the spiritual poverty of the age. Searching for belief is evidence that vitality, the crude energy that O'Flaherty admired in the Russians, is already gone. Vital peoples have no need for belief. They act. And when this vitality is gone, lost through an excess of intellect, it cannot be recovered, because a man cannot reason himself back to unquestioning life. Life is revived only through another race or class who live unquestioningly for the sake of life itself. Thus, Krutch said, even the Russian resurgence and the new life being built there could offer no hope for Western man, where skepticism had too deep a hold ever to be replaced by faith. Man cannot make himself simple again; he is forever within the cultural tradition whose values he shares. If his tradition has exhausted its vitality and brought itself to the asking of ultimate questions that lead to despair, then that is the condition that must be faced.

O'Flaherty could not be a Communist, whether he willed or not. It was not a choice he could make. He could not choose not to be a member of Western culture. He could not choose not to be tortured by doubts and questionings about the meaning of life. That which he most admired about the Russian Communists in *I Went to Russia* was exactly what he could not have or participate in: their unquestioning dedication to work, not for a reason, but as an end in itself, possessed of "the earth's electric force." He saw, exactly as Krutch did, that our civilization had reached its climax: "It is degenerating. Its force is spent. There are no fresh hordes within it to be trained, no fresh human resources to be exploited" (p. 94). And the conclusion that he reached for himself was the conclusion that Krutch reached for Western culture in general.

O'Flaherty's relationship to communism must be understood in this spiritual sense. He was not at all concerned with communism as a new and better economic system. He has the greatest derision for the Norwegian Communist for whom revolution is "not of a dynamic force, a spiritual renaissance, but a cold, mercenary exchange by calculating mobs of one system of economy for another" (p. 90). He saw communism as a religion because this is what he wanted—a spiritual home, an all-absorbing principle that would absorb his being, a refuge from despair. And regardless of his despising the one and admiring the other, the same gnawing intellect that convinced him that the Christian God was dead kept him from being a part of the communism he thought to be alive.

After the Rotunda affair, O'Flaherty felt that an almost irreconcilable split now divided him from his countrymen. At his return in 1924 his intentions were more to advance his own cause as a writer than to support any Irish cause, but as he joined with the young radicals it seemed that these interests might coalesce. As he had imagined himself singing a wild song of revolt in the Communist cause, a celebrant of a new wave of vitality, so this appeared possible for him in relation to the Irish. In this spirit he wrote the articles in *The Irish Statesman* urging Ireland not to use passive resistance but to be proud of its gunshots and attacking *The Irish Statesman* itself, the platform for George Russell, one of "the old fogies," for lacking this wild vitality. O'Flaherty called it "non-Irish," "bourgeois," for the "well-fed middle man," "submerged beneath a rotting mound of British traditions." But the younger generation, he said, is tired of this, tired of "bravado and mountebanks." As a member of the younger generation he felt he was one of those who would determine if Irish civilization would be a force in Europe.

There was no denying the force of the Russian Revolution, but O'Flaherty's efforts to create this same kind of force in Ireland were doomed to failure. In February, 1927, George Russell discussed, in an editorial the Report of the Committee on Evil Literature, a movement that would end in a censorship bill that would ban most of O'Flaherty's books in Ireland. Sean O'Casey, one of the best hopes for the new Ireland that O'Flaherty envisioned, left the country, sick of the literary cliques and the priestcraft and the reaction to his plays. O'Flaherty wrote to *The Irish Statesman* on December 17, 1927, that he was no longer much interested in the regeneration of the Irish people "too hopelessly sunk in intellectual barbarism to be capable of being saved by a single man."

In *Shame the Devil* O'Flaherty once more considered himself an outcast from the Irish people. He met a countryman named O'Donoghue and engaged in an argument with him. O'Donoghue expressed what O'Flaherty believed to be the general Irish reaction to his works. O'Flaherty's books were "obscene." "You defame your nation," he said. "You are one of a long line of degraded writers bought by the English to defame the Irish race" (p. 183). O'Flaherty could not but admire this passion which made O'Donoghue a "mouthpiece of his race": "I felt that I too was one of that race, that their passionate hatred was also mine and that its intensity made it beautiful. I could see why they were angry with me, believing that I did not appreciate their sufferings, or the struggle they were making to overcome their torturers. They believed that I mocked them, instead of fighting side by side with them and using my voice to state their case before the world. They believed that instead of singing them on to victory and peace I was harrying them with gibes and ill-timed criticism of their defects" (p. 184). It was not that O'Flaherty did not wish to belong to this race or this movement, but he could not make of Ireland what it was not—a force in the world—or of himself what he was not—one who could be a participant in any religion or political movement. As strong as was his desire to belong, he could not be other than the on-looker, the artist, "a man without the right to love or hate."

O'Flaherty's disillusionment with the Irish is set forth most scathingly in a little satirical tract, *A Tourist's Guide to Ireland* (1930).[10] Here O'Flaherty lambastes everything Irish—all the existing causes and creeds, all the social classes—in a way that would antagonize every-one. In the manner of eighteenth-century satire he writes what pur-ports to be a general guide for foreign tourists to enable them to make their way about the country most advantageously. In order to get any pleasure from a country which seems bent on eradicating pleasure, he says, an understanding of social conditions and controlling social structure is needed. His book goes on to explain.

No aspect of society is immune from his attack. The priests use religion to enslave the people. The parish priest has a finger in every pie, exacting his tariff "from the first yell at birth until the sod falls on them in their grave" (p. 21). His whole concern is his own power, and he is opposed to all ideas and culture as a threat to this power. Even the state is an enemy because it has usurped temporal power from the Pope. These parish priests, of greedy peasant stock, dominate country life. And the fearsome religious priests, Jesuits and the like, dominate educa-tion and the intellectual life. They cover the country with 'the heavy, hairy garment of Puritanism," opposing all pleasure and extolling "the lamentations of the damned" "as the only fitting cry for an unfortu-nate human being" (pp. 49-50). They oppose all writing that might challenge their concept of the universe and, through their great influence with the middle classes, can stop any periodical that appears to be non-Christian or intellectual. O'Flaherty must have had the short-lived *To-Morrow* in mind when he noted that "on rare occasions, when groups of citizens have tried to publish periodicals of that sort these periodicals have come to a sudden end" (p. 54). The whole country is on the verge of becoming a "clerical kingdom," and O'Flaherty sees Ireland "as a beautiful sad-faced country that is being rapidly covered by a black rash" (p. 56).

This is the dominant influence, and it is so powerful that nothing else can be taken seriously. Politics takes its tone from religion, and politicians make of Ireland a living woman—a Kathleen ni Houlihan or Roisin Dubh, or the Old Woman of Beara—a kind of mystical entity to which love and loyalty are due, but only with the intent of preying upon her. They concern themselves with the soul of Ireland, rather than her body, and preach "that Holy Ireland is above such coarse ambitions as wealth, culture, bathrooms, tooth brushes, and machinery" (p. 71). For O'Flaherty, parties and programs are equally foolish and ineffectual. The Civil War over the wording of an oath was an incredible foolishness that resulted in nothing: "the position is exactly what it was before the war and the argument" (p. 74). The attempt to revive the Gaelic language is a political gimmick; and though the native speakers continue to emigrate until it appears that none will be left, "the government have hired a few men in Dublin to manufacture Irish words according as they are needed" (p. 81). The revolutionary groups are without leaders and clear programs:

> Their passwords, their secret movements and their hair-raising programmes must be taken with a smile because they mean nothing of it. Here again he [the tourist] will see the result of the priestly culture of the art of conversation, for the activities of these groups never lead any further than conversation, unless it be some utterly purposeless act committed by what Dostoievsky called the "Contemplatives": those fellows who meditate for years and then suddenly, for no apparent reason, burn a house, murder a man, or go on a pilgrimage to Lourdes or Jerusalem. (p. 86)

Only with the peasant is there any hope, and though O'Flaherty says he likes him—"the only natural type of human being in this country that I consider an honour to the country and to mankind" (p. 109)— he says nothing to endear himself to the Irish peasant. The peasant is "like a mangy dog" that needs to be rid of the parasites of priests and politicians. O'Flaherty chides "those literary hirelings that still dishonour our country by trying to persuade us that the peasant is a babbling child of God" (p. 110), for it is not the peasant's natural innocence and ignorance that O'Flaherty commends, but his potential. "Peasants, as compared to civilised human beings, are children" (p. 113). He admires those qualities they share with children—their laughter, their simplicity, their lack of vulgarity, their uniformity with nature. But the peasant must grow from this childhood, and on every side "rapacious rogues" surround the stupefied peasants; they "fall upon every little morsel produced by the peasants and tear it to pieces in their ravenous beaks" (p. 131).

O'Flaherty's pessimism is not complete. Though no hope for leadership exists among the priests or the priest-ridden politicians, or the ineffectual revolutionary groups, here and there is "a sign and portent of salvation, some brave soul standing up and crying out the gospel of revolt and salvation" (p. 133). "These voices crying from the depths of hell shall bring up great forces of revolt, armed with the great wisdom of the damned, and they shall spread over the land and inhabit it with free men and women, free from usurers and sooth-sayers" (p. 134). When he was among those who seized the Rotunda, O'Flaherty must have seen himself as a "brave soul," "crying out the gospel of revolt and salvation." And when he returned to Ireland in 1924 and took an active part in the literary movement, it was with this spirit that he wanted to infuse the young radicals opposed to priest-craft and to the established well-fed bourgeois he thought to be dominating the literary circles. Even when his most objective view tells him that there is no hope for a new civilization to arise from the native spirit of Ireland (as he saw arising in Russia) still he hopes.

O'Flaherty is not a systematic thinker nor is there any reason to demand that he be. Frank O'Connor believed that O'Flaherty's forte was "instinct, not reason." [11] There is little consistency about O'Fla-herty's intellectual position in regard to the makeup of the universe or man's proper social organization. He made no effort to achieve reasonable objective formulations of any world view. His concern was with himself and his relationship to the world, to the universe. It was harmony not truth he sought, for to him the *truth* was obvious, if truth is measured by the intellect: Man is a pompous little creature that has somehow appeared on the face of a planet careening blindly through space. He behaves selfishly, greedily, and foolishly, yet with his intellect he can better his condition immeasur-ably if he will throw off superstition and achieve what he is capable of. But regardless of his aspirations and achievements, he will die. And in the end, all is motion without purpose. Sometimes O'Flaherty dwells on one or the other aspect of this truth, but the one truth which dominates all is the final truth that intellect presents and O'Flaherty must battle to accept—that man must die and in the end all is motion without purpose. In the face of this all arguments about man as a social being appear shallow and irrelevant.

O'Flaherty's novels are built from the materials of his own life, as all writing must be, and so his novels are about the Aran Islands and Ireland, politics and revolutionary intrigue. But—and this is the most important consideration—O'Flaherty's main characters are built from the materials of his spiritual life, and their deepest concerns, like his, are not the objective situations that they are in, but how they might effect some kind of harmony between themselves and the awesome universe. O'Flaherty is not an objective thinker who looks out at the world to find truth as if truth could exist apart from him. First he is an individual with a desperate subjective need to make meaning out of his own existence. This is the standard of truth—truth is that which gives his life meaning. Ideas and theories do not exist apart from him but become aspects of his own personality. The world is an extension of himself. To solve the world's problems is to solve his own problems; to solve his own problems is to solve the world's problems.

The fundamental pattern of O'Flaherty's life and ideas being quest, he must find what he must do and what he must be. His concern is not for art, but what it means for him to be an artist; not for communism, but what it means for him to be a Communist; not Ireland, but what Ireland means to him. His quest does not take him out from himself to explore with curiosity this way of life or that, this theory or that, but always deeper into himself to find who *he* is. This is the overwhelming question beside which all others pall. O'Flaherty's life and ideas are the stuff of his art, but his ideas must be seen as intensely subjective qualities of his life; his life must be seen not as a series of events that molded and modified his opinions but as an intense and desperate search for a way to come to terms with the burden of his existence. This is the dominant quality of his art. Sometimes he can look at his characters, in his novels especially, and see them as no part of himself. But then there is no sympathy or no understanding, and the characters appear as harsh, brilliant satirical portraits, at which O'Flaherty is a master, or, in the case of women, as objects of desire lacking any real inner being.

When O'Flaherty moves into a character, however, when he views him with sympathy, the character becomes an aspect of himself. The character does not think, but is possessed by ideas which are more akin to feeling-states. And at the root is the overwhelming question of the meaning of his own existence. For O'Flaherty this is the ultimate fact. This is the source and goal of all thought and all striving. He can understand life in no other terms.

∽∽ III ∽∽

Into the Destructive Element

BECAUSE it gives the most forthright statement of the spiritual crisis which forms the basis for his creative expression, *The Black Soul* (1924) is perhaps O'Flaherty's most interesting novel. *The Black Soul* is about Fergus O'Connor, the Stranger, who comes to the bleak island of Inverara, off the western coast of Ireland, to regain his physical and mental health. Although the simple life of the island, the stimulating sea air, and the life close to nature begin to restore the Stranger to physical health, his black soul lies at the root of his problems, and until this part of his nature is restored to health, his complete recovery will be impossible. For the black soul—the intellectual, cynical, civilized force—destroys all values and renders life hopeless and meaningless.

Black soul is a spiritual state, a sickness of the soul, and a way of describing a vast and overwhelming cosmic uncertainty. The Stranger had been in Dublin "burrowing in the bowels of philosophy, trying to find consolation one day in religion, next day in anarchism, next day in communism, and rejecting everything as empty, false and valueless." Finally, "despairing of life, flying from it as from an ogre that had been torturing him, he had come to Inverara" (pp. 32–33). He seeks an answer and sense of permanence and belonging. His answer could not be found in religion because his intellect had convinced him that Christianity is one of the relics of the childhood of human thought. And he curses God for giving him a strong intellect until he remembers that there is no God and becomes still more depressed at having no one to blame. He feels sorry he cannot pray without losing his self-respect, because it would be "such a comfort to throw himself on the mercy of some Being that was stronger than nature" (p. 83).

In the grip of his soul sickness, nature for Fergus O'Connor is a terrifying thing, especially the sea. He listens to the voice of the sea, envisioning it crashing, rolling, returning. "Ha! It moved without purpose. That is life, motion without purpose." In the light of this discovery he has a vision, "for his brain had a weird faculty for presenting things to him vividly, as clearly as if they were filmed" (p. 87). He sees fat-bellied businessmen and the lean-faced men "with anger in their eyes and hunger in their stomachs, shouting ideas of revolution and liberty. All a farce. Does the sea have a purpose, the wind ideas?" (p. 88). He sees a man with a manuscript, and reading "he saw vermin crawling on the beautiful heroine's corpse even before she had fallen into her lover's arms in the last paragraph." He sees scientists and dictators, but all their actions are pointless, for "then the whole world froze up and skidded off through space. Another planet had collided with it" (p. 89). Nothing was assured "but the air, the earth, and the sea." The cormorants sitting stupidly on the Jagged Rock seem to speak: "We have lived here five hundred years . . . and we have heard it all, all before now! but tell us what does it end in? In ashes and oblivion" (p. 90).

This is the problem that the mind of man creates and the mind of man is powerless to solve: the awareness of our littleness amidst the vastness, our mortality overshadowing all our hopes or triumphs. There can be little doubt that the Stranger is in the midst of a religious crisis classical in its pattern. This is the "Sickness Unto Death" that Kierkegaard describes, the despair and the world-weariness, the intellectual frustration, the conviction of the futility of human endeavor. And this despair Kierkegaard sees as a necessary spiritual step, and William James shows over and over again as a common experience of those who at this juncture undergo a vast spiritual change most often described as "being born again."

So it was with Fergus O'Connor. Driven to the depths of despair, even to the point of physical death by the blackness of his vision, his gnawing intellect reduced to zero, other forces begin to work. Looking at the same sea that had inspired the vision of horror, he is possessed by a new spirit. He sees in the sea "real life, unchanging life." And "the meaning of life flickered across his mind, vanished, leaving wonder and awe behind it" (p. 185). Meditating on nature—the cliffs, the sea birds, and the sea—a "delicious sorrow" rose up within him. He felt he wanted to write a great poem about the cliffs and the sea—that he knew something no one else knew, that he was "scratching at the door behind which the secret of life lay hidden" (p. 211). All other writing about the sea or nature or life appeared superficial to him. In this mood he clings to nature, humbly. He becomes intimate with every wave on the bay, feels a kinship with the fishes of the sea. He has been born again.

This spiritual struggle and duality of nature ascribed to the Stranger in *The Black Soul* are really O'Flaherty's. Inverara, which becomes for O'Flaherty what Yoknapatawpha County is for William Faulkner—his real home cast into convenient literary form—is, of course, in the Aran Islands. And Fergus O'Connor's own life history has more than a passing resemblance to O'Flaherty's. Fergus at twenty was a brilliant student maintaining himself on scholarships at the University. He spent three years in the war with a memory of horror. After the war he spent two years wandering, trying to find somewhere to rest—Canada, the Argentine, South Africa. All these are familiar details to the reader of *Two Years*. His life in Dublin, his communism, parallel O'Flaherty's accounts of his own life. And both the Stranger and O'Flaherty come to Inverara to seek their spiritual peace. O'Flaherty has drawn heavily upon himself and his own experiences in creating the character of Fergus O'Connor; the spiritual struggle presented so forthrightly in *The Black Soul* is a recurrent O'Flaherty theme that appears again and again in various forms in his later works.

O'Flaherty's deep personal involvement in this novel is seen clearly in his letters to Edward Garnett during the period *The Black Soul* was being written. When he tells Garnett of the guilt he feels at breaking off his engagement to Miss Casey (the daughter of the woman who befriended him when he came to London) he thinks in terms of what he is writing: "Truly I have a black soul," he writes (June 6, 1923). In the same letter he tells Garnett he is following his instructions and "giving free rein to feeling and emotion." All that he is is being poured into the book: "If there is anything in me it's going into it. So you can see my bare soul and measure its worth when you read." Later, struggling to perfect the book, he reaffirms to Garnett its meaning to him: "It hurts me as much now as the first day I thought of it. . . . It is only the things one loves that hurt" (June 23, 1923).

The change of soul that is the fundamental topic of *The Black Soul* is represented in the story line by the Stranger's vacillation between two women. Kathleen O'Daly is the intellectual. The daughter of a strong, garrulous, capricious Irishman of the old school, she represents the attractions of culture and civilization. When the Stranger first comes to call, she is playing the violin. She is a devout Roman

Catholic with a great respect for the traditions and discipline of the Church. She is slender, refined, cold, appealing, but emotionally sterile. On the other hand is Little Mary, the peasant woman in whose house the Stranger lodges. The model for Little Mary was Mrs. Morris, the woman he met at Quaker farm while writing the book, and the one who caused O'Flaherty to break his engagement with Miss Casey. Like Little Mary, her mother was what O'Flaherty calls a peasant woman. But her beauty, like Little Mary's, came from her father, and O'Flaherty has a theory that fathers hand down the characteristics of race or type and the women hand down the characteristics of genius. O'Flaherty was greatly taken by Mrs. Morris at this time and wrote their affair into the book: "You will find our first embrace depicted truthfully in the middle of Summer of the Black Soul," he wrote Garnett (May 9, 1923). Little Mary is a passionate, full-breasted woman, full of the fire of life. Because of her great beauty and her lineage (she is said to be the illegitimate daughter of an English gentleman) she feels greatly superior to her peasant husband, Red John. She represents the darker forces of elemental nature. Fearing the Stranger's death as he is rendered feverish and delirious by his black soul's influence, she takes out a Druid charm, a stone covered with inscriptions written in old Druidic writing. And, the author comments: "Who knows? One thing is as certain as another and nothing is reasonable. All men and women fashion their own gods and they are all omnipotent" (p. 68).

Although the Stranger feels that Kathleen O'Daly represents the higher part of himself and his responsibilities to his own intellect and civilization, the forces of nature prevail. They are attracted to each other, but she is too weighted down and inhibited by culture and tradition to give herself freely. He gradually overcomes the pride that put him above Little Mary and his sense of guilt and jealousy that she is married to a man so crude as Red John. Yielding to her great appeal, in a scene reminiscent of D. H. Lawrence, the Stranger's intellect becomes subdued and his body obeys the mysterious feeling without reference to the brain. In a "mystical, indescribable experience . . . His body did not unite with hers, but his life. He had lost his individual being" (p. 142).

Such a pattern of love, overlaying, more or less, the more basic spiritual crisis, is the effect, no doubt, of the strong influence of Edward Garnett on this novel. Edward Garnett, who was D. H. Lawrence's publisher, took an interest in O'Flaherty because he sensed in O'Flaherty the same sort of relationship to nature that he considered important in D. H. Lawrence's work. In *Shame the Devil* O'Flaherty describes bringing *The Black Soul* to Garnett page by page for his suggestions and approval (p. 44). Though we are not told what suggestions or modifications resulted from these conferences, this attempt to merge sexual fulfillment with spiritual rebirth (especially in so strong a Lawrentian scene) would seem the obvious outcome. Moreover, the contrast between the two women is much like the contrast in *Lady Chatterley's Lover,* with Kathleen having the function of Sir Clifford and Little Mary that of the gamekeeper. (Even Little Mary's lineage being above her peasant surroundings is paralleled in Mellors' being superior to his station.)

On May 14, 1923, O'Flaherty wrote to Garnett that he had an idea for a new book on Aran peasant life from reading *The Fox,* even though he says "I don't like that fellow Lawrence's way of writing." *The Fox* is more a spark than a source in relation to *The Black Soul* because the triangle represented in Henry Grenfel, Jill Banford, and Nellie March is hardly recognizable in Fergus O'Connor, Kathleen O'Daly, and Little Mary. *The Fox* is more delicate, more subtle, more concerned with the essence of man-woman relations. And it is Nellie March who cannot give herself, lose herself completely to Grenfel's masculine power even after Jill Banford is killed. Yet the same pattern of choice is there. March must choose between Grenfel, who exerts a power deeper than her intellect, and Banford to whom she thinks she is obligated, as O'Connor must choose between Kathleen, who appeals to his civilization and intellect, and Little Mary whose appeal lies in dark irrationalities. And overlaying these fictional choices must be the choice O'Flaherty himself was involved in—his obligation to Miss Casey and the physical appeal of Mrs. Morris. But aside from this pattern of choice the essential themes of *The Fox* and *The Black Soul* are very different. March must choose to be a woman, must stand as a woman in relation to Grenfel and not as a man in relation to Banford. The story is about what it means for her to be a woman, and in the end her inability to give up her strenuous independent consciousness, her wakefulness and inability to sleep in him is her failure and their tragedy. O'Flaherty's essential theme is very different. He is not concerned with what it means to be a man or a woman on the human level regardless of the meaning this has for life. Fergus O'Connor's choice involves what it means to be a man on the existential level, not in relation to a woman but in relation to the totality of life. O'Connor must make a cosmic choice *before* he can choose Little Mary, and his choosing her, his giving himself to her, is not the choice but the consequence of the choice. March's inability to cease being a self is rooted deep in her being, but it is not caused by any black soul whose nihilism prevents her. If *The Fox* inspired *The Black Soul*, it also imposed an alien pattern upon it.

This alien pattern causes a distortion in *The Black Soul* because, despite superficial resemblances, D. H. Lawrence and O'Flaherty are entirely different in their essential views. This contrast serves as an important insight into O'Flaherty. If the identification of Fergus O'Connor with O'Flaherty is valid, the difference is apparent. There is no cosmic uncertainty in Lawrence, none of the sense of sin and guilt, futility and doom, of enormous despair in the face of cosmic immensity—all elements that are basic to this novel. For Lawrence belongs to that group which William James labels "the once born," men who have accepted life immediately as being good, without going through the throes of despair and rebirth. Life is basically good only if accepted fully and passionately without the distortions of intellect and abstractions. His theme is not rebirth after despair, but awakening to the essential goodness of life that civilization and intellect hide and dull but that lies waiting to be tapped from our deeper passionate natures. The "mystical, indescribable experience" of the Stranger and Little Mary would have for Lawrence a great significance, because this love relationship is the finding of what was lost or hidden. It is the revelation of the vast, deep resources of life. But it is not the answer to the question of man's destiny, and this is the fundamental question of *The Black Soul*.

The spiritual death and rebirth theme is so important to O'Flaherty's intention that real spiritual peace is impossible for the Stranger (even after his awakening to nature and his mystical blending with Little Mary) until a more complete and significant crisis has occurred. This is represented in the Stranger's life-or-death battle with Red John on the rugged sea cliffs. At this moment, when the Stranger "came face to face with the reality of death, the reality of life assumed a meaning for him" (pp. 248–49). This comes as a second climax, weakened and confused by the effect of the first. For O'Flaherty spiritual peace could not be found by yielding to the dark and mysterious forces of his being, because for him these forces did not exist as they did for Lawrence. In O'Flaherty's work we do not find the refinements of love and sexuality. For him passionate sexuality never leaves the plane of the popular novel, and a beautiful woman is seldom more than a sex object. This kind of love could not be the answer to the cosmic questions that tortured his soul. But the Lawrence influence gives a

Lawrence answer to a spiritual problem utterly alien to Lawrence's spirit. O'Flaherty can give the easy and unconvincing love answer at the end of *The Black Soul* because the general direction of the love relationship has taken the problem almost out of his hands.

Indeed O'Flaherty himself felt that the end of the novel as he had written it was unsatisfactory. In a letter to Garnett dealing with the ending he says that in his initial conception he saw the Stranger die. Here, apparently, Garnett disagreed because he thought, as O'Flaherty writes, "we can't afford it yet." But O'Flaherty has a "dream" way which he prefers. In this ending the Stranger dies in a death grip with Red John, "with the peasants watching on top, with the wind, sea, sun, air, etc. changing, clashing, moving, with the soul of the whole piece contracting into an intense moment of fierce beautiful endless immaterial melancholy sadness—then Little Mary casting herself down —a shriek from the peasants—and the curtain—The Black Soul was dead" (October 16, 1923). O'Flaherty, although almost forced by Lawrence's influence to make the love theme central, cannot find a satisfactory close in the fulfillment of that love. His real theme is spiritual conflict, with a man tormented by a black soul who can find no peace until the black soul is extinguished.

The Black Soul is the most revealing and therefore the most important novel in the study of O'Flaherty's genius because he put all of himself into it. His self-identification with the main character may not result in the greatest art, but it does supply the most information and insight to anyone seeking to know O'Flaherty. Not only does this novel give a detailed study of the kind of spiritual conflict that gnaws at O'Flaherty, but it also shows most of the themes and techniques that will be used in almost all of his future work. The most important theme is the turmoil of the soul in a godless world. This will recur in almost every subsequent novel. "I am afraid I will never again write anything but Black Souls," O'Flaherty writes to Garnett (October 16, 1923). And with this theme comes a fundamental pattern—the novel as the psychological and spiritual study of a single dominant character with a single dominant consciousness. Because this character is constituted out of strongly personal elements (as is the case with *The Black Soul*) the pattern also poses an artistic problem.

In *The Black Soul* O'Flaherty attempted to present and give an answer to the overwhelming question. The strength of the novel is the intensity of the asking. The weakness is the weakness of the answer. There is no set, articulate answer, nor was O'Flaherty able to make the love interest of the plot an adequate conclusion. But the novel does have within it the answer as it is for O'Flaherty—an answer that is not pat doctrine or formula but more akin to mystical vision. This sort of vision is so like lyric poetry—so intense, of short passionate duration—that it was not possible for O'Flaherty to express it in novel form. This mystical vision, awakened by his brooding over the sea cliffs, that caused a delicious sorrow to well up within the Stranger is the informing spirit of the short stories. There the Stranger attempts to express the secrets of life that "flickered across his mind . . . leaving wonder and awe behind them." There he tries to communicate the kinship he feels with the waves and the fishes of the sea. This mystical vision will be of the greatest importance in the study of the short stories.

Another technique and characteristic of *The Black Soul* that will become an O'Flaherty trademark is the short, sharp character sketch, pinning and classifying a character with one swift stroke. The doctor in *The Black Soul* is "officious, proud of his littleness, setting himself above and apart from the peasants, affecting the manner of an English gentleman, disdainful and condescending, face set in an expression that he had studied in the Dublin hospitals when he realized that his abilities would never allow him any higher than a practice among peasants or in the slums" (p. 77). This incisive portrayal is a by-product of O'Flaherty's concentration on what are for him higher things. Viewing the world and life in relation to his overwhelming cosmic uncertainty, he is impatient with characters whose concerns are worldly and petty. Characters like the doctor he can dismiss like a man swatting a fly. In O'Flaherty's novels it is most often a happy result.

And in the character of Red John, Little Mary's peasant husband, O'Flaherty has conceived a character and a way of presenting him that will later become O'Flaherty's solution to the problem of objectivity and self-identification—the inarticulate protagonist: a stark, cold, fearsome character portrayal of someone in the grip of passion. But this will be discussed more completely later. O'Flaherty's knowledge of his own soul is his greatest resource—knowledge of the utmost import gained through the intensity of his spiritual crisis. And closely connected with this crisis and this knowledge is his conception of his role as an artist. The black soul, the mocking destructive intellect that keeps Fergus O'Connor from participating in life, is another representation of O'Flaherty's creative genius, that part of himself that he sees standing apart from life, above life, making all of life material for artistic expression and keeping O'Flaherty the man from participating in life. His most intense spiritual conflict is resolved only when the black soul is dead. Yet over and above this most momentous experience is O'Flaherty's creative genius making of the conflict material for his art. That malign spirit that must be destroyed before O'Flaherty can find spiritual harmony is also the spirit that must be reawakened if he is to turn his most significant knowledge into art. As long as he is the subject of his art, he must undergo the spiritual torment his creative genius feeds upon.

In the novels that follow the black soul pattern,[1] it is a torment his creative genius inflicts upon him, however reluctantly O'Flaherty the man undergoes this torment. And it is a pattern he is continually trying to escape. In the black soul novels the only consciousness that exists is his own because it is the intensity of the spiritual conflict that gives consciousness and life. But O'Flaherty is continually trying to escape this trap by attempting to create another consciousness, genuinely alive, but somehow other.

O'Flaherty's next novel shifted from the country setting of *The Black Soul* to Dublin and to a cast of Dublin characters. *The Informer* (1925)[2] is about Gypo Nolan, a hulking, fantastically strong brute with only the glimmerings of intellect, who on the impulse of the moment informs on his partner in the Irish revolutionary organization, Frankie MacPhillip, in order to collect a £20 reward. This unleashes all the fury of this secret group whose members search out the informer, the worst kind of evildoer. Gypo becomes terrified at the consequences of his act and drinks up or gives away the money in a wild orgy. But the revolutionary organization, with Dan Gallagher as its brains, suspects Gypo, brings him to trial, and sentences him to death. He escapes and runs, but the routes from the city are blocked. He seeks out the lodgings of Katie Fox, his occasional mistress, who gives him shelter but betrays him as he sleeps. Gypo crashes through his executioner's bullets in a fantastic display of strength, to die, confessing his guilt to Frankie MacPhillip's mother, in a church nearby.

O'Flaherty gives two widely different accounts of the circumstances surrounding the creation of *The Informer*, one in his correspondence with Garnett before and during composition, the other in retrospect in *Shame the Devil* in a view nine years removed. The difference is extreme. In *Shame the Devil* he makes *The Informer* the product of a deliberate, cynical scheme to fool the reading public and thereby create a popular success. It was in Oxfordshire, he says, while living in a cottage belonging to A. E. Coppard, that he thought of trying out his "trick on the public" (p. 187). He, J. B. Priestley, and Coppard were talking about the difficulties of a writer gaining a living by his work, and Priestley argued that because of the tremendous competition, the writer must do something spectacular to call attention to himself. This angered Coppard who cursed those who had schemes "for tickling the mountain's rump [popular opinion] and so making it roar out: 'He is a man of genius. I'll make him a best seller'" (p. 188). O'Flaherty agrees with him but nevertheless decides to try this himself. In Dublin he worked out the plan of *The Informer* which he thought of as "a sort of high-brow detective story" with "its style based on the technique of the cinema." "It should have all the appearance of a realistic novel and yet the material should have hardly any connection with real life." O'Flaherty thought he would treat his readers "as a mob orator treats his audience and toy with their emotions, making them finally pity a character whom they began by considering a monster" (p. 190). With this plan, with his tongue in his cheek, he began. And according to O'Flaherty, the plan worked. "The literary critics, almost to a man, hailed it as a brilliant piece of work and talked pompously about having at last been given inside knowledge of the Irish revolution and the secret organizations that had brought it about." O'Flaherty calls this nonsense. "Whatever 'facts,'" he says, "were used in the book were taken from happenings in a Saxon town, during the sporadic Communist insurrection of about nineteen twenty-two or three." But his trick succeeded, even though he thought it endangered him by bringing the masses too close, and "those who had paid little attention to my previous work, much of it vastly superior, from the point of view of literature, to *The Informer*, now hailed me as a writer of considerable importance" (p. 191).

But O'Flaherty's account of *The Informer* to Garnett is not at all cynical, and his predictions for its reception not at all optimistic. In a letter of April, 1924, he tells of starting on a Dublin story, "The Vendetta," which will be a "shocker" and a "thriller." In July of that year he is deeply engaged in the story and tells Garnett about his character, Gypo, his "beautiful monstrosity" (July 28, 1924). By September the plans of the book are complete, and in a long letter to Garnett on September 18, 1924, O'Flaherty lays out the entire plan and asks Garnett to judge it "not so much for what it is by itself" as for what he has "set out to make" and what he has "succeeded in making." O'Flaherty believes that "the mob," the mass of readers, who "never know anyway" will bring all sorts of "eccentric things into the scales—

morals, god, politics etc." But he wants Garnett to trace out the development of the book from the initial dream:

> It is on these lines, following from an initial dream through its
> changing fortunes as other circumstances mould and redirect it to
> a conclusion in a way unexpected from such beginnings that I
> have tried to build The Informer. I have envisaged a brutal, im-
> mensely strong, stupid character, a man built by nature to be a
> tool for evil-minded intelligence. The style is brutal at that stage,
> without finesse, without deviation, without any sweetness, short
> and curt like a police report. Then as other characters appear on
> the scene the character of the man changes gradually. Elements
> of cunning, of fear, of struggle that is born of thought, appear in
> him. The style changes to suit this, almost imperceptibly. More
> and more characters appear. The character is no longer brutal.
> Sympathy veers around and stands in the balance, for him or
> against him. He is now a soul in torment struggling with evil in-
> fluences. At this point the style becomes definitely sympathetic,
> lengthens itself out, softens, strikes a note of joy in the eternity
> of nature. Scenes of horror and sin present themselves.
>
> Then with gathering speed The Informer is enmeshed by his
> enemies. His vast strength crumbles up overwhelmed by the gath-
> ering waves of inconquerable intelligence. He stands alone, with-
> out the guidance of a mind to succour him, seeking an outlet for
> his useless strength, finding that it is no longer strength but a
> helpless thing, a target for the beings that press around to harass
> it. Intelligence, evil intelligence is dominant and supreme, civilisa-
> tion conquers the first beginnings of man upwards.
>
> The Informer makes a last effort to escape. Here the style com-
> pletely changes and becomes like a wild storm, cascading, aban-
> doned, poetic.

From there, O'Flaherty says, the style rises to a climax, and he
quotes what will be the beginning of the last chapter, a vision of horror, of "endless wandering through space." Then he says he strikes a
note of pity and finishes it. He does not know what success he has
had in his execution of the plan, but he has hopes.

By January, O'Flaherty, who had been sick and very depressed, is
not at all optimistic. He told Garnett (January 20, 1925) that those
who have read *The Informer* say it is much inferior to *The Black
Soul*, and "I believe it myself now." He predicts that the reviews will

think that it is a pity that he has not duplicated "the beauty, the high moral tone, the chaste simplicity" of *The Black Soul*. And on January 24, 1926, he writes that he is hard-pressed financially because "*The Informer* has been a failure."

Whether O'Flaherty created the novel cynically or seriously, whether he thought it was a success or a failure, two things are clear from his accounts: the novel is about a person, a man who is put through an ordeal; and the novel is not a serious attempt to write about Irish politics or the secret Irish revolutionary organization. O'Flaherty does not talk about what is most interesting about the novel: the pattern of the torment that Gypo Nolan undergoes—what causes torment, what happens to "a soul in torment struggling with evil influences." For when O'Flaherty attempts to represent evil intelligence and plumb the depths of a soul in torment, he is involved in the same theme that motivated *The Black Soul* and the same theme that dominates his own autobiographies.

Although *The Informer* seems to represent a marked change from *The Black Soul*, the change is mainly in the setting. With some rearrangement the same forces appear, and the same pattern. In *The Black Soul* O'Flaherty has concentrated the conflict in Fergus O'Connor with Red John the mindless character driven entirely by instinct and impulse. In *The Informer* the mindless character, Gypo, is central, and his central conflict is with Dan Gallagher, who is the power of intelligence. What was concentrated in Fergus O'Connor is now divided between Gypo Nolan and Dan Gallagher.

The main function of Gypo Nolan's being an informer is not to tell about informers but to introduce an accepted device to cut him off from society, to isolate him as the black soul was isolated, turned in upon himself without society to support him. When the consequences of his act seep slowly into his thinking, Gypo avoids his old haunts. He walks down the streets passing people "like a being utterly remote, a unique creation" (p. 33). But he cannot exult in this remoteness, trying, rather, to lose it in drunkenness and in sexual pleasure. The force of intelligence represented by the revolutionary organization and concentrated in Dan Gallagher is the cause of the remoteness. This is what Gypo fears—not what he can get his hands on but what he cannot understand. When it is obvious that his guilt is known, the "unspeakable terrors crowded into his mind." For a moment he resolves to fight, but "the dreadful fascination of Gallagher's cold eyes sucked his passion clean out of him" (p. 132). And when Gallagher speaks out his guilt, Gypo collapses:

The sight was fearsome even to the callous men that surrounded him. Even THEIR hardened souls saw a vision of a strange life just then, an unknown and unexpected phantom that comes to some once in their lives and that never comes to many, the phantom of a human soul stripped naked of the covering of civilization, lying naked and horror-stricken, without help, without hope of mercy. They forgot for the moment their hatred of him. . . . They only knew . . . that he was a poor, weak human being like themselves, a human soul, weak and helpless in suffering, shivering in the toils of the eternal struggle of the human soul with pain. (pp. 133–34)

This is the point to which Fergus O'Connor is driven by his black soul; but whereas in *The Black Soul* O'Flaherty presents this extreme soul state from an inner view, in *The Informer* he presents it from an outer. Here is the soul's crisis.

From this nullity Gypo slowly emerges. "When blundering reason flees, instinct, that is fundamental and unerring, rushes to the defence of life" (p. 145). When Gypo escapes from his cell and attempts to flee the city back to the country and nature, "the rocky passes and the swift flowing rivers" which offer "freedom, solitude, and quiet" (p. 162), his way is blocked by revolutionary organization guards at the bridge. "Gallagher's cold, glassy eyes were on the Bridge. He could not pass" (p. 163). The force of intellect still pursues him. He flees to Katie Fox's room as a haven and falls exhausted in a nightmarish sleep on her bed, with visions of "yawning abysses full of frozen fog," "endless wandering through space," "everything without shape or meaning" (p. 178). Betrayed by Katie, he awakes with a start as his executioners enter. He charges through them, almost ignoring them, almost ignoring the bullets from Gallagher's gun that convulse his body. "It's no use," he says aloud. In his death throes, his mind dead, he enters a church, where "sad, haggard, hungry faces" are "wrapt in the contemplation of infinity" (p. 181). With his last breath he confesses his guilt to Frankie MacPhillip's mother and asks her forgiveness. In an obvious parallel she forgives him: "Ye didn't know what ye were doin.'" A great joy fills him and he becomes "conscious of infinite things." At the end "he stretched out his limbs in the shape of a cross," "shivered and lay still" (p. 182).

This is the black soul pattern of spiritual crisis and regeneration repeated, in this case with more objectivity, but nevertheless O'Flaherty is building with the stuff of his own nature. The dark forces of intellect are embodied in Dan Gallagher whose revolutionary views parallel O'Flaherty's: "Civilization is a process in the development of the human species. I am an atom of the human species, groping in advance. . . . I am impelled by the Universal Law to thrust forward the human species from one phase of its development to another . . . I am a Christ beating them with rods" (p. 73). O'Flaherty makes Gallagher faintly ridiculous, having all of his theories end in confusion and uncertainty, but expressing through Gallagher the sort of theories he states, and rejects, in *Shame the Devil* about communism and world revolution.

And he tends to build his characters with a spiritual terror at the root of their being. Crank Shanahan, a local political fanatic and philosopher, "was given to fearfully morbid thoughts that caused him to lock and bar himself in his room and sleep with the blankets right over his head" (p. 87). Aunt Betty, the madam, had the peculiar habit of stopping, wild-eyed, even in the middle of a conversation, "as if she were afraid of some dread spectre being in pursuit of her" (p. 94).

"I can't write about characters. I can only talk about them or create them," O'Flaherty complains in a letter to Garnett (July 31, 1925). This is essentially the problem O'Flaherty tackles in *The Informer*. How can he write about characters and make them different from himself when at their root, in the only way he can understand them, they are like himself? He had poured all of himself into the black soul, Fergus O'Connor. And when he got past the surface description of Red John, when he tried to understand him, it was in terms of a kinship that Fergus can feel with Red John as he sees his own potential insanity mirrored in Red John's eyes. Yet Red John, this character type, offered one possibility of artistic detachment, for he was not possessed by a dark intellect that would drive him to brooding and despair. The root of Red John's being would be instinct, passion, and impulse. He would express himself in action. O'Flaherty would not be likely to get the workings of that kind of mind tangled with his own. Gypo Nolan is such a character, a creation that O'Flaherty can look *at*, not through. Not having a complex mind, he does not cause O'Flaherty to deal with the problems that O'Flaherty believes every complex mind must deal with. In *The Informer* this kind of mind is separated and objectified in other characters that can be looked at. Thus Dan Gallagher is that aspect of mind. He is the black soul, but without the spiritual depth and passion that would drive him to a personal crisis. Because of this he is shallow and a little ridiculous, and O'Flaherty can mock his own views in him.

In each case where Gallagher goes into a theoretical discussion, on marriage, on property, on the nature of life, he echoes O'Flaherty's own arguments in *Two Years* and *Shame the Devil*. Gallagher, for example, attempts to explain to Mary McPhillip the nature of belief. He believes in nothing fundamentally, he says, because "nothing fundamental that has consciousness capable of being understood by a human being exists." If he could believe in something fundamental, he could comprehend the whole superstructure of life. But then life would resolve itself into intense contemplation, and action would be impossible. When he observes, however, that "men seek only that which offers no explanation of itself" he is entering spiritual ground, and O'Flaherty pulls him up short in what comes to be a characteristic tag line: "I haven't worked that out fully yet. It's only in the theoretical stage yet" (p. 73). And Dart Flynn, the revolutionary, "a man to stalk ahead of the bulk of humanity," "born with a curse upon his brow," "anathema to the mass of beings who always seek tranquility and peace at any price"—in other words O'Flaherty's ideal revolutionary, what he has often imagined for himself—is given a fantastic philosophy "based on the premise that each human being shares his soul with several different animals" (p. 142). In this way O'Flaherty keeps him at a distance and objectifies him.

Perhaps it is this aspect of *The Informer* that O'Flaherty looks back on with distaste in *Shame the Devil*. In mocking himself he has betrayed himself. Instead of pursuing his thought and accepting the consequences, he has held his thought up for ridicule, as an exhibition for the mob. But O'Flaherty was trying to solve a problem of art, a problem of artistic technique. He was attempting to create characters that would have a life of their own, trying to extricate himself from the web of himself. He did not solve the problem here, though in the character type of Gypo Nolan he went some distance in solving it by creating a character whose mental processes were different from his own. But the characters, even if objectified, are still too much O'Flaherty objectified and extremely limited because of the way that objectivity was achieved. The pattern of spiritual quest is still the O'Flaherty pattern. Essentially *The Informer* is still a novel about himself.

In the final estimate one thing is certain: whether or not O'Flaherty wrote *The Informer* as a serious literary effort, it is a novel about a soul and not about Ireland or Dublin or revolutionary intrigue. All the latter are incidental. Donagh MacDonagh lays great stress upon the meaning of being an informer in Ireland, and he sees the novel as showing up "the smudged fifth or sixth carbon copy of the revolution" with "ideals that have sunk to the brothel level." [3] But MacDonagh looks at the novel as an Irishman, and what he sees as central is only background. Gypo Nolan is made an informer to cut him off from society, to launch him into frenzied action and conflict that will lead to his destruction. It is his being cut off and not his being an informer that is central. And if the revolutionaries, as represented by Dan Gallagher, are less than noble, it is the way that O'Flaherty has objectified the force of evil intelligence, to separate himself from his own ideas. *The Informer* is about Gypo Nolan, and Gypo is essentially a human soul driven by evil intelligence until it is "stripped naked of the covering of civilization, lying naked and horror-stricken, without help, without hope of mercy."

O'Flaherty's efforts toward objectivity and detachment, represented especially in a central character like Gypo Nolan in *The Informer*, continue in his next novel, *Mr. Gilhooley* (1926).[4] Lawrence Gilhooley, the central character, is of the same mold as Gypo. O'Flaherty tells Garnett of this next novel, tentatively called *The Firebrand*, in which the main character is an "intelligent Gypo," a man who is "hounded" and "chooses to be hounded" (January 18, 1926). O'Flaherty attempted to achieve objectivity with Gypo by depriving him of intellect, by making of him a character that could be described almost entirely by his overt acts. Whatever small ideas he has are converted almost immediately into action. His fears and triumphs play over his face; his agonies of spirit are reflected in the contortions of his body. O'Flaherty can stand on the outside and read him. But Gypo's simplicity gives the novelist very little scope. What O'Flaherty needed was not a character without intelligence but a character with a different order of intelligence, whose mind O'Flaherty could understand without becoming himself intellectually involved in that mind. This is the sort of character O'Flaherty attempts in Lawrence Gilhooley.

Gilhooley is a different kind of person from O'Flaherty. He is not young, he is not sensitive, he is not highly intelligent. Gilhooley is essentially a stodgy conservative. He is fifty-two years old, balding, well-made but gone to seed physically. His clothing is unkempt, not because Gilhooley lacks money (he is a retired engineer with a comfortable 700 pounds a year income) but because he is indolent. When a slight heart ailment brought him back to Ireland, even when completely cured he did not return to South America where he had worked for twenty years. For him, his work was done, and he turned to a life of idleness among other idlers whose sole interest is to pass the time amusingly. In politics he is conservative, opposed during the Irish

Civil War to the Revolutionaries whom he associated with bolshevism. He reads the stock market quotations diligently every day to keep track of his holdings. He is very concerned with his own self-respect and is mortally afraid of being publicly shamed. And most important, he is precisely defined as being a voluptuary, given entirely to his own sensual pleasure. This is the whole key to his character. In other words Gilhooley is almost everything O'Flaherty is not.

Such a character fulfilled for O'Flaherty a very distinct function and need; and if he could not find a model in himself, he could make a character out of the opposite of himself. However, a model for this type did exist. On July 31, 1925, prior to writing *Mr. Gilhooley*, O'Flaherty wrote Garnett that he was reading "nothing now but Joyce and Dostoievsky and Gogol" and the similarities between Gilhooley and Dostoevsky's Svidrigailov could very well stem from that reading. Not that O'Flaherty has chosen a direct model—there are many differences: Svidrigailov is sinister, Gilhooley is open; Svidrigailov is diabolical, Gilhooley is essentially good-hearted. But in one respect they are essentially the same—both are voluptuaries. Neither fills any useful social role. Pleasure—selfish perverted sexual pleasure— becomes their whole reason for being when nothing else in the world interests or titillates. If Svidrigailov gets this pleasure from seductions and from young children, Gilhooley gets this kind of adventure from prostitutes or from the cinema where in the darkness as he lets his hand slide over a woman's knee his "self-centered passion" merely toys "with the subtlest form of lust, which does not depend on the object desired, but on the suggestions brought to bear on the subject" (p. 27). And both—Svidrigailov with Dounia and Gilhooley with Nelly—are undone by becoming obsessed with a passion that cannot be gratified and end their own lives.

As Svidrigailov and Raskolnikov are not strangers but share a knowledge of one another deeper than words, Gilhooley, though not O'Flaherty, is understood by O'Flaherty on a level far deeper than their superficial dissimilarities. For Gilhooley stands to O'Flaherty—the black soul—in much the same pairing as Svidrigailov stands to Raskolnikov. O'Flaherty the artist understands Gilhooley the voluptuary, because looking into his own soul he believes he knows what lies in Gilhooley's soul. He has an insight into the voluptuary in *Mr. Gilhooley* as later he will have into the assassin and the puritan in novels to follow. At the root is a common pattern: When a man is cut off by his mind or his actions from the common life of society that can involve him and shield him from himself, when he becomes merely himself, a naked soul facing the terror of his own existence, this is the ultimate crisis. This is what a man flees from, builds theories and philosophies to protect himself from, and tries to escape from through sexual pleasure. Echoes and forebodings of this terror become the wellsprings of his being. He is projected into life with passion and intensity, searching or fleeing, striking out violently or cringing in a cowardly lump. No terror or violence of a physical order has any meaning in relation to this ultimate terror. Fergus O'Connor in *The Black Soul* faced this terror, was extinguished by it, and experienced a spiritual rebirth. Lesser souls—like Gilhooley and, later, the assassin and the puritan—are driven to insanity or suicide or both.

This is the pattern of *Mr. Gilhooley* into which O'Flaherty pours his understanding of the human soul in crisis. Lawrence Gilhooley, as the book opens, is going to seed. This life is not happy, nor is it profound. "He would soon go to pieces like a disused hulk, unless something forced him to change the course of his life" (pp. 5–6). That something was Nelly Fitzpatrick, a mysterious, provocative girl who intrudes herself into his life. At a streetcorner she begs his help. She is without shelter. Reluctantly, but with "a strange sensation of pity" he befriends her, and his life is changed. For Nelly is the embodiment of the most subtle sexual pleasures, the personification of lust without love, who can be enjoyed but never possessed. She is not a creature of the earth, not a full-breasted womanly woman, meant for procreation. She is slight, refined, a merry sprite. She is pure, civilized sexuality, removed from procreation; pure pleasure, for the moment, without attachments, without consequences. She smiles, and "in the smile there was now some precocious knowledge, a knowledge of bacchanalian joy and of feminine subtlety" (p. 47). She tilts Gilhooley from his even keel and precipitates him on a course from which he cannot return. He sneaks her into his rooming house to give her shelter and falls under "her strange power." In almost a dream, without his intending, she goes to bed with him. He lies perfectly still "thinking rapidly without thinking anything. Then he felt her hands, as it were mechanically, begin to fondle his person" (p. 70).

The first change occurs. Always concerned with his self-respect, afraid of being shamed, now he is evicted in shame from his rooming house for having the woman in his room. He leaves in a state of "abject terror." "With the immovable and unreasoning fatalism of the voluptuary, he firmly believed that he was in the hands of an evil spirit . . . moving towards some inevitable catastrophe" (p. 93). His "insane passion" for her, "for the memory of that drunken excitement of the night, her eel-like body," fills his mind with terror. He feels that he is slipping "over the brink of a precipice," over the edge of which he had been hanging for the three years since he had returned to Ireland. A vision of terror returns, a man with a club, grinning, haunting him (pp. 94–95).

But Gilhooley forgets his shame and takes her as a mistress. They move to a disreputable rooming house, and in another ecstasy of drunken passion he finds peace: "They were united in a perfect intimacy by the common delight of humanity at escaping from the consciousness of existence and the fear of death, through lust and drunkenness" (p. 105). As the life that had become numb in him for his past three wasted years quickens, the need for Nelly becomes greater. The intensity of life brings with it an intensity of consciousness. At the rooming house Gilhooley becomes jealous and brawls with a little disreputable jockey. Normally a jovial, even-tempered man, Gilhooley is agonized by the change brought about in him by his insane passion. He feels that he is in the power of some disease and that he is threatened by the indefinable horror of something remote:

> The thing remote and indefinable was connected in his mind with vague superstitious fears, with ideas of God and eternity, with the rotting of the limbs and a slow paralysis of the mind. It was an irresistible force slowly surrounding him and about to overwhelm him. . . .
> The joyous days of lust and dissipation he had spent with her in the lodging-house had ended suddenly in a misery even worse than his former misery. For this love which he felt burning within him was not the form of ideal love of which he dreamt but its opposite. (pp. 122–23)

His ideal dream of love was of peace, of children, of nature and the country, blending himself into a harmony that contained all goodness. But this love is the opposite because instead of absorbing self it intensifies self, instead of letting him escape time it makes time and the ravages of time even more ominous. He is more detached and alone than ever because he is more aware than ever. He watches a parade of unemployed workers and feels indifferent yet envious: "The ambitions, prejudices, woes and joys of his fellow-citizens had already ceased to have any interest for him. In fact, feeling a great movement of people about him . . . he felt envious. He felt there was a mass of people near him . . . cooperating for some purpose and therefore eluding the thought of death by fixing their minds on some concrete human enterprise. And in that they were happy, lucky, and filled with hope . . . whereas he was alone, without hope, with his mind fixed on death" (p. 125).

This is the pattern of the impending crisis in which O'Flaherty sees Gilhooley involved: the longer Gilhooley is with Nelly the more are his passions awakened; and as his passions awaken, he becomes more and more aware of himself in time—his age, her youth, impending death —in a growing horror. But the greater the horror the greater his need for her, the more intense the passion needed to forget the horror, all in a cycle of increasing tension. Even the flat into which they move is related to this, with decorations so artificial as to give "an air of remoteness from primitive life . . . where the growth and decay of nature, moving conjointly, temper human joy with a grim realization of death" (p. 164). Here the hand of nature had been stayed by "refinement," "civilization," and "soft charm" very like Nelly herself.

Michael Friel, a young house-agent acquaintance of Gilhooley's who has procured the flat for them, brings this cycle to a climax. He is a libertine—vigorous, vital, attractive to and attracted by women. Gilhooley contrasts himself with Friel and grows more aware of his age. It is a threat to his relationship to Nelly. A thought passes through his mind which soon became "a fixed contemplation of some final act that would forever keep him with her" (p. 193). And the thought of killing her and himself whirls in his mind until he is nearly insane. When Friel leaves to take Nelly for a ride in his car, Gilhooley passes through his final torments. Horrible pictures come before his eyes. He attempts to pray, to confess his sins. And then comes a sound like Gypo Nolan's final nightmare "the despairing cry heard by all living things when the evil of death approaches with slow, silent feet. . . . It was the roar of disbanded oceans spilling in great foaming cataracts through the universe. It was the cracking of the earth and the hissing of volcanoes in the sun, when the great white star becomes disembowelled. . . . And through this wrack of sound he heard the cry of all humanity crying out for help. . . . What help?" (p. 228).

Nelly and Friel return drunk, and Gilhooley learns that Nelly can never love him and that Friel has made love to her. Everything falls to pieces. In a trance Gilhooley strangles her, not aware of what he is doing. He staggers around the streets, delirious: "In terrible agony he searched the heavens for a God, and finding none he sought devils to destroy the universe and make a void." Finding nothing, he is forced back to the earth" to contemplate the kind that pursued him." They are not beings, with names and personalities, but "living parts of himself" and "in all faces he saw his own face, horrible with the mark of guilt" (pp. 286–87). In a final frenzy he climbs the river embankment, looks into the water and denies everything: "There is nothing. Nothing at all." And he topples into the water and drowns. "Whither? Whence?" (p. 288). O'Flaherty ends the novel.

This is the one dominant action of *Mr. Gilhooley*. O'Flaherty is concerned mainly with the struggles of a soul in crisis, as in the previous novels. And the pattern is a familiar one, built out of his own deepest spiritual awareness. The man who seeks life passionately, with his mind, with his actions, must come face to face with the terror of existence in a universe that seems to offer no solace or meaning. This is the specter from which men flee, the man with a club that haunts Gilhooley. The refinements of civilization, the artifice and decoration, all human activity can be explained in relation to that specter. Weak men huddle together in causes in order to forget, and society is arranged to make this forgetting possible. But a man on his own, forced in upon himself by his character or circumstances, must face that vision of terror. And when he does, it becomes the fundamental fact of his existence.

In *The Assassin* (1928) [5] O'Flaherty dropped all efforts to create a central character who would be other than himself. Michael McDara, the assassin, is O'Flaherty thinly disguised. He is thirty-one years old, just O'Flaherty's age at the time the book was written. During the war in Europe he had served in the trenches and was discharged for shell-shock. After the war he had knocked around the world a few years as a seaman. Like O'Flaherty he is of peasant stock, his native village on a rock-bound coast. In his youth "he had been drawn away from primitive, peasant thoughtlessness by a thirst for knowledge" (p. 165) which separates him from his people. And more important than the external details of his life is the order of his consciousness. Like O'Flaherty he has the same kind of inner division. He is aware of being two people, and the description of this duality parallels exactly the duality ascribed to Fergus O'Connor in *The Black Soul* and more specifically to O'Flaherty himself in *Shame the Devil*, as discussed previously. One person is "terror-stricken, eagerly watching for enemies, acutely conscious of the most minute details of life, smelling, looking, listening, reacting to every touch in an abandoned manner" (p. 50). This is the side caught up in life, the body, and the senses. The other personality is masculine, "a scoffing, arrogant, contemptuous one. With a bold callous will, it caught and crushed every idea and suggestion that was offered to it . . . plundered what was useful and cast out the remainder." This personality exists in the body "like a foreigner" (pp.

50–51). It despises the body. This duality in McDara drives him into the same kind of spiritual turmoil that beset O'Flaherty.

The reason O'Flaherty reverted to this kind of central character probably stems from the circumstances surrounding *The Assassin*. In June, 1927, Kevin O'Higgins, prominent and popular Irish political leader, was assassinated by revolutionary terrorists. A.E., in *The Irish Statesman* (July 16, 1927), eulogized O'Higgins and interpreted the assassination as the expression of political hatred of ignorant and passionate men who would not abide by the election results. And he notes that "there are some people who by nature are terrorists." The subject of *The Assassin* is topical, and it is an attempt to answer the questions that always arise when a political leader is struck down by an assassin's bullet: Why did he do it? What motivates men like that? O'Flaherty attempted to respond to any popular demand that might exist by quickly turning out a book on the subject. His dedication— "To my creditors"—gives some clue to his urgent financial needs.

But O'Flaherty is not a journalist, whatever the immediate motives prompting the book. If there was a question about the mind of the assassin, O'Flaherty felt he had a special knowledge of that mind. The main theme of *The Assassin* is not the fact of a certain assassination as an event in Irish history, but the mind of the assassin in any society at any time. As he argues with his fellow conspirators about the job to be done, McDara, the assassin, says, "But I'm not an Irishman. I'm simply a man" (p. 191). O'Flaherty feels he understands the assassin because he understands the assassin in himself. It is the universal quality that interests him. In *A Tourist's Guide to Ireland*, when he mocks the spiritual and intellectual bankruptcy of Irish revolutionary groups, he observes that the activities of these groups never lead any further than conversation "unless it be some utterly purposeless act committed by what Dostoievsky called 'The Contemplatives': those fellows who meditate for years and then suddenly, for no apparent reason, burn a house, murder a man, or go on a pilgrimage to Lourdes or Jerusalem" (p. 86). McDara is one of these "Contemplatives," and through his understanding of himself and his understanding of Dostoevsky, in a compound of the two, O'Flaherty believes he knows what sort of experience lies at the root of a consciousness that might either murder a man or go on a pilgrimage to Lourdes or Jerusalem.

The Assassin derives from a fusion of O'Flaherty and Dostoevsky, but Dostoevsky as O'Flaherty knew him, the interpreter of the sick soul as O'Flaherty knew that sick soul in himself. The assassin can be understood, as can the voluptuary, in terms of an intensity of spiritual experience or vision, whether it be morbid or otherwise, that brings the man alone and terrified to the meaning of his own existence. Without that specific meaning all is meaningless, all is fantastic. The voluptuary is driven deeper into his passions to escape this terror, but as he is driven deeper his terror increases in a cycle that ends in insanity and suicide. The assassin strikes out in violence. He kills not for a cause or a reason but from the terror of his soul, to find meaning, to make meaning, to define himself against the lack of meaning, to do anything in a positive gesture, to relate himself to something that is fundamental, to defy God, to challenge God, to determine if there is a God.

McDara is carefully distinguished from the other conspirators in the assassination. Their function in the novel is to show what an assassin is not. Kitty Mellett is a confused "mixture of sex and idealism" which O'Flaherty notes as "so strange a characteristic of women revolutionaries" (p. 37). For her the assassination has meaning. In a state of ecstasy "She was contemplating the vision of a female spirit in flowing robes, Ireland, whom she was about to free from bondage." And mixed up with this are her frustrations at being a member of a group that had dwindled from a large, romantic women's army during the revolution against England to "a tiny organization of one hundred disgruntled old maids" (p. 65). The assassination vindicates her dedication. But hers is not the character of an assassin.

Nor are Gutty Fetch and Frank Tumulty true assassins. Gutty Fetch is a cold-blooded killer, "an automaton," who kills for the love of killing. He has no soul, no guilt, no ideals, no mind. He is an instrument, but he is not an assassin. And Frank Tumulty is not an assassin because he has belief. For him the assassination is to cause a revolution that will lead to a better world. When the act is done and he learns that McDara intends no revolution, he feels betrayed: "Now ye've ruined me, but, be Christ, we're going to get even with ye. I'm no assassin in cold blood. I swore an oath to be faithful to my country and to liberate her, with arms in my hands. I'm a soldier" (p. 263). But he is powerless to act further.

McDara is the true assassin. When Tumulty falls into a delirious sleep after the assassination, McDara envies him, despite the fact his "dreams had grown old in his brain," because "he still believed" and thus remained innocent. "I am evil and you have remained innocent," McDara says, but he cannot confess his envy. "He realized with horror that it was impossible for him henceforth to bow down before any man because he was proud of knowing evil" (p. 273). Gutty Fetch is sub-human and incapable of evil. Kitty and Tumulty have ideals to which the assassination is related and they remain innocent, unaffected in their deepest natures. Only for McDara can the assassination be evil, but this is no relative evil. It is an absolute, ultimate evil. It is the forbidden knowledge of the Garden of Eden, a knowledge gained through the act. It is the evil of T. S. Eliot's statement that "it is better, in a paradoxical way, to do evil than to do nothing: at least we *exist*."

For O'Flaherty assassination in its essence is not a political but a spiritual act, as certain murders were for Dostoevsky. And McDara is like Raskolnikov. The idea lies deep-seated in his brain, like Raskolnikov's idea, but grows and becomes a mental torture as the plan develops. The reason for the act is not clear. Sometimes he has the theory that it will advance the cause of humanity, "to create a superior type of human being" by killing off a strong man who sucks the power of the mass into his being and free the individual who then "becomes a living force, groping forward, unimpeded" (p. 97). Sometimes it is individual: "I am doing this because I want to be free. To cut every cord. It's only when a man cuts every cord that he approaches nearest to being a God. Supposing, then, a man arises, who is so far beyond the comprehension of his mates, in fearlessness, in bru—" (p. 142). This is an echo of Raskolnikov's theory. The assassination is related to God and the meaning of existence.

O'Flaherty interprets McDara in part through Dostoevsky, but basic to his understanding of McDara (and Dostoevsky) is his own spiritual turmoil. McDara is cast into the pattern of the black soul, the informer, and Mr. Gilhooley. He is cut off from society and conventional social aims and goods and made most intensely an individual soul, at one time exulting in the strength of his aloneness, at another terrified at his own existence. Like O'Flaherty, Fergus O'Connor, and Lawrence Gilhooley, in his weakness he has terrifying visions of death: "Then he saw death, on all sides, engulfing man and a horrible void beyond, terrible with fierce cries of anguish, with hands clawing the emptiness and fleshless lips constantly murmuring: 'Where? Where? There is nothing'" (p. 57). This is what O'Flaherty and his main characters must define themselves against. It drives Fergus O'Connor to despair and spiritual regeneration. It drives Gilhooley deeper and deeper into passion and selfhood until he has no course but insanity and suicide. And it drives McDara to assassination.

McDara is not easily explained. He does not operate according to any clear-cut theory. He cannot explain himself to himself, nor can O'Flaherty explain him. But O'Flaherty understands him because he understands the awful terrors of the naked soul writhing in spiritual agony for whom some momentous act, even if it is evil, represents an escape from awful uncertainty and meaninglessness. McDara does not know why he acts. He only knows he is driven to act by the spiritual turmoil within him. His two-sided nature drives him through a cycle of torment. Part of him finds happiness in an acceptance of nonexistence, "a melancholy acceptance of the futility of endeavor" (p. 160). As a thinking man he feels doomed "to go on and on thinking, trying to reach the end of a road that only led to the brink of a precipice" (p. 162).

But death, as a reality represented by the finality of assassination, cuts short this melancholy happiness. The reality of death awakens and terrifies the other side of his personality which clings to life. "Now he wanted to hide under the bed and remain there until he became an old man with white hair and toothless jaws; just for the delicious pleasure of being alive and able to think" (p. 164). He wishes to live "quietly, without effort, obeying other wills." But then the first part of him reasserts itself and despises the cringing coward. His mind traces his life back from primitive vitality and acceptance as a peasant through knowledge to "the chaos of unbelief" (p. 165). When McDara says "In one stroke I'll free myself" (p.165) he sees the assassination as an escape from this cycle of torment. The act will establish who he is. But even this is not clear. Prior to the act he despairs of the meaning of the act: "I expected to find here a new revelation of life and an explanation of the purpose of my existence." Instead he finds himself in a dirty slum room with two trivial fellows and no meaning at all. Still he will go through with the act: "I know that and yet I am going to do it, although it means nothing and it will have no effect, neither for the purpose of explaining my life nor for any other purpose" (p. 202).

When the assassination is over, nothing is clearer. He is still divided. Part of him experiences a sublime ecstasy. He is raised to a lofty peak from which he can look down on and understand the whole universe. Part of him conjures up the vision of his dead mother, and the reality of death drives him into a terror of loneliness. He abandons himself "to a feeling of submission" to the crucified Christ (p. 221), until the mocking self reasserts itself. In the end, in a delirium of despair, he becomes aware that he is going to meet Kitty Mellett and afterwards kill himself. "That is extraordinary. There is no use struggling then if I can't kill my conscience. Is there a God then? Some unknown Being, of whom I never dreamt?" (p. 286). And the novel ends.

When Y.O. reviewed *The Assassin* for *The Irish Statesman* (June

16, 1928), he found the book less effective than O'Flaherty's previous novels because it contained "hardly a shred of intelligible impulse." His view can certainly be sympathized with, especially if he expected to find expression of the the reasoning behind the O'Higgins assassination or the logic of any assassination. For O'Flaherty there is no intelligible impulse that can be explained. He knows in himself the spiritual condition that could seize upon the violence of assassination and attempts to portray this in McDara. He understands with an understanding deeper than words an impulse that is not intelligible, because it is a part of his own spiritual makeup.

Although *The Puritan* (1931) [6] is not O'Flaherty's next published novel in chronological sequence, it is best discussed here because it forms, with *Mr. Gilhooley* and *The Assassin*, a distinctive group of novels written under a strong Dostoevsky influence. In addition to the strong internal evidence of these novels there is an abundance of direct and circumstantial evidence to show that Dostoevsky played a prominent part in O'Flaherty's thought. *Shame the Devil, I Went to Russia*, and *A Tourist's Guide to Ireland* refer repeatedly to Dostoevsky, as we have seen. And of course there is the direct reference in his letter stating that he has been reading "nothing but Joyce and Dostoievsky and Gogol." In addition there would be every reason to believe that Edward Garnett, who played so strong a part in O'Flaherty's development in the period 1923–26, would call O'Flaherty's attention to the works that his wife Constance had recently completed translating. The impact of these translations on the English literary scene is well-known. There is no reason to believe that Ireland could remain isolated from this influence, although Sean O'Casey tells in *Inishfallen* of an interesting episode regarding Yeats and Dostoevsky that occurred around 1925. Lady Gregory told O'Casey of giving copies of *The Idiot* and *The Brothers Karamazov* to Yeats, and O'Casey is surprised that Yeats had read nothing by Dostoevsky up to that time. When he visits Yeats a week or so later he finds Yeats, already a Dostoevsky expert, making the grandiose pronouncement: "O'Casey, you are the Irish Dostoievsky." O'Casey is ashamed of Yeats for this statement, made from such slim knowledge, and O'Casey is not proud of this comparison. He wants to be no one but himself (pp. 210–11).

O'Flaherty would have a far greater claim to this title even if O'Casey had not rejected it. When O'Flaherty read Dostoevsky the effect must have been almost overwhelming. Consider the impact of such novels as *Crime and Punishment, The Brothers Karamazov*, or *The*

Possessed on a man subject to the spiritual upheavals revealed in *The Black Soul*. O'Flaherty found such a kinship of the soul with Dostoevsky that in addition to an over-all effect, *The Puritan, Mr. Gilhooley*, and *The Assassin* are in essence the adapting of *Crime and Punishment* to an Irish setting. Considering the makeup of the writer of *The Black Soul*, it is not surprising that a novel like *Crime and Punishment*, with its central religious theme, should be his most influential model. In many ways the Stranger of *The Black Soul* is created in the Raskolnikov pattern, especially in the psychosomatic effect of guilt and despair that drives each to illness and almost to death. It is not essential, though, to determine what elements are native to O'Flaherty and which are derived from Dostoevsky. If the borrowings from Dostoevsky are extensive, it is because Dostoevsky seemed to express what was latent in O'Flaherty.

One aspect of *Crime and Punishment* that would certainly find a sympathetic reception with O'Flaherty is the character of Raskolnikov. Always an admirer of passion, violence, outrageous opinions, himself subject to fits of melancholia, extreme emotional ups and downs, and aware of a duality in his own nature, O'Flaherty must have felt a strong identification with Raskolnikov. Also the concept of the novel as the spiritual history of one man in the grip of his characteristic passion is well illustrated in *Crime and Punishment*. This was to become O'Flaherty's most usual form, appropriate to a writer whose strongest impulses are in the direction of spiritual quest.

But the strongest effect of *Crime and Punishment* is in its analysis and working out of Raskolnikov's religious experience. From *Crime and Punishment* one can derive a whole philosophy of psychology or psychology of religion based on the premise that a man's relationship to the world is determined by his relationship to himself and that his relationship to himself has at its basis his relationship to God. Raskolnikov's plight was not based upon his poverty, nor was the murder the calm execution of a theory. His psychology is a complex of pride, godlessness, and guilt. His salvation consisted not in the rational working out of social or material problems but in the momentous acceptance of Sonia's cross—his humility and resignation—and mounting the stairs to the police office to confess. It is an illustration of the Dostoevsky thesis that O'Flaherty recalled from *The Possessed:* that man must choose and that the logical choice of a man without God is suicide. In the novels of the Dostoevsky group this is to be the essential theme: the puritan, the assassin, and the voluptuary are individual manifestations and aberrations of a common spirit that has its basis in their relationship to their god. Not finding the salvation of humility and acceptance, their fate is madness, despair, and suicide. *The Puritan* is most nearly the translation of *Crime and Punishment* into a Dublin setting with an O'Flaherty twist in the theme. Francis Ferriter, the puritan, is a young ne'er-do-well journalist obsessed with an idea. Like Raskolnikov's, his idea has been put into the form of a treatise which will become the basis for a contemplated action. *The Puritan* is about that action and its consequences for Francis Ferriter.

Francis Ferriter's obsession is with the flagrant immorality that he sees around him. His treatise deals with the hordes of the Antichrist marching under the red banner who have stayed the advance of Christianity. Christians are powerless because they have become corrupt. Materialism has spread even into the church; the state has taken over many of God's prerogatives. Now, he says, a violent shock is needed. "We must purify ourselves by pouring out the blood of sinners" (p. 191). Inflamed with this idea he plots the murder of Teresa Burke, a prostitute living in his rooming house, as the kind of bloody example that is needed.

Like Raskolnikov, his execution of the act only approximates the plan. He stabs the girl and returns to his room, but in his nervousness he fails to remove all the evidence as he had planned; now fear and confusion of his motives in the act drive him alternately to escape or confession. John Lavan, the chief superintendent, is the Porfiry Petrovich of the novel. He too had become interested in Francis Ferriter from a former book-burning episode and immediately suspects him, but he cleverly allows Ferriter enough freedom to let his own inner tortures implicate him completely.

Like Raskolnikov, Ferriter is completely confused about his real motives. Was this a real "sacrifice of blood" or was he impelled by motives of lust and jealousy? He makes the rounds of those whom he believes to be equally guilty—those whose words if carried to their logical conclusions would justify the act. But Mr. Corish, the editor of the Catholic middle-class *Morning Star,* is more interested in business than in sins. And Father Moran, editor of the *Catholic Vanguard,* is more interested in his career than in any possibly dangerous spiritual crusade. Ferriter rereads his manuscript and is overcome by fear and guilt. He goes to church, but the church appears different. A spirit within him hostile to God raises the question: "Does God exist? Has man got a divine destiny?" (p. 201). He goes to confession and tells the whole story, trying to make the priest understand his motives. The vulgarity and stupidity of the priest antagonize him; and when he learns that only a bishop can forgive the sin of murder, he revolts against the Church and haughtily, Lucifer-like, leaves the church. He then goes to the slums, gets drunk, and resolves to give his innocence to a miserable prostitute as an atonement for the murder. But the prostitute, horrified by the confession, runs away. At this point Ferriter begins to rave and is taken into custody by Lavan's detective assigned to follow him. As Lavan gets the full confession, he attempts to get Ferriter to implicate others in the puritan movement. But Ferriter accepts the whole guilt for the murder not as a holy act but as a crime of passion and jealousy. In his own hand he adds: "By this confession I have proved to myself that in taking this life I was not inspired by cowardice, but that I finally made a gesture of complete revolt against a false idea of God by destroying that which is considered most sacred and yet surviving. There is no God, but man has a divine destiny. It is the duty of each man to become God" (p. 313).

Aside from the many details reminiscent of *Crime and Punishment*—the bloody glove like Raskolnikov's bloody sock, the masterful detective, the written theory, the mysterious strangers following, the confusion of motives, the seedy rooming house, the ugly backdrop of city squalor, even the confessions in which both Ferriter and Raskolnikov give personal, selfish motives as the cause—the most important parallel is the insight that at the root of both Ferriter's and Raskolnikov's motives is a pride that has cut them off from humble acceptance. But when Ferriter is precipitated toward a classic religious crisis after his confession, "All the common dead things that had become a part of himself now being stripped—soon nothing left but this frail body to meet the noose and then eternal silence without movement" (p. 194), he, unlike Raskolnikov, cannot accept his cross and be restored to the path of spiritual regeneration. His final lot is raving madness.

O'Flaherty's is a free adaptation of the insights and techniques of *Crime and Punishment* to his own purposes. *The Puritan* is much more the dramatization of a specific idea than the exploration and presentation of a whole character. The reader never has an ambivalent relationship to the main character, who is immediately set aloof and apart. Whether by accident or design or the limitations of O'Flaherty's powers as a novelist, there is a narrowness and thinness about *The Puritan* far different from the complexities of *Crime and Punishment*. O'Flaherty, reacting against the Censorship Act, was attempting to show the psychological workings of an extreme puritan mind. And after Ferriter has worked himself into such a fever pitch in the tortures of his God relationship that he no longer functions as a social commentary, through an anonymous lawyer O'Flaherty expresses a view also expressed in *A Tourist's Guide* that the puritans have driven out all real intellectual life: "I feel I have to make some gesture of revolt or go insane. I visit this slimy catacomb as a gesture of revolt against the intellectual stagnation forced on me by the damned horde of Puritans of which you are a member. I'd rather be at a good theatre, or in my study with a good book, or in bed with a woman I loved. . . . It's not I but you and your kind that bring brothels and whores into existence, shebeens and slums and crime and disease" (p. 275).

O'Flaherty begins *The Puritan* as a ruthless study of a fanatical Irish puritan. His initial intention seems to be social criticism. But then, when his creative mania becomes awakened (as he explains in *Shame the Devil*) and he rises above mere social concerns, when he writes in what he considers to be his true role as an artist, when "human controversy about right and wrong is like the anarchic screeching of the wind above the overwhelming sea," then whatever motives of social criticism he had at the beginning of *The Puritan* become lost in his artistic absorption in the main character. At this point when O'Flaherty identifies a part of himself with Ferriter, his insight into his own relationship with God gives him a special understanding of the puritan mind he had been presenting. Ferriter's confession, his arrogance with the stupid priest, reflect typical O'Flaherty attitudes, and Ferriter's final confession is curiously similar to O'Flaherty's own ideas in *Shame the Devil:* "But we are preeminent in our power to imagine a state of perfection which we call God and which we are trying to reach" (p. 88). In the same book O'Flaherty has a conversation with a former steel millionaire where he calls God "a varying symbol of perfection," and says that "human happiness is a struggle against environment toward omniscience" (p. 128). In *The Black Soul* O'Flaherty's own spiritual crisis underlies the story. In *The Puritan* O'Flaherty projects the overwhelming significance of this crisis to make it the basis of action and motive of a character more objectively presented. In each case, however, the main theme is religious experience, and the main insight is O'Flaherty's knowledge of his own soul.

Although the novels just discussed seem to follow the pattern of *The Black Soul* and to abandon attempts at the kind of objectivity sought in *The Informer* and *Mr. Gilhooley,* this sort of objectivity continued to be one of O'Flaherty's major goals. This striving for objectivity reflects the complexity of his divided consciousness torn always between detachment and participation. Part of him watches—aloof, mocking, above humanity. This is his conception of the artist beyond good and evil. Yet when he had to give his characters life, which for him meant penetrating the surface of their consciousness to the roots of their being, it was always his own life that became the ultimate model. When he set a character in motion impelled by its own conscious vitality, spiritual crisis was inevitable because this was a part of the meaning of conscious vitality. Looking into himself, he saw spiritual crisis as the essential quality in being alive. It was as if he could not conceive of life without this crisis, that characters (or people) without this crisis were not really living. Thus, regardless of his artistic detachment which would have him standing above, observing life, he found himself drawn in, participating to the depths of his being as the source of life to be observed.

Thy Neighbour's Wife (1923),[7] his first novel, is a good example of how O'Flaherty's creative consciousness operates in the detached, superior observer attempting to bring into the same view the petty and colorful life of the natives of Inverara (Aran) and the torment of a young curate whose vocation is imperiled by the return to the island of the woman he had once loved. The novel opens in a bantering tone as O'Flaherty the artist looks down with amused detachment on his native island. Kilmurrage, the capital of Inverara, had no streets properly speaking, but what streets it had were on seven different levels, "which was a great achievement for a small town like it." The badge that hung over the R.I.C. barracks had fallen to one side as if it were drunk and disorderly, and though some said this was an advertisement for drunkenness to give the police something to do and a chance of promotion, "the police themselves were a sufficient advertisement for drunkenness without the harp" (p. 10). The wooden hut which had served as a cinema theater had been wrecked by one of the natives who, coming in drunk, mistook the action on the screen for real and attacked the villain who had murdered the heroine. The same bantering, mocking tone is taken toward the large gallery of local eccentrics who come across the pages of the novel. Mr. Wilbert, the Protestant vicar, whose main interest is Greek literature, has had his intellect turned into incipient idiocy by his residence on the island, "and if the stories told about him were even in part true, the idiocy instead of being incipient was highly developed" (p. 14). John Carmody, the local socialist and agnostic, eats his bacon only on Friday mornings, flaunting the odor of his cooking through the streets to show his disdain for the rules of the Church. Mrs. Connolly is always on the point of dying because she believes the oils of Extreme Unction are good for her rheumatism.

There is no personal involvement here. O'Flaherty's wit plays over the surface of things, amused, gently mocking. But also there is no life in the O'Flaherty conception of life. His intellect can swiftly strike off the clean lines of caricature without in any way affecting O'Flaherty the man as the source of life. This same detachment can be extended to more detailed character analyses, provided that the characters are defined in terms of their motives. Again intellect can play, as in a game, to ferret out the self-interest that forms the basis of an act. Thus postmaster Pat Coleman's extraordinary religious piety is to compensate, in an excessive display of Roman Catholic devotion, for his being in the employ of the hated British Crown. And the parish priest, Father Reilly, the most powerful figure on the island, can be explained entirely in terms of his personal greed and lust for power. O'Flaherty brings to this kind of analysis the same order of intellect that operates in *A Tourist's Guide to Ireland*, and indeed Father Reilly is the very kind of parish priest that O'Flaherty presents in that work. Characters that can be so explained, however, do not live. They exist as impersonal forces in the world of O'Flaherty's novels as the caricatures exist as ornamentation.

These ornaments and forces exist as a background against which the essential drama is enacted—the struggle within Hugh McMahon to find meaning in a vocation that has cut him off from the warmth of physical love. This struggle cannot be explained in terms of self-interest which O'Flaherty's detached intellect can discover, because the self-interest itself is the issue. McMahon himself is aware of the forces that pull him. As he says Mass before a congregation which contains the woman who tempts him, "He knew that his soul was filled with desire, unconquerable desire for Lily McSherry, and he knew that he was a priest and that she was 'His Neighbour's Wife'" (p. 58). He can see himself almost as O'Flaherty sees him and, most importantly, he exists apart from his motives. He is a man, a soul, not a vector of contending forces. He escapes the analytical powers of O'Flaherty's intellect—which can circumscribe him, measure him, weight him as it does the lesser characters—and becomes the life that is the essential subject of O'Flaherty's art.

With the vital force out of his intellect's control, which can only describe, O'Flaherty must now draw upon himself, as he exists apart from intellect, as the resource through which the struggle can be resolved. For O'Flaherty only one pattern is possible. The question of a choice of this nature which is beyond reason becomes the ultimate question of the meaning of existence which is beyond reason. Over and above this stands O'Flaherty the artist describing the inevitable drama that O'Flaherty the man is compelled to enact. It is not a role that the man willingly plays. He is driven to it by the artist "who would cut off his hand for the sake of a phrase" as O'Flaherty describes this relationship in *Shame the Devil*. Nor is the division between the man and the artist so precise that their boundaries can always be established. Often the struggle between them is projected into the novels. The man often threatens to escape the control of the artist. Or the man and the artist join—as if to let the man escape by fixing the entire spiritual conflict in a character, once and for all—with such detachment that both the man and the artist can stand superior and aloof. This seems to be the case with Hugh McMahon.

Father Hugh McMahon is what O'Flaherty is, what his mocking intellect scoffs at, and what his genius drives him to rise above. By embodying in McMahon all that he is, O'Flaherty attempts to transcend himself, to transcend even his mocking intellect which is bound together in an ambivalent relationship with his creative genius. Through the character of McMahon, O'Flaherty attempts to anatomize himself. McMahon is a "man of strong passions and with a highly sensitive nature" (p. 24). He is a poet with Republican sympathies. And he is possessed of an intellect that continually acts to separate him from what he considers most valuable or most sacred. Because of his intellect he cannot be a peasant, and his intellect scorns the calm stupid faces, the greed, the superstition. He is separated from the clergy because he can see that the church has no sympathy for intellect but is like Father Reilly, the parish priest, obsessed with maintaining power and acquiring material possessions. No part of him is in sympathy with the gentry or business people "too intent on their yardsticks and their beer measures, their silly code of etiquette and their bigotry to understand life as the curate wanted it to be understood" (p. 144). His intellect tears him from all sympathies and all causes, because he can see the greed, the pomposity, and the foolishness behind all human activity. He is alone, except for God, and his intellect annihilates this last refuge. He is trapped between belief, which his intellect sees as a delusion behind which his personal fears cause him to hide, and unbelief, which would mean that there is "no purpose to his actions in life, no cause for anything but fantastic theories that were incapable of comprehension or of being examined even by reason" (p. 257). As these forces war, McMahon is buffeted by "a perfect chaos of impressions"; "a perfect whirlwind of thought [floats] around his brain in confusion" (p. 262).

Here is the spiritual turmoil that O'Flaherty attempts to put into perspective and to bring under intellectual and esthetic control in his novels. In *Thy Neighbour's Wife* he attempts to stand above this turmoil by mocking it, by making Hugh McMahon weak, ascetic, and even ludicrous. The young curate dramatizes himself. He is Paul and Augustine, and his sainthood will be even greater because he has pulled himself from the pit of sin. He has delusions of grandeur, riding his spiritual fervor to a triumphant conquest of the Chinese through his poetic skill and missionary zeal. His last spiritual test, emulating the legends of ancient Irish saints who proved their own virtue by setting themselves out to sea in oarless curraghs, is motivated by drunkenness and jealousy as well as by his concern about his soul. In the end, it seems that a new Hugh McMahon will arise from his bout with the sea, when O'Flaherty has him undergo a transformation: "The curate died. The intellectual died. The visionary died. The drunkard died. The lover died. The pious, shrinking, conscientious priest, fearful of himself, torturing himself with doubts and temptations, they all died. There remained but Hugh McMahon the man, the human atom, the weak trembling being, with the savage desire to live, to save himself from the yawning chasm of death that was opened up about him by the storm" (p. 331). But McMahon is allowed no such transformation. Unaccountably, except that O'Flaherty wishes to keep the character subordinate and under the control of his intellectual, mocking view, McMahon immediately turns back to the Church and pledges his devotion if his life will be spared. The novel ends with McMahon standing dripping wet and incongruous, announcing to Father Reilly that he is going to become a missionary to China.

In *Thy Neighbour's Wife* the dominant tendency is toward detachment. All is to be brought under the control of the detached artist, who dispassionately records man's foibles and passions. If O'Flaherty is entirely involved in the character of McMahon, it seems to be in an effort to free himself, to write himself out of his art. In the final crisis in the boat when O'Flaherty and McMahon fuse into almost a common soul and it seems that McMahon will emerge as a new being, O'Flaherty shakes himself free by having McMahon instead throw himself back into the Catholic Church. It is as if by that gesture O'Flaherty sets himself apart from even the most profound experience to which a man can be driven, so that every aspect of life then comes under control of the artist.

If in this novel the artist declares his independence of the man, in *The Black Soul*—the novel that follows—the man sets himself free from the artist, the intellect that stands superior to life. In *Thy Neighbour's Wife* it is O'Flaherty the man who ceases to be, taken out of life and the inevitable spiritual crisis of life by the artist who stands above life. In *The Black Soul* it is the black soul that dies and the man who emerges into a new life as a result of the crisis. The former attempts the greatest detachment, the latter the greatest participation. In both O'Flaherty stretches himself to his furthest spiritual limits. It is no wonder he can write to Garnett that these two novels "will stand out as far greater and of more spiritual importance than anything [he] may do" (May 23, 1924).

These two novels represent the two tendencies of O'Flaherty's art —participation and detachment. *The Black Soul, The Informer, Mr. Gilhooley, The Assassin,* and *The Puritan* follow the former course in that they are marked with the imprint of O'Flaherty's own spiritual conflict. In *The Black Soul* he attempts to resolve this conflict through Fergus O'Connor by allowing him the transformation and spiritual rebirth denied to McMahon. The conflict is represented externally in *The Informer* with the warring elements embodied in Dan Gallagher as the destructive force of intellect and Gypo Nolan as the naked human soul driven to destruction. In *Mr. Gilhooley, The Assassin,* and *The Puritan* O'Flaherty uses the knowledge of his own spiritual make-up as an insight into specific character types.

That this pattern of spiritual conflict is O'Flaherty's own there can be no doubt. Even if the autobiographical elements and his deep personal involvement in *The Black Soul* are discounted, his direct autobiographical statements in *Two Years* and *Shame the Devil* show him caught up in the same pattern to the extent that it becomes the focus of his existence. It is an essential part of his creative genius, which he conceives of in *Shame the Devil* as a demonic spirit possessing his body; it is this genius that drives him from belief, that cuts him off from the joys and consolations of human fellowship and precipitates him into the bleakest despair. His genius feeds on him, destroys all his complacency, mocks all his hopes, lays bare the humanity in him to the gravest spiritual torments and makes of his writhings the material of his art. Yet it is only through his genius, the cause of the torment, that the torment can be transcended, for when O'Flaherty's creative fire is burning he ceases to be a man but achieves in his creative enthusiasm a state such as he possessed in writing *The Puritan* when, he tells in *Shame the Devil,* he can look at his mother's grave "looting the scene with fierce, avaricious eyes, impervious to remorse, gloating over the majesty of the human intellect that can transcend the tragedy of death and turn it into ecstasy" (p. 16).

This is one direction where O'Flaherty immerses himself in the destructive element, turns in on himself, and projects the turmoil he sees there into his characters. The subject is always spiritual conflict. The essential action is inner, within the soul which is living because it is in crisis. One figure dominates the scene, one consciousness, and everything is related to that consciousness. The consciousness becomes more and more directed toward itself, intensified, rubbed raw, tormented, until it screams out for help in terror and despair. In comparison to this, all outer action is insignificant, having no meaning in itself except as it is an expression or reflection of the inner state. The external violence that characterizes these novels is not real. The bullets that crash into Gypo Nolan are nothing compared to his nightmare of "frozen fog," "screeching winds," and "endless wandering through space." Gripped by his soul terror, Gilhooley strangles Nelly without being aware he is doing it. The agony of his soul, the haunting vision of the man with a club, the phantoms of his own consciousness drive him to act, and the act is in proportion to his terror. O'Flaherty's sordid slums, toothless withered prostitutes lurking in the shadows, and foul and dingy rooms are mirrors of soul states. The realism is subordinate to the expression. The quality of the central tormented consciousness is everything.

The central character embodying this intensity of consciousness is not in conflict with society. He is cut off from society. Society ceases to have meaning for him. He is in no way caught up in social momentum or concerned with social purpose. He is absolutely and terrifyingly alone. If he strikes out—as McDara and Ferriter strike out—in a violent act, it is not against society that he strikes but to find meaning, to escape his own inner horrors by a gesture of sufficient intensity to establish a point of meaning outside himself. O'Flaherty does not measure this consciousness against society. The informer, the puritan, and the assassin are souls, not social forces. That their acts have social implications is incidental, like the violence and the realism that characterize the novels. Although they have a local habitation and a name, it is not the habitation or the name that is central but the fact and quality of their being. In these novels O'Flaherty's subject is not Irish society or Irish politics, censorship bills or revolutionary organizations. The subject is a dominant consciousness which intensifies, becomes alive, precisely because it is cut off from society, alone, turned in upon itself, unrelated to social organization or social values.

In a sense the novels in this group could be called psychological studies, as they commonly are, but not without qualification. When William York Tindall describes O'Flaherty as entering the field of the psychoanalyst and pathologist to depict "violent souls, possibly mad, certainly neurotic," [8] he attributes to O'Flaherty a clinical quality that does not exist. As O'Flaherty's souls are not measured against society, they are also not measured against normality. Gilhooley and Ferriter are not driven to their spiritual crises because they are insane; they become insane, rather, because they can find no other relief from the unbearable intensity of the spiritual crisis. And if O'Flaherty's characters are neurotics, it is in no way a judgment of the truth or the value of their experiences. As William James argues so well in *Varieties of Religious Experience*, the source of a psychological experience cannot be used as *prima facie* evidence for its merit or lack of merit. Because the characters are maladjusted they are driven to unusual intensities of experience. O'Flaherty's focus is on the intensity of the experience and not the maladjustment. Only in his interest in the deepest experience of the psyche can O'Flaherty be called a psychologist, and his knowledge of the psyche comes from his knowledge of himself.

As has been said, in the novels that follow the pattern of *The Black Soul* O'Flaherty looks in and feeds upon himself. But latent in *Thy Neighbour's Wife* is the strong tendency for him to want to look out, to free himself from the painful bondage the artist imposes on the man. Although the setting and the minor characters serve no functional importance in Hugh McMahon's crisis, which becomes the central issue of the novel, there is an interest in these for their own sake. In this novel O'Flaherty turns out toward the world. He takes an obvious delight in describing the annual games of the Gaelic Athletic Association —the footrace, the wild and wonderful dancing of Michael Corbett "with his tangled beard and his eyes grinning devilishly beneath his bushy eyebrows" (p. 301), the race of the curraghs, the whole scene. As the artist, the detached observer, he wants to see and understand everything. And even if he cannot create life without projecting himself into the life, he pulls himself sharply away to observe even that and put that within the scope of his understanding.

The problem for him in *Thy Neighbour's Wife* is to create characters that have a life of their own. The quality of life he seeks is so close to the kind of spiritual conflict he sees in his own life that no other seems possible. Mr. McSherry, the middle-aged profligate (a retired engineer from South America, like Gilhooley), whose consciousness O'Flaherty attempts to penetrate more than any other (except, of course, McMahon's), is led to contemplate his soul: "He had forgotten that he had a soul, any kind of soul—a religious soul, or a moral soul, or a soul capable of appreciating goodness or beauty, or nature or art. He had forgotten it. He had lost it, and he began to wonder whether he had ever had one; or, if he had one, where had he lost it?" (p. 270). For O'Flaherty this appears to be the road down which all consciousness leads.

While O'Flaherty's own spiritual torments were his greatest resource in creating novels like *The Black Soul*, they also constituted an artistic trap, because they seemed to preclude his creating a consciousness other than his own. In the black soul novels, with the conflict within one character, there was no problem. But to create an objective conflict, the kind he could view with the detachment he sought in *Thy Neighbor's Wife*, he needed to create objective characters who could be in conflict. And whether or not O'Flaherty believed that all consciousness when quickened by intellect and passion ultimately must go through the pattern of torment and despair, he was continually trying to create characters that would be genuinely *other*, into whom he could breathe life and whose consciousness he could penetrate without having the consciousness turn out to be his own. His intellect could *see* characters, sketch them brilliantly, pin them with their shallow motives, devastate them. But it could not set them in motion. They were formulated, without potential other than the equation to which they were limited. As such they had to be minor characters, a part of the background against which the major drama of the single soul was enacted. They are the glitter, but not the life. And it was life that O'Flaherty was interested in—not the surface clatter but the very source. Yet whenever he asks: What drives a man who is not an automaton trapped within his own motives? he seems to get the same answer and the same pattern of spiritual crisis.

To escape this pattern, whether to escape himself or to expand the boundaries of his art, O'Flaherty had a continuing interest in a sort of "middle" character as an alternate source of consciousness. Characters that were young and sensitive and intellectual must inevitably be some embodiment or echo of himself. One way to avoid this was to continue to explore the possibilities of a character who was not young, sensitive, and intellectual, in the line of development of McSherry, Red

John, Gypo Nolan, and Gilhooley. And whether or not a new direction was needed to escape from himself—as if in creating a character other than himself he could shift the burden of consciousness from himself—it must have been apparent to O'Flaherty that he had about exhausted himself as a resource in the black soul novels and that some new areas must be explored as a possiblity of expression or his novels must continue to be variations on a single theme. Having exhausted the possibilities of participation, O'Flaherty turned toward detachment in his subsequent novels.

∾∾ IV ∾∾

Toward Objectivity

IN THE NOVELS that follow in *The Black Soul* pattern O'Flaherty explores the human soul, projecting himself into the characters and seeing his own spiritual conflict as the essence of consciousness and the depth and intensity of his own experience as the key to the secrets of all tormented souls. *Thy Neighbour's Wife*, however, indicated another possible approach where, instead of seeking deep within himself for the life and consciousness with which to infuse the novel, he would attempt to transcend himself, to limit and define himself in an effort to move outward from himself, to set the limits to his own individual consciousness in order to be able to create characters other than himself. The *House of Gold* (1929) [1] is an attempt to return to that approach, another effort to look at characters instead of projecting himself into them.

The scene of *The House of Gold* is essentially the same as in *Thy Neighbour's Wife*—not in the Aran Islands, however, but in an Irish provincial town across the bay. Life is so different. The same kinds of characters appear—the priest, the doctor, the local shopkeepers and publicans, and the colorful and eccentric peasants. And with these characters come the same concerns and conflicts—the scheming for money and power, social and political ideals perverted and distorted for one personal reason or another, and a beautiful, unhappy woman married to a man she does not love. But where in *Thy Neighbour's Wife* the conflict was concentrated in the character of Hugh McMahon, in *The House of Gold* four main characters embody the conflict, each in some way picking up a thread of what tore at McMahon. Father Considine, the alcoholic priest, is driven between his lust and his religion. Jim Fitzpatrick, the doctor, has McMahon's rational tendencies and his alternate impulses to assert himself or humbly submit. Francis O'Neill, whose external life is modeled after O'Flaherty's, is the impulse to achieve ideals through direct action. And Ramon Mor Costello, who contrasts directly with Fitzpatrick, is passion and energy without intellect.

As in *Thy Neighbour's Wife* it is a beautiful woman who precipitates the conflict, in this case Nora Costello, who has a relationship to Ramon Mor much like Lily McSherry's to her husband, whom Ramon Mor somewhat resembles. But Nora is more a force than a woman. She is a symbol of beauty, earthly pleasures, culture, civilization, of all those things that drive a man into life; she takes on a different meaning to each of the characters drawn to her. To herself she is a conscious personification of beauty. Life for her is a "glorious tragedy" in which she is always the heroine, "always dogged by men who struggled for her caresses, men driven to despair, men exalted, men damned" (p. 229). This is exactly her role in the novel, and O'Flaherty penetrates no further into her consciousness. Her importance is not what she is but what she stands for, how she enters into the minds of the main characters.

As the effort was in *Thy Neighbour's Wife* to objectify himself in the character of Hugh McMahon, so O'Flaherty creates characters in this novel that objectify aspects of himself. Francis O'Neill, for example, is the external O'Flaherty, not idealized but seen with a dispassionate, even mocking eye. Like O'Flaherty, he is a young man in his early thirties (O'Flaherty's age); he is of peasant origin but has run away from the peasant life. His family had collected money to send him to a seminary to become a priest, but instead he ran away to become a revolutionary. After that he went from one job to another. His last project was a newspaper that he started (an idea that O'Flaherty toyed with but rejected when the plan was proposed by his brother in America), but when the newspaper went bankrupt, O'Neill was forced to return, defeated, to the country to live with his aged peasant father, who is very like O'Flaherty's own father as he describes him in *Shame the Devil* when he recalls visiting his home some years after his mother died (pp. 61–68).

But O'Neill is confined to external action. He does not brood. His desire for Nora does not drive him to introspection. For him she is a beautiful, desirable woman, representing in some way the ideals that he has ineffectually pursued, in some way his spiritual salvation. He is poor and powerless and ashamed of his poverty. Without money he lacks the means to take Nora away with him, and he robs to get this money. But he is as ineffectual in this as in his other endeavors, kept from Nora not by any inner obstacles but by his own weakness and bungling. When he gropes his way to what was to have been their final assignation and finds that she has been extinguished (symbolically, by the priest, the enemy of life and beauty), all value is lost and he has to be led away.

This is O'Flaherty as he can see himself from the outside, kept from possessing all that Nora represents not by the crises of his soul but by his own personal weakness, his lack of ability. And because he cannot save Nora from the forces of commercial greed or priestly extinction, he, like O'Neill, can be looked at as a powerless nothing. But O'Flaherty does not pity O'Neill or sympathize with him. He looks at him. He makes him a character and in this way rises above what O'Neill is and represents. By fixing his position in a character like O'Neill, O'Flaherty can keep track of himself. This part of him, established in a definite relationship to the action without having his own particular consciousness involved, lets him create other characters separate from himself. O'Neill objectifies O'Flaherty's outer life, making it something that can be dealt with, manipulated, and looked at. In the same way O'Flaherty attempts to look at his inner life, that which is almost his constant concern in the black soul novels, the soul in torment, driven deeper and deeper into self-consciousness until confronted with the insuperable burden of its own existence. This is O'Flaherty's special knowledge, and as such this too must be objectified to free him from it. Part of this knowledge appears to be madness and part vision, often so tangled at the depths to which O'Flaherty plummets as to be inseparable. In *The House of Gold* he brings this to the surface to be examined as O'Neill is examined.

Father Considine is clearly mad. Already driven to drink because of his involvement in Ramon Mor's machinations to bring the town under his control, Nora's coming is more than he can stand. She represents for him all the temptations of the flesh, all that is in conflict with his religion that contemns the flesh. Yet she lures him so powerfully that it seems he must destroy her to save his soul. He loses all sense of proportion, whirled in the chaos of his own imagination, which becomes "peopled with the changing and dread phantoms that madmen see" (p. 160). His madness is pathological, presented objectively, unlike the madness of Gilhooley or Ferriter whose visions of horror are the inevitable consequence of the intensity of their spiritual experience and who become distraught because the burden of their individual existence without a God is more than their spirits can sustain. In the black soul novels O'Flaherty concentrates on the experience, madness or no. With Considine, O'Flaherty is concerned with presenting a character who is mad. His delusions are clearly delusions, symptoms of his madness, and it is in his madness that his mind confuses God and the Devil, until "Despair, a hunchback with one eye in the centre of his forehead, carrying a great flail, flogged God and the Devil and sent them shrieking out of sight" (p. 160). Then his mind ceases revolving and fixes on the attainment of his one desire regardless of consequences. Following Nora from the church up the desolate Black Cliff where she is going to meet O'Neill, he attacks her in a fury of agony and ecstasy, biting at her golden hair which appears to him as golden snakes, tearing their heads off, kissing them, until he sees them fall and disappear, "creating by their disappearance a vision of a palace among the clouds, of a myriad women, waiting in wanton postures for their lovers, who became one and identical with himself, armed with the amorous qualities of countless men, which . . . he simultaneously squandered, thus abolishing by one enormous effort the will to love" (p. 318). In the black soul novels the characters strike out as a consequence of their terror, to find meaning. In *The House of Gold* O'Flaherty objectifies this kind of spiritual experience in the character of Considine by looking at its psychological roots in sexual frustration.

But there is another kind of madness which O'Flaherty separates from pathological madness—the madness of Tommy Derrane, a character like the Fool in *Lear* or Lear himself in his madness—the madness which gives more than earthly wisdom. "They say that madmen can read a man's character better than those that are supposed to be in their senses," O'Flaherty has one of the characters say (p. 205). If O'Flaherty, looking deep into himself and remembering his war trauma and his psychological discharge, can suspect a pathological madness at the source of his most intense spiritual experiences, he still cannot reject the validity of these experiences. He does have a special knowledge. He has been where others have not been and seen a truth that others have not seen. He objectifies this, too, in the character of Tommy Derrane, "the wild man from the islands," whose vision of truth it would take a madman to bear. Derrane addresses Ramon Mor: "Fools curse you but I bless you, for it's nothing to me that you sucked the blood of the villages and the islands. It's the nature of a hawk to pounce on a mouse, and for an eagle to steal the lamb from its mother's teat. Take the bread out of our mouth. God bless you. We'll all be equal one day. Death, I say. The Devil is waiting for us all. It's between God and the Devil who'll have us. A man is no more than a cow to be bought and sold at the crossroads between Heaven and Hell" (p. 120).

As O'Flaherty has embodied his own external life in the character of O'Neill, and has distinguished pathological from prophetic madness in Considine and Derrane, so he portrays his own inner, rational life in Dr. Jim Fitzpatrick. O'Flaherty uses a myth to explain the doctor's personality: "Away, away beyond the reach of the imagination flows the great, red river of the human soul, . . . guarded by an unknown spirit who makes strange experiments as he pours a drop into each womb where seed is germinating. Sometimes he joins to an uncouth and servile body an alien soul, whose dreams are a torment to the flesh that covers it" (p. 214). The Doctor is trapped in a provincial town with the "barbarous food, barbarous companionship, an entire lack of social morality, of culture and intellectual tolerance" that "cause a melancholy that corrupts the strongest mind" (p. 78). A weak man, and an idealist, for him Nora is the symbol of the perfection that his mind seeks but his body is unable to accomplish. Forced to defend Nora against Ramon Mor and Father Considine, representing to him the forces of greed and superstition that are the chief obstacles to the perfection of society, his soul and body war with one another. O'Flaherty enacts, within the Doctor, the same conflict of soaring intellect and frail humanity that he describes within himself in *Shame the Devil*. But he does not plunge into the doctor's being, as he does with the souls in conflict in the black soul novels. He understands him. He sets him within limits. And at the same time he describes in the Doctor a crisis and cycle of experience that culminate in O'Flaherty's ideal of artistic vision.

The Doctor contrasts Nora's ideal beauty with his wife's child-worn shabbiness. He sees Ramon Mor's power and the "rough and cunning zest for life" of the townspeople in contrast to his own delicate body. As much as he despises the priest "who followed a disgraceful profession and whose mind was in darkness," he also fears him, "the awakening of his childish awe of the mystical powers of the priesthood" (p. 218). He longs to submit, sees the beauty in being a person "without the instinct towards revolt, a weak acceptor, living a dull life" (p. 224). "He began to feel afraid of God, in whom he did not believe" (p. 219). In this mood he loves his wife and children wildly, and Nora becomes "a dangerous woman" who would wreck his life. He longs to kiss the priest's hands, to accept and believe. But no one understands him. He resents his wife's doing her housework "when his soul was suffering from a crisis" (p. 216). When he tries to explain to the priest, the priest is too distraught with his own obsession with Nora to understand or care about the Doctor's spiritual vision. Yet the Doctor has a momentous inarticulate insight that he wants understood. He rejects the word *religion* to describe what he has to say as "so ill-used as to mean nothing but fetish-worship." He tries to explain: "But there are times, if you understand what I mean, living in a barbarous state of society, I hope you understand clearly what I mean, when one has a vision above the ordinary, when the very form of the human soul, to use now the expression and symbolism which passes for reality in your church, excuse me, I mean to say . . ." (p. 225). The priest interrupts him and he cannot continue to say what he cannot say, what seems to escape being said. Then he curses his own cowardice, the priest, the abominable town, and his own sordid life tied to a wretched woman.

The Doctor's conflict is not resolved until his mind soars away "into that vague place that the mind always soars when it contemplates the universe" (p. 289). Then all sounds become identical, and "pain became identical with pleasure, sorrow with joy, anger with love," all balanced in a beautiful harmony. His whole situation is projected into a struggle he observes between a spider and a reptile, in which it is uncertain whether the reptile is attacking the spider or the spider tricking the reptile into its web. In the town square crowds are gathered listening to arguments about farmer cooperatives to free them from the power of men like Ramon Mor. To the doctor the warring insects and the folly of his own life are more interesting. "Pursuit and conquest," he concluded "were really worthless compared to the subtle pleasure of understanding" (p. 292). Now he becomes interested in the activity in the square, not for itself, the argument, but for "the full mental and sensuous pleasure" which he derives; and he understands that this pleasure to be derived "by means of wonder, was probably the main instinct in life" (p. 292).

Standing apart and indifferent, "being gifted with the powers of universal observation," he is able to appreciate the speaker and the crowd. He then understands his previous failures. Because he has a "creative faculty" in "a human organism too weak to give it expression," he has not truly enjoyed and understood life. He had directed himself wrongly in trying to change and perfect society. He is better equipped for "the analytical life, for accepting reality and for influencing his fellow creatures towards the pursuit of beauty by moving inwards on his own soul" (p. 294). All his efforts to help Nora, to side with the people against Ramon Mor, and to fight priestly superstition have been misdirected. All these things are to be appreciated for their "intellectual and sensuous interest," because they "gave pleasure to the contemplative mind" and so are justified in their existence. Even

Ramon Mor was merely following the creative impulse in himself, the law of his own nature.

Now everything is beautiful for the Doctor as all is brought into reasonable proportion: "the beauty of growth against the struggle for existence, with its attendant cruelties," "life was beautiful and good in all its manifestations," "evil would cease to have meaning," "all human beings became beautiful and lovable, each after its kind," some for their gentleness or courage, others for their contrast in cruelty or ugliness, or for being "diseased, criminal, insane, perverted." And all their activities became beautiful. And "after them came the animals, the birds, the insects, the earth itself, the sea, the firmament . . . waiting for the spark of life." It does not matter from whom this spark comes, because to his mind, "ruminating on beauty, right to the dissolution of his existence, his disembodiment, his decay, his return to the earth, the earth's bursting, becoming spawn . . . waiting for the spark of life," the circle is complete and has no beginning (p. 297).

In his ecstasy, the Doctor rises superior to and indifferent to everything, and his conflicts are resolved, except that O'Flaherty represents this triumph as something less than admirable or ideal: "He shrugged his shoulders, continued his journey, passed out of the square into Railway Street, and out of Railway Street into his home, disappearing, utterly indifferent to the welfare of the town, to the welfare of the people, to the welfare of humanity, to justice and really, if the truth were known, to beauty itself" (p. 298).

Toward the end of *Two Years* O'Flaherty tells of a change he underwent as he began to realize that he was without the power to bring about the changes that his lofty imagination envisaged for a mankind moving toward a godlike perfection. As he realized that he was fit to be no more than a drummer in the war of world revolution, he saw what he believed to be his role: "Now I saw the world and its laws, its wars, its prophets, and the quickly changing countenance of its philosophy as a drama filmed on a globe beyond my being, but turning to my hand and subject for the exercise of my observant vision" (p. 349). His role would be to "mime the outer strength" he lacked "with wordy subtlety" (p. 350). Like Jim Fitzpatrick, it is his lack of power, of will, that changes him from trying to be an actor to accepting his role as an observer.

O'Flaherty traces out in the Doctor his own inner life. When O'Flaherty began his career as a writer, he too made the decision that he might influence people toward the pursuit of beauty not by direct admonition but by "moving inwards on his own soul." The vision that

Fitzpatrick had "above the ordinary," when he was aware of something momentous and inarticulate about "the very form of the human soul" is like the vision of Fergus O'Connor in *The Black Soul* when out of his despair there came a mystical insight that he found himself incapable of expressing. O'Flaherty tells in *Shame the Devil* of the conflicts within himself like Fitzpatrick's where, "when the fire is out," he alternately longs to submit and find peace or throw himself into a cause or crusade that will absorb his whole being. Finally, when out of the struggle a peace comes, it is the kind of peace that Fitzpatrick achieved—a rising above the struggle, a flight of powerful confident intellect where he is indifferent to man's wars and his politics, to whether "workmen are driven to slaughter one another by Fascist chiefs or Communist commissars. . . . It is the movement that counts, provided there is movement" (p. 298).

Then he realizes what a "hypocrite and scoundrel, judging him from a humanitarian point of view," the artist must be. He recalls Garnett's saying that "to the artist, everything that exists justifies itself by the fact of its existence" (p. 230). From this exalted vision gained by turning inward upon his own soul come the black soul novels where O'Flaherty shares with Fitzpatrick the esthetic that all human existence is beautiful, each after its kind, even the "criminal, insane, perverted" —McDara, Gilhooley, Ferriter. And from Fitzpatrick's insight comes an awareness of the beauty of everything, all activities, the animals, the birds, the sea, the firmament itself. This is the vision that lies behind the majority of O'Flaherty's short stories.

O'Flaherty creates this character with an order of experience like his own not to penetrate to any new depth of experience or truth, but to define and look at the character and thus to stand apart even from himself (as he does from the external view of himself in Francis O'Neill), to transcend himself as he attempted to do through Hugh McMahon in *Thy Neighbour's Wife*. He makes of Jim Fitzpatrick a character as Fergus O'Connor or McDara are not characters. His inner experience is not important for itself but as it defines him as a character. O'Flaherty does not plunge into the depths of the Doctor's being to explore the human soul as he does with Fergus O'Connor or Gypo Nolan or Francis Ferriter. He stands off from the doctor and in so doing stands off from himself, the ultimate in detachment.

In the black soul novels, O'Flaherty, willingly or reluctantly, was confined to exploring his own consciousness and his own vision. By making that subjective consciousness and vision objective in the characters of O'Neill, Considine, Derrane, and Fitzpatrick—by making them, and himself in them, objects of contemplation—he freed himself from his confinement and made it possible for himself to create a character that was really *other*. The character he creates is in the pattern of Red John, McSherry, Gypo Nolan, and Gilhooley, but is created by artistic skill and not torn from his being. Such a character is Ramon Mor Costello, a magnificent creation, terrifying and beautiful, like "an aged oak," as O'Flaherty describes him, "whose twisted massive branches and naked, scarred roots are full of majesty" (p. 50).

Ramon Mor is a gombeen man, that hateful kind of huckster-merchant-usurer that drew O'Flaherty's wrath in *A Tourist's Guide to Ireland* as being, along with the priests, the most malign force preying on the Irish peasants. O'Neill hates him, hates his power, hates his having Nora, hates the humiliation he remembers when as a child he saw his mother bowing and scraping before him out of fear. But O'Flaherty draws him, not as an object of scorn but as a center of force and terrifying beauty. With a craftsman's skill he notes the significant detail—the way Ramon inspected his room each morning lest something of value be left, the hair he refused to crop closely "lest he might waste a part of himself," the way he swept the crumbs into his hand and swallowed them after slicing the family's bread and butter rations (p. 75). He sees him as Tommy Derrane sees him, as an eagle or a hawk whose nature it is to prey on the weak and, as Fitzpatrick sees him, as something of "intellectual and sensuous interest" who in following the creative instinct in him "gave pleasure to the contemplative mind."

Yet for all his colossal exterior and eccentricities of avarice Ramon is not a monster or a caricature. He has feelings, fears, doubts, but in keeping with the character of a person who by force of will has raised himself from poverty to wealth and power. He has a weakness, which O'Flaherty describes as "the weakness of the non-intellectual man when confronted with the problem of universal harmony" (p. 162), but this weakness does not drive him to a spiritual crisis. He too fears death, "the mysteries of what was beyond earth," and the priest whom he trusted to defend him against those mysteries. But he does not submit. He defies the priest, defies death. For him avarice will "gobble up all rival passions and lay waste with its golden fires those menacing doubts that drag men from the banquet of desire" (p. 163). Ramon is the antithesis of the Doctor—all strength where the Doctor is all weakness; all action where the Doctor is all contemplation, all practical, self-serving scheming in contrast to the Doctor's ineffectual idealism. Only in their love for Nora do their lives cross; and as the Doctor abandons Nora when he abandons the life of action, Ramon Mor destroys himself in trying to possess her.

Even though he is married to Nora, she is always out of his reach. She coldly submits herself to him and he is loathsome to her. He is impotent, and his impotent passion torments and infuriates him. Yet he is driven toward her as he is driven toward gold, and her golden hair and the gold that he has devoted his life to acquiring blend together. As his avarice is fruitless so is their marriage. What she represents to him is vague, like that which has impelled him to sacrifice everything in his mania for wealth and power. But even though he believes that his desire for her will lead to his destruction, he will not cast her out. Until the end he is driven to possess her. With his bare hands he crushes the life from the priest who has killed her, and when death overtakes him it is her golden hair that is focused at the diminishing center of his consciousness. At the end he achieves a grandeur beyond that of any other character: "The moonlight poured into the hall upon the wailing women, upon the kneeling men, upon the old woman tearing her hair, upon Ramon Mor's enormous corpse, stretched stiff upon the mattress, and upon his eye that stared, unblinking, at eternity" (p. 348).

L. Paul-Dubois called *The House of Gold* the best constructed and the most finished of O'Flaherty's novels,[2] and he is right. O'Flaherty in this novel is most consciously the craftsman, most concerned to achieve with form what his previous novels had achieved with intensity and power. Prior to this his novels were constructed from his own passion, took their intensity and violence from his own inner turmoil. The scorn for form and the admiration of violent energy were a part of the esthetic of the young radicals whom he joined when he returned to Dublin in 1924 and who considered a perfect style suspect. In *The House of Gold* his novels begin a conscious turn from that esthetic toward novels that will be constructions, made by his knowledge and skill, and impersonal, not wrenched from his soul. In this novel, by delimiting himself in characters who could be looked at, he in effect wrote himself out of his work. And by doing this he created the grand character of Ramon Mor by means of his own skill. He had freed himself from the black soul pattern, and only *The Puritan* reverted to that manner among the rest of the novels. Whether this move was toward the frank commercialism that Tindall suggests,[3] an escape from his own spiritual conflict, an effort to break out of a fully exploited pattern, or a new understanding of himself as an artist, whether this move was for better or worse it marked the direction that O'Flaherty henceforth would take.

V. S. Pritchett, reviewing *Skerrett* in the *New Statesman and Nation* (July 23, 1932), gave as a serious limitation to O'Flaherty's novels the fact that "his creatures have no minds." Looking across the whole sweep of the novels, from *The Black Soul* to *Insurrection*, a reader would be inclined to agree with Pritchett's observation—with characters like Red John, Gypo Nolan, Gilhooley, Ramon Mor, Bill Gunn, Skerrett, and Bartly Madden as particularly conspicuous illustrations of mindless creatures. However, to call this a limitation is to impose upon O'Flaherty a requirement that is not related to his esthetic ends but reflects some preconception on the part of the critic as to what a novel should be.

O'Flaherty's mindless, "middle," characters are very deliberate artistic creations designed to fulfill a definite esthetic role. O'Flaherty had chosen for his patron the Great God of Passion, and for his theme wild tragedy which for him was the highest form of beauty. As an artist his role was to portray the beauty of passion, and the highest passion was that of men passionately engaged in life. *The Black Soul* illustrates the artistic problem that existed for O'Flaherty. The central character, Fergus O'Connor, engaging life and the meaning of life directly, is kept by his intellect from full commitment and participation. The world exists for him as a logical problem. He "burrows in the bowels of philosophy" to find the truth or attempts to find truth in a cause like communism.

But for O'Flaherty there is no truth. In *Shame the Devil* he begins with the premise that all intelligent men are convinced that the attempt of Christianity and the civilization founded upon it to find truth or the meaning of truth has been a failure (p. 9). This is the conclusion to which all intellectual quest must lead. The intellectual man in the modern age cannot shatter himself against life like a Faust who is unwilling to accept any limit to human reason. There is no truth for which he can barter his soul. At the furthest reaches of his mind there is only the barren emptiness of chaos. Existence is motion without purpose. Those characters built out of his own spiritual substance, like Fergus O'Connor and the other tormented souls of the black soul novels, must share with O'Flaherty this ultimate vision of reality, and it is a vision that precludes what he calls in his study, *Joseph Conrad* the most beautiful of human expressions, "the terrible madnesses of men and women crashing their bodies and their minds against the boundary walls of human knowledge" (p. 8). They can lash out, as do McDara and Ferriter, in a violent act, but the act is more a futile protest than a gesture of defiance. They are tormented, but they are passive. The exquisite writhings of their minds and bodies supply material for the artist, but it is material of a lower order.

The character type of Red John offered an alternative to this. Red John embodies the most elemental passions unrestrained by intellect. He is moved by the most primitive forces of life. Driven by jealousy and frustration, cut off from the elemental society in which his life has meaning, he reacts directly and physically. He drives his sheep from one side of the fields to the other in his inarticulate frenzy. He tears off his clothes, his limbs twitch uncontrollably, he becomes the instrument of expression for all the elemental passions over which he has no control. So possessed, he engages in the last fierce combat with O'Connor until his heart bursts in the last effort of his madness. This is the full expression of passion, not a whine but an active protest of the full animal forces of his being.

Neither the thought-tormented Fergus O'Connor nor the passion-possessed Red John was adequate for O'Flaherty's highest tragic expression. O'Connor's black soul keeps him from passionate engagement, and Red John is not as much a man as the embodiment of elemental forces that possess men. It is fitting that in O'Flaherty's alternate ending they destroy one another, intellect being destroyed by passion and passion by intellect, for it is only together that they form the man for whom tragedy is possible. Much the same division between intellect and passion is made in *The Informer* between Dan Gallagher and Gypo Nolan, but Gypo, despite the dullness of his intellect, is a man in a way that Red John is not. Red John had neither intellect nor physical power. He was frustrated because he lacked the strength to assert his rights, and he had neither the mind nor the imagination to raise his protest to the human level. Gypo has the strength and stature to contend with all physical obstacles. He will accept the challenge of anything he can reach with his bare hands. Only the nameless terrors that lie hidden behind intellect haunt him. He has the imagination to be aware of forces greater than he is, terrifying because he cannot come to grips with them. His last fearsome charge into the hail of bullets is a defiance of the powers of earth, but his last gesture is a submission to the powers beyond the earth.

In Gypo Nolan O'Flaherty is moving toward a solution of the problem of creating a character of tragic stature in the modern world. The character must be a man of great strength and passions capable of heroic gestures. But his intellect must in some way be limited to allow him the full extravagant engagement that the brooding intellect will not permit. Yet he must be a man with the consciousness of a man, aware of himself against the background of human existence. And he must be motivated, set in motion by a force that gives him a credible, independent being and that has the power to propel him strongly into life. Red John, though not the central character of *The Black Soul*, embodies the sort of intensity O'Flaherty sought. Gypo Nolan is an extension of this and a more deliberate effort to create a specific character type. But Gypo achieves his motivation only through the external force of Dan Gallagher's evil intellect and the nameless terrors it conjures for him. Without this he is inert. There is nothing within him strong enough to face the nightmare of chaos. That which drives him wakes in his imagination the force to which he must submit. His ending is magnificent, terrifying, but has not the wild beauty of tragedy which for O'Flaherty meant the greatest force of man contending against the greatest force of the universe.

This character type held a continuous fascination for O'Flaherty, a challenge to his highest ideals of art, but it was beyond his achievement until he could escape from the confinement of his own consciousness which limited him to a repetition of the black soul pattern. It was not until he could transcend himself in *The House of Gold* and put his own spiritual turmoil into a manageable perspective that he could turn again to the strong character and attempt to create that separate consciousness of a stature capable of tragic grandeur. Ramon Mor evolves from Gypo Nolan as Gypo evolved from Red John. He combines the elemental passion of Red John with the physical strength of Gypo, but he is modified and given independent life by his drive for gold and power which is the natural expression of his being. His intellect is limited—deliberately limited. He has a mind, but he is not an intellectual. He is aware of himself as a man, but his expression is action, not contemplation. The terror of existence does not drive him to despair but to defiance. When he shatters himself against life, it is a full expression of all that he is, and in this expression he approaches O'Flaherty's tragic ideal.

O'Flaherty's middle characters are deliberate esthetic creations to achieve a deliberate end—the tragedy of which the brooding intellectual is incapable. For O'Flaherty the beauty of life is expressed in passionate action which it is the artist's function to record. Insofar as mind interferes with that action, he limits mind. It is not a defect in his work but a necessary choice in a world in which the intellect's highest flights must bring only a view of meaningless chaos.

The Return of the Brute (1929) [4] is notable for little but O'Flaherty's continued interest in the strong, nonintellectual character driven by some force to expend himself fully. The setting is the trenches during World War I, O'Flaherty's only use of his wartime experiences in fiction. The manner is rather like Robert Graves's *Goodbye to All That* in that the aimlessness and confusion of battle dominates. The common footsoldiers slough around in the mud and the darkness, lost, bewildered, almost abandoned to death. Among the nine men in the section on which O'Flaherty centers is Bill Gunn, a giant of a man like Gypo Nolan, with the same restricted intellect. He has reached the limit of his ability to tolerate the kind of battle that has him sitting in the mud deprived of food and sleep, fighting an unseen enemy and tolerating the incessant chipping of the section leader. His mind begins to conjure strange images, savage brutes with clubs whom he both fears and identifies himself with. Then something snaps and explodes within him, compelling him to act, and at the same time "in some remote part of his body, very distinct and faint," he hears "a chorus of birds . . . singing in beautiful harmony" (p. 182). He attacks the section leader with blind ferocity and strangles him. Then he charges toward the enemy trenches until a machinegun cuts him down. "Riddled with bullets, he died, bellowing and clawing the earth" (p. 187).

In a way *The Return of the Brute* is an experiment to see if tragic effects are possible with a character devoid of brooding intellect. There are no intellectual forces in this novel either within Gunn or external to him. The emphasis is on the unthinking man stripped of his humanity and driven by external circumstances to his final passionate act. Except for this intellectual vacuum, Gunn is like O'Flaherty's other middle characters. Like Gypo he has unusual physical strength. His singing birds are reminiscent of Gypo's bucolic yearnings. Like Gilhooley's his nameless terrors are represented by men with clubs. His violent death effort, the blind charge into the bullets, is like that of Gypo (and Bartly Madden in *Insurrection*). The main difference is that only Gunn is the case study of an overwrought mind—or rather, brain, for Gunn is more a collection of nerve ends than a significant mentality.

The terrors of the other middle characters have a spiritual dimension. Gilhooley's man with a club, though imaginary, is expressive of his spiritual state and foreshadows his ultimate spiritual terror. Gunn's hairy brutes with clubs are the delusions of a deranged mentality, symptoms of his condition and not expressions of a spiritual state. As Gypo and Gilhooley are driven by intellect they become naked souls. Their last violent gestures are not individual distortions but universal expressions as they become aware of the terror of reality. Gunn is merely sick; his last gesture is a spasm. His madness is without meaning. Lacking a spiritual dimension he fails of universality, and his final act is pitiful, not awesome. The brooding intellect desperate for meaning is essential for the tragic effect O'Flaherty is seeking, and though mind could be limited, as in the case of Gypo and Ramon Mor, to make possible the violent expression, it could not be eliminated or the expression would lack tragic meaning.

When O'Flaherty wrote Garnett (March 8, 1932) that he had "undergone a rather stupid cycle of experience" to arrive at a clearer consciousness of what he wanted to do and set himself to his task ("Now, it's coats off, and to do it"), it was *Skerrett* [5] that he was writing. And *Skerrett* is representative of the new direction that O'Flaherty's novels take, with O'Flaherty as a consciousness outside the novel and not having his consciousness extended into a character in an act of personal exploration that forms the real subject of the novel. In *Skerrett* O'Flaherty turns outward from himself and also away from himself in time—*Skerrett* is set in the past, beginning ten years before O'Flaherty was born and ending thirty years back from when O'Flaherty was writing, in contrast to the black soul novels which were essentially contemporaneous.

Turning outward and away from the theme of spiritual conflict, O'Flaherty created a conflict outside himself in two strong men with opposing wills and opposing ideals. The source for the main character, Skerrett, was a short story called "The Bladder" included in O'Flaherty's early *Spring Sowing* collection. In that story a strong but rather ridiculous schoolmaster who persists in telling the peasants how to improve themselves finds in the peasants a practical knowledge that puts his theoretical knowledge to shame. After he is unable to cure his heifer swollen with a surfeit of water she has drunk, but has her cured by the old peasant remedy of whiskey, he is given the nickname, the Bladder, for his habit of blowing off advice to everyone.

In *Skerrett* the general outlines of the character are the same, as are many of the details. The unnamed schoolmaster is fleshy, bearded, with a little bald patch at the rear of his skull, like Skerrett. His wife drank until she died of delirium tremens like Skerrett's wife, who was committed to a lunatic asylum because of drink. And like Skerrett, who also came to be nicknamed the Bladder after his strength began to fail, the schoolmaster began to preach against drinking. But the schoolmaster is a ridiculous person and Skerrett is far from that, because it is the strength of Skerrett's will that O'Flaherty focuses on. Opposed to that will is Father Harry Moclair, the parish priest from the same mold as Father Reilly from *Thy Neighbour's Wife* and the parish priests of *A Tourist's Guide*. Dedicated to extending his own wealth and power, he quickly senses in Skerrett's strong will a force that threatens his own; relentlessly, using all the powers at his command, he sets out to destroy him.

Skerrett comes to Nara a cruel and imperious man, hobbled by a whining and ugly wife who symbolizes all his frustrations. The school he comes to is a wreck, the previous schoolmaster driven to insanity, but Skerrett is not daunted and determines to beat civilization into the unruly islanders with a birch rod. By strength of will and muscle he creates a measure of order and even wins a grudging respect of the peasants. But then his fortune turns. His young son, whose birth softened Skerrett even toward his wife, is killed in a fall. His wife begins to drink, and Moclair begins his systematic persecution. Skerrett meanwhile turns more and more toward the islanders, even adopting their manner of dress and teaching Gaelic in his classroom. All things seem to conspire against him. His cow dies from drinking too much cold water. Then his fishing boat and the entire crew is lost in a freak accident, making the peasants believe he is cursed. His wife becomes more and more unmanageable with her drinking, until she grows completely insane. In a last gesture she strikes Skerrett in the head with the fire tongs, starting him on a quick physical decay. At this point Skerrett is at a low ebb, tied to a lunatic wife, scoffed at by the peasants, persecuted by Moclair at every step: "There he was, in spite of his force, conquered by the island which he had tried to dominate." It had toyed with him, giving him a promise of greatness. "Now it was crushing him into a weak, defeated thing, a subject for the most common man to mock" (p. 186).

Skerrett was yet to show his true measure. Up to this point he is a character, involved in society, with his aspirations centered in society. Now he begins to emerge as a man dependent only on his own spiritual resources. No gnawing intellect weakens him or drives him to despair as is the case with the black soul characters. O'Flaherty gives him stature. When he knows that he will be driven from his classroom after a government inspection prompted by Moclair, Skerrett rises to almost his full spiritual height. He sees the naked rocks glittering about him and they appear to him as the eyes of devils grinning at him. Suddenly he thinks the earth is a living being, making fun of his defeat:

> All was so silent and mysterious and unapproachable. He thought how puny and weak was man, wandering haphazard on this cruel earth, pressing its face with his feet, burrowing in its bosom and then passing to his death, when the vain quests of his life have dissolved in horrid annihilation. And it was made manifest to him as he watched this glistening crust of sun-baked rock, beneath its dome of sky, that there was no God to reward the just or to punish the wicked, nothing beyond this unconquerable earth but the phantasies born of man's fear and man's vanity. And he began to laugh softly to himself. (p. 249)

This is a height no other O'Flaherty character reaches, before or after—the awareness of the black soul coalesces with the strength of Ramon Mor. There is no spiritual crisis, no despair. The black soul undergoes a spiritual change at this moment and becomes one with the life of the universe. Lesser men lose their sanity or commit suicide. Skerrett laughs, rising superior even to an awareness of his own annihilation. His "arrogant soul" takes "wing into complete freedom" for the first time. Nothing, not even a belief in God, will make him subservient to Moclair again. "Rather sink into the bosom of this grinning unsympathetic earth, to which all beings were the same, the bones of the wicked and the bones of the just, than mount into a fantastic paradise on the passport of Moclair" (p. 249).

Skerrett is the triumph of O'Flaherty's detachment. Trapped within his own consciousness, he could create only tortured souls like his own, as if genuine consciousness could produce no other pattern but spiritual crisis when detached from social momentum and faced with the awful awareness of its own existence. In *The House of Gold* O'Flaherty for once was able to transcend himself and free himself from that pattern by embodying himself in characters who could be looked at as mere men among other men, not the only form of consciousness possible. And Ramon Mor emerged as another consciousness, by strength of body and strength of will superior to the petty forces of life, driven by his passion to destroy himself. But his eye that "stared, unblinking, at eternity" is already dead. He had not reached the tragic heights and peered over the brink of chaos in the true tragic grandeur that was O'Flaherty's ideal. But Skerrett did. He stared unblinking at eternity and laughed.

It matters little that after that, his body ravaged with illness, boycotted by those peasants who obeyed Moclair's promptings, he attempts to lose himself among the wilder peasants who show some independence of Moclair. When they in turn are cowed by Moclair, he remains his own man, refusing to take their aid in secret. Now everything is lost, "everything he held dear . . . taken from him . . . until he now stood alone in this tiny cabin on a lonely crag, by the edge of the ocean" (p. 269). And still he will strike out. Despite his feeble health he sets out to attack Moclair. He is intercepted, struck down, and begins to rave. Despite the fact that he recovers his senses Moclair's enmity causes him to be committed, and in the asylum his proud heart breaks after six months. But his last words were still defiance: "I defy them all. They can't make me bend the knee" (p. 273). In an epilogue O'Flaherty comments on the legend that Skerrett had become on the island: "The nobility of Skerrett's nature lay in his pursuit of godliness. He aimed at being a man who owns no master. And such men, though doomed to destruction by the timid herd, grow after death to the full proportion of their greatness" (p. 274).

It is puzzling to try to understand what Vivian Mercier is talking about when he says that "not until we have closed the book do we realize that Skerrett symbolizes Nature rather than Man—perhaps it would be most accurate to say that he is the Natural Man—and that once again Nature has triumphed, as she does in almost every work by O'Flaherty." [6] Skerrett is, rather, Promethean man, a man capable of tragedy. He is man raised to the highest level, and still a man, with the faults and the weakness of a man but, above all, the grandeur of a man. Skerrett is not the triumph of nature but the tragedy of a man who had risen to such heights as to be capable of tragedy. His tragedy is man's triumph—and O'Flaherty's.

Although *The Martyr* (1933) [7] looks back eleven years to the last days of the Civil War, the novel is not as much a historical picture as a representation of the conflict of certain basic forces in Irish society and, as much as this, another objective portrayal of those forces that O'Flaherty sees in conflict in himself. The action takes place in the small western provincial village of Sallytown, in 1922. During that period the new Irish national army—which represents the government that has accepted the oath of allegiance to the British and the split of Ireland—is mopping up the fragmented Republican army—which represents the idealists who will settle for nothing less than a free, independent, and united Ireland. The military action is of little consequence. A small force of the Republican army occupies Sallytown, much to the chagrin of the local business interests who want stability and an end to the fighting. Units of the Free State army are approaching. The Republicans attempt to set an ambush, but because of lack of discipline the whole plan fails; the town is occupied, and the Republicans either scatter or are captured.

The personalities involved in the conflict, and the tendencies they represent, are O'Flaherty's main interest. The Republicans are a mixed group, opposed to a common enemy but for entirely different reasons. Brian Crosbie, the Republican commandant, is a fanatic idealist whose dreams for a united Gaelic and Roman Catholic Ireland go far beyond political and economic goals. It is Ireland's soul that he wishes to save, and Ireland's mission, to "save Europe from the devil" (p. 192). For him Ireland's ideal mission is religious, and his aim is the "purification of the national soul" to make Ireland the ideal Christian religious community that will make her a source of inspiration and leadership for Europe and the world (p. 24). Jack Tracy, the second in command, though no less an idealist, has humanistic, not religious goals. He is a socialist and a worshiper of the machine; "steel an' combustion" are his God. "I want to make our people drop the craw-thumping God and take to worshippin' this new God" (p. 91). The rest of the Republicans —Catholics, communists, and adventurers—are opposed for one reason or another to the national betrayal which they see as merely substituting for the tyranny of the English the tyranny of the upstart Irish middle classes.

The staters are no such idealists but are best represented by Paddy Hunt, the corpulent commander of their group, who has taken advantage of the new Free State government. Nothing before, now he is a colonel in the new army, proud of his rank, passionately addicted to the bountiful life for himself, and dedicated to preserving the status quo which has made this good life possible. The order he seeks is shared by the town merchants, the publicans, the banker, and even the parish priest, Canon McElroy, who are all puzzled and perturbed by what they consider the fanaticism of the Republicans. Only the sinister Joe Tyson has any long-range goals and dedication. For him the Republicans are not a disturbance to be put down but an enemy to be ruthlessly purged. He sees the misguided idealism of men like Crosbie and Tracy to be the real hindrance to Ireland's progress, and with such idealism Ireland must learn to be ruthless: "That's what we must learn to do in Ireland. To kill in cold blood whoever stands in the way of progress. To own no God above the state" (p. 282).

In *A Tourist's Guide to Ireland* O'Flaherty describes the society that emerged after the Civil War and the tendencies of the Irish people making that society what it was. These same ingredients exist in *The Martyr,* and with the same importance, foremost of which is Ireland's tendency toward mysticism. O'Flaherty says that that tendency originates in Ireland's mist and fog; and as long as the climate remains what it is, "there will always be a vast proportion of the population under the influence of mystical dreams and mystical terrors" (pp. 16–17). As a result, there is common an "extraordinary psychological disease" from which the politicians suffer to the greatest degree: "the attempt to unite mysticism with reality" (p. 66). This disease manifests itself mainly in the belief that Ireland is a living woman, a beautiful unfortunate creature that the politicians love and wish to save. And as the priest regards the soul as of greater importance than the body, so the politicians "regard the soul of the nation as of greater consequence than the mere welfare of the nation's citizens" and say that Holy Ireland is "above such coarse ambitions as wealth, culture, bathrooms, tooth brushes and machinery" (p. 71).

This mysticism, especially as it is manifest in Brian Crosbie, is one of the main themes of *The Martyr;* and Crosbie exhibits all those tendencies just stated to an extraordinary degree. Angela Fitzgibbon (whom Tindall believes is modeled after Constance Markiewicz) identifies herself with Dark Rosaleen, an apotheosis of the living spirit of Ireland, a role in which she sometimes believes but more often uses for her own amusement. In *A Tourist's Guide* O'Flaherty has no sympathy for this kind of mysticism, the "business of managing the state" being "altogether different from the business of regulating the affairs of the Heavenly World," and "nothing concerned with the state should be a mystery or hypothetical" (p. 67).

Until O'Flaherty's attitude toward that which Crosbie represents is clear there might be a tendency to make him the hero of the piece and Tyson the villain as an unbelievably cold-blooded and ruthless murderer. But in *A Tourist's Guide* O'Flaherty's hope for Ireland is in "great forces of revolt, armed with the great wisdom of the damned, and they shall spread over the land and inhabit it with free men and women, free from usurers and soothsayers" (p. 134). Tyson is the only character in *The Martyr* with a realistic view of the situation and of what needs to be done. He hates Crosbie for the "fetish" that he worships, "idealism in general, everything that is mawkish and feminine and gushing" (p. 281). And though he does not hate Jack Tracy personally, he sees his socialist idealism as a part of the same error that motivates Crosbie, "a form of Christianity, without Christ" (p. 192). Tyson has the "great wisdom of the damned" needed to make a civilized country of Ireland, coldblooded as his methods might appear. He sees immediately the error in detaining Angela Fitzgibbon and giving her the attention she seeks, and he predicts exactly what will happen if the remnants of the Republican army are not tracked down and punished—the sniping that does occur when Paddy Hunt chooses to establish peace and order rather than finish the job.

The central conflict of *The Martyr* is between Tyson and Crosbie, with Tracy in a measure of opposition to each; and as much as these characters represent tendencies in Irish society, they also represent forces in conflict within O'Flaherty himself. Tracy, with his idealistic socialism, his gospel of communism, God, and the machine, preaches exactly what O'Flaherty preaches in *Two Years*, when he discovers the power the machine could have to shape a new society, and what O'Flaherty preaches in *Shame the Devil* when he expounds on the new god replacing the old who is dead. Tyson cannot despise the man who has this view but thinks of him as being out of date, "invaluable in another age, or under different circumstances." But with no "Spanish galleons for him to loot," Tracy is an Elizabethan out of step with the times which can tolerate no such lack of discipline (p. 192). And for Tyson, what Tracy represents stems from the same mawkishness as Crosbie's mysticism. Both through some grand gesture, want to give their lives for a cause; though Crosbie thinks that Tracy, who wants to fight rather than submit, is opposed to him, they are both merely opposite sides of the same coin.

The tense drama of the weasel and the rabbit that Crosbie and Tyson play is the drama played in *Shame the Devil* between the alternating sides of O'Flaherty's personality. O'Flaherty the man is like Tracy and Crosbie, looking for salvation by losing himself in something larger than himself. Crosbie exemplifies one extremity of this compulsion for personal sacrifice carried to its logical conclusion—a compulsion for martyrdom, not because of any theories about a better world but from a personal desire to save his own soul. Crosbie accepts the cross that Tyson has built for him not because he is constrained in any way by Tyson. Tyson is armed only with the demand that Crosbie choose to live. But like Kafka's hunger artist, Crosbie's talent is not for life but for death. His crucifixion by Tyson is a voluntary act—

what always has been latent in him. When the blazing cross hurtles over the precipice, O'Flaherty has one of the characters say, "It's only a rabbit caught by a weasel" (p. 286). The weasel is one of O'Flaherty's favorite symbols for that strong, cold, superior part of himself that stands above life—the snake's eye, the goat's eye, the Satanic element—haughty, damned, and proud. This is his creative genius which is above human frailties. The other side is the rabbit, what O'Flaherty regards in *Shame the Devil* as his weakness—"a sentimental craving for being in love and being loved and cared for and protected against life"—that even tries to make him afraid of God (p. 76). It is the desire for submission represented in Jim Fitzpatrick's wanting to kiss the priest's hands (just as Crosbie kisses Tyson's hands). When O'Flaherty attempts to shake himself from his despondency in *Shame the Devil* and reorganize his strength, he vows to weave cunning plots to thwart his enemies "and to appear once more with shining eyes, a weasel to hypnotize the rabbits, who shall be forced to give me bread for my dreams" (p. 13).

The Martyr is O'Flaherty's most Irish novel in that it holds central conflicting viewpoints which are more Irish than universal. Brian Crosbie is an Irish martyr in a way that McDara is not an Irish assassin or Gypo Nolan an Irish informer. His compulsion for martyrdom is not that of a man who happens to live in Ireland; it is, rather, something characteristic of the country that O'Flaherty knew, so characteristic that Crosbie is more an embodiment of a special Irish tendency than a man in his own right. He *is* that tendency toward resignation and mysticism that O'Flaherty thought was the chief obstacle to Irish progress. Crosbie wishes to speak with Tyson "like two brothers who have fought bitterly for the love of one woman and then have been drawn together by purification of that love" (p. 197). But O'Flaherty says in *A Tourist's Guide* that "the love of a mystical woman like Caitlin Ni Houlihain does untold harm" (p. 87). Crosbie loves Ireland for "her wild earth and the air above her, sweetened by her fragrance. . . . Her night gowns of pale mist and the sunlit dew in which she bathes her green cheeks on awakening . . . the soft music of the wind that plays her lullabies" (p. 198). O'Flaherty warns the tourists to keep a grip on their purses and their minds "lest they be induced by the whispering winds that float about our beautiful mountains to see spirits in the air." There is where, he believes, "Irish mystical patriotism originates." The antidote that O'Flaherty prescribes is that the tourist "should mock and jeer our mysticism until he shames us out of it" (p. 88). This is what Tyson attempts to do to Crosbie, laughing at Crosbie's "beastly, sentimental tosh" about his love for Ireland (p. 198).

Crosbie believes the issue at question between him and Tyson deals not with politics but with religion. But Tyson sees no difference. For him "the nation's religion is not something apart from the social life, something standing above the state." Religion for him is "the poetical expression of the people at large; their impulse towards immortality and the conquest of the universe" (p. 191). When Crosbie proclaims that Ireland will rise again under the banner of Christ, Tyson takes this as an indication that Crosbie no longer believes in the Irish Republic for which he has been fighting but has become a monarchist giving his allegiance not to Ireland but to the Kingdom of Christ." Tyson abhors Crosbie's slave morality, his feminine weakness. "Slaves should die," he says, "lest they might breed slaves." He advocates "triumphant action" which transmits to the soul "a fine arrogance, which is the direct opposite to the craving for martyrdom" (p. 187).

Tyson's view is O'Flaherty's, and Tyson stands in relation to Crosbie as O'Flaherty believes he stands in relation to Ireland and to that mystical Irish tendency in himself. In his "National Energy" letter to *The Irish Statesman* he criticized the policy of passive resistance for Ireland in favor of violent action, which he believed more in harmony with the desired national character. O'Flaherty's position in *A Tourist's Guide* toward Ireland almost exactly parallels Tyson's toward Crosbie. Tyson's definition of religion as people's "impulse towards immortality and the conquest of the universe" is like O'Flaherty's idea that God is "a state of perfection" which man imagines and strives toward, and who calls man's divine destiny "the struggle towards the perfection of his species to a state of godliness."

In *I Went to Russia* O'Flaherty says that those who have spent their lives in prison (as Crosbie has spent much of his) "become infatuated with the idea of self-torture" which is "a form of sadism . . . a miserable and disgusting form of selfishness." O'Flaherty is against all this: "I hate mummies, tombs, martyrs" (p. 169). Tyson's hate for Crosbie is intimate "as a man hates a woman he has once loved." "Not that I ever loved you personally," Tyson says, "but what you represent" (p. 281). As Tyson had excoriated from himself all Crosbie's weakness, which he hated as he once loved, so O'Flaherty represents in Crosbie all his own tendencies toward submission which he constantly struggled to rise above.

Herbert Howarth quotes a letter from Yeats to Mrs. Shakespeare in which Yeats recommends that she read *The Martyr* "which is very mad in the end." Howarth interprets this dismissal of the climax as mad as a refusal on Yeats's part "to acknowledge the Messiah he had promulgated." Howarth puts Crosbie's choice as one between martyrdom and persisting in Civil War and says that Crosbie dies on the cross believing that his martyrdom will re-Christianize Europe. For Howarth, Brian Crosbie represents the Messianic spirit which arose in Ireland after the death of Parnell and which was fostered by poets like Yeats in the literary renaissance.[8] In a way this is true. Crosbie does see Ireland and himself in Messianic roles, but if Yeats refuses to acknowledge this Messiah, O'Flaherty much more explicitly condemns him. Crosbie's choice in the last issue is not between martyrdom and persisting in Civil War but between martyrdom and life, and he dies dreaming that he will achieve personal salvation and not that his martyrdom will have any effect on Irish destiny. In *The Martyr* Crosbie does not represent hope for Ireland but a weakness in the Irish national character that must be ruthlessly expunged.

The Martyr is an Irish novel and a personal novel because it is built from the contending forces of O'Flaherty's own persona, in this case projected into Irish affairs. He sees the conflict in Ireland in terms of the conflict he sees in himself. As he sees the mystic and also the crusader in himself as part of his weaker nature that exists when his creative fire is out, that part of himself that wants to lose itself in submission or in a cause, so he sees Crosbie and Tracy. In one of the hallucinatory dialogues in *Shame the Devil* the artist chides the man for believing that he has rehabilitated himself by identifying himself with an ideal cause: "You are merely a coward, prepared to attach yourself to anybody when danger threatens" (p. 217). This is the weakness of Crosbie and Tracy. But in Tyson he sees himself as he must be —cold-eyed, ruthless, "armed with the great wisdom of the damned," the ideal that he set for himself in his essay on Joseph Conrad, "the fearless, cold-eyed adventurer who curls his lips at all that has been" (p. 10).

Despite this self-projection, however, *The Martyr* differs extremely from the earlier novels with titles cast in the same form—*The Informer, The Assassin, The Puritan*—because it is developed in the objective mode of *Thy Neighbour's Wife, The House of Gold,* and *Skerrett.* The novels in the black soul pattern are subjective. The author enters into the consciousnesses of the main characters to show the spiritual terror at their bases. The informer, the assassin, and the puritan do not represent characteristic Irish tendencies. They begin as

Irishmen, perhaps, but they end as souls. Whatever their beginnings, O'Flaherty enters into the black soul characters to achieve understanding, and the ultimate spiritual crisis is his own. In the objective mode of *The Martyr* no such relationship to the main character exists. O'Flaherty looks *at* Crosbie. He understands him as an intellectual concept and is detached from and superior to him. Crosbie's character is fixed: he has no spiritual conflict, no terror brought on by the vision of chaos to which the black soul characters are driven. His only doubts or questions are about his ability to endure his martyrdom. He is not a living soul, which for O'Flaherty is synonymous with spiritual crisis, but represents a tendency or trait both of Ireland and of O'Flaherty's own weaker nature. What Crosbie represents is central, and this is what O'Flaherty the artist detaches himself from and rises superior to. This detached view is reinforced through Tyson, who represents genius as genius is described in *The Ecstasy of Angus*, and Tyson stands to Crosbie (and Tracy) as O'Flaherty the artist stands to the Crosbie and Tracy in himself.

It is ironical that *Famine* (1937),[9] the one novel least typical of O'Flaherty's manner of seeing, is the one that most critics single out as his best. In his "Don Quixote O'Flaherty" article Sean O'Faolain calls *Famine* "the Irish Exodus," "almost Biblical," "magnificent," and notes particularly that in *Famine* O'Flaherty has somehow suppressed his cynicism, his hatred, whatever it is that leads O'Faolain to call him an "inverted romantic," and by his sensitive and sympathetic treatment of the peasants and nature has lifted the theme out of the rut of despair. He sees this as the one novel in which O'Flaherty does not lash out almost blindly at all that offends his romantic concept of beauty but enters into the subject with understanding and sympathy. In the same way Frank Hynes in the *Saturday Review of Literature* (May 25, 1946), contrasting *Famine* with the novels that preceded it, notes that O'Flaherty had a "tardily developed sense of pity and compassion for the downtrodden and dispossessed" and that *Famine* is the first to reveal this latter quality, which he regards as genuine advance in O'Flaherty's development as an artist. Vivian Mercier calls *Famine* and *Skerrett* O'Flaherty's best novels because in these he is dealing with his true subject, man and Nature.[10] Benedict Kiely calls *Famine* O'Flaherty's finest novel and one of the best Irish novels. He attributes this to a difference from everything that precedes because for once the Dark Daniel side of O'Flaherty is counteracted by another character, Thomsy Hynes, whom Kiely considers a symbol of "humility and charity and hope." Kiely calls the moment when Thomsy returns home after his search for Martin and his hearing the message of hope of the Young Irelanders "the wisest moment in all the books that Liam O'Flaherty has written." "It is a vision of raggedness and hunger leaping up to salute liberty or the hope of liberty, of love hungering for love and knowing the hollowness in the heart of hope, and knowing also that in the whole chronicle of man on earth no story has ever been told to the end." [11]

These are the Irish critics, who like O'Donoghue, the Irishman O'Flaherty tells about in *Shame the Devil*, feel somehow that O'Flaherty up until *Famine* has betrayed his Irish trust. When O'Flaherty wrote *Shame the Devil* he of course was aware of the popular Irish reaction to his work, even without the effect of the Censorship Act which banned his novels in Ireland: "I could see why they were angry with me, believing that I did not appreciate their sufferings, or the struggle they were making to overcome their tortures. They believed that I mocked them, instead of fighting side by side with them and using my voice to state their case before the world. They believed that instead of singing them on to victory and peace I was harrying them with gibes and ill-timed criticism of their defects" (p. 184). Yet his own esthetic precludes his taking sides: "I must only listen and reproduce their passions," he said, regardless of "how cold it is standing in the wings, watching the miming of the actors" (p. 184).

If *Famine* is successful for the reasons that the Irish critics assert, then it would appear that after *Shame the Devil* O'Flaherty changed his entire artistic position of detachment, abandoning that role of artist which cost him so much loneliness and torment and which represented the dominance of creative genius over O'Flaherty's human frailty. Not all critics agree that *Famine* is successful, however. Kelleher notes that *Famine* represents a change, O'Flaherty "uniting for the first time the furious speed and brutality of the other stories with the living sensitivity of the short stories." But Kelleher, who does not take the native Irish point of view, takes exception to O'Faolain's contention that O'Flaherty has lifted the theme out of the rut of despair. He believes that the Irish read into the book what is not there, that the hopes that Kiely sees generated by the hint of the Young Irelanders is a hope that the Irish read into the book, and that the end of the book, when Mary and Martin escape to America, is a *deus ex machina* device which fails of universality and does not have the forceful significance the author intended. Kelleher believes that the book is not successful because O'Flaherty is "so moved by the suffering of his own people that he too often lets brief indication support what explanation should

carry," that O'Flaherty is so personally involved as an Irishman that
he fails to be an artist, and that the Irish critics respond to the Irishness
they read into the book rather than the art, which Kelleher feels is
defective.[12]

The question about *Famine* is whether O'Flaherty had found himself
when he discovered a social consciousness (as the Irish critics seem to
infer) or whether with this social consciousness he had lost himself,
as his conception of the role of the artist presented in *Shame the Devil*
would indicate. Or had he previously betrayed Ireland for the sake of
art and in *Famine* betrayed art for the sake of Ireland? In *Shame the
Devil*, written to tell the truth about himself, he had reaffirmed his
necessary role of detachment, seen that the malign snake's eye was a
part of his creative genius and that his task was not to escape it but
accept it as his gift and curse, to "put it in harness" (p. 250). This
was in 1934, just three years prior to the publication of *Famine*. Yet
Benedict Kiely says that *Famine* is O'Flaherty's best novel because the
Dark Daniel side which is also the black soul side—the scoffing detached intellect which recognizes no social values—for once has been
offset by a character embodying humility, charity, and hope. But
this malign snake's eye which O'Flaherty came to recognize as his own
is the black soul side. Between 1934 and 1937 either he must have
undergone a complete change in his whole concept of art and his role
as an artist, in effect denying everything that he had striven for up to
that time, or he did not write *Famine* as a serious attempt at art, at the
truth, which was his sacred obligation as an artist, regardless of personal consequences.

The external evidence to answer this question is slim, but perhaps
significant. Between 1934 and 1937 O'Flaherty had sold the screen
rights to *The Informer* and gone to Hollywood to assist with the
script. The success of the movie is well-known, and though he was
paid only $5,000 for the screen rights, the success of the movie must
have been a great boost for the sale of his books. The dust jacket
blurb of *Famine*, making capital of this, proclaims that O'Flaherty's
previous work had been "appreciated for many years by critics and
discriminating readers," but it took the prize-winning movie version of
"his last book, *The Informer*" (written ten years before the movie)
to make his name known to the masses. Now, it goes on to say, "an
imposing array of producers and stars is bidding for the privilege of
screening *Famine* in the hope it may duplicate *The Informer's* success."
Famine is dedicated to John Ford, the director of *The Informer*. *Famine* was never made into a movie, and *The Informer* was O'Flaherty's

only Hollywood venture. The Hollywood adventure is one fact. The other is that O'Flaherty, who had written eleven novels, four volumes of short stories, two autobiographies, a travel book and a biography in the years preceding *Famine* (and he was only forty) with a novel almost every year, did not publish another book until 1946, nine years after *Famine*.

About O'Flaherty's Hollywood experiences little is available except —and the exception may be very important—*Hollywood Cemetery* (1935),[13] published immediately on the heels of his experiences. In this novel there appears an O'Flaherty-like Irish author, Brian Carey, who has sold the screen rights of a novel and who has been hired at five hundred dollars a week for three months to go to Hollywood and assist with the scenario. *Hollywood Cemetery* is primarily a lampoon of Hollywood, a predecessor of Waugh's *The Loved One* and in the same spirit. It is interesting mostly because it gives O'Flaherty's view of Hollywood and a cold-eyed objective view of a version of himself in Brian Carey who is made a little ridiculous, but in the way Jim Fitzpatrick and Francis O'Neill of *The House of Gold* are ridiculous, or Hugh McMahon, from *Thy Neighbour's Wife*.

Carey is a highbrow writer who has a grievance against society caused by the poor sale of his novel. "Led astray by the critics, who over-praised it on its publication four years previously, he had become afflicted with the mania of genius and got to hate humanity for buying no more than four thousand copies of his masterpiece" (p. 13). Mortimer, the producer who has come to Ireland, describes him as a "goddam Irishman that turned his back on his own country . . . a has-been, a washed out highbrow scribbler that couldn't sell dirt to a tabloid newsrag" (p. 33). Carey himself feels a measure of artistic pride, but this is easily assuaged with money. He feels he has sold himself and should resign but grows enthustiasic about the adventure of Hollywood, which is described to him as an "insane phenomenon." In an O'Flaherty manner he rants: "I had grown stale, impotent. A man can't live always in a mountain-top. . . . Let's go down into the pit and wallow like pigs" (p. 52). He speaks the familiar O'Flaherty phrases—"You adventure on earth. I adventure in heaven." "Now God is dead"—and self-condemnation—"God gave me great talents. I abused them. I sold them for a mess of pottage."

The book however, is not primarily about Carey, but a satire on Hollywood and motion-picture making in which the naive and bumbling Carey has been unwittingly involved. The essence of the satire is Hollywood's artificiality, the necessity of "fixing" everything, so that an Irish village in Ireland would never be as convincing on the screen as the Hollywood version of it, and the Irish girl that Mortimer imports could never be as convincing as the version of her he has created. And that is the main theme of the novel. Biddy Murphy the flesh-and-blood Irish girl Mortimer brings to Hollywood is only the idea of the girl he wishes to create into a love goddess. The perfect Angela Devlin—the name he devises for his creation—who is "Adapted for the screen . . . with the closest possible regard for the original" is a female impersonator, much more tractable than the original Biddy Murphy. Through his imitative talents and the aid of a Dr. Zog, the impersonator becomes the perfect love goddess for Hollywood with qualities that the original herself did not possess, most notably an expression of "barren ecstasy." At her appearance the mobs explode into a Dionysian orgy, intoning again and again, "She is. She is." Hollywood's most perfect success is its most barren imitation.

O'Flaherty obviously was not pleased with everything he saw in Hollywood, and if his experiences were anything like those of Brian Carey (who escaped, married Biddy Murphy, and was purified by love from his sin against the Holy Ghost) he was not pleased with what was done with *The Informer*. Everything about Hollywood was corrupted by money and the public taste; even the good people, the intellectuals like Bud Tracy and Sam Gunn, the director and screen writer (who might well have been John Ford and Dudley Nicolas who performed these functions for *The Informer*), who, though they realize they have been corrupted, are too enslaved by their large salaries to escape.

This is the book that intervenes between *Shame the Devil* and *Famine*. It is comical and it is bitter. O'Flaherty portrays himself in it as a "highbrow" who is bitter because of the poor sale of his books, and who, comically here, is enamoured of his own creative genius to which he must be true. Brian Carey is pompous and shabby. Because he can earn three thousand dollars easily by writing an exposé, he deludes himself into believing that it is a noble act. And in the same breath he condemns Hollywood for driving him to it: "This Hollywood is but a manifestation of the modern hatred of the human intellect. Man, tired of the struggle for the perfection of his divine intellect, has created this factory . . . for the destruction of all that is beautiful . . . by using the beautiful as raw material for the manufacture of Black Masses, at which lust and ignorance are worshipped" (p. 202). This is the sort of thing that O'Flaherty could have said, in the same words, in *Shame the Devil*. But he rises above the version of

himself he gives in *Hollywood Cemetery*. He is detached from and
amused by Brian Carey. Is he at the same time looking at the O'Flaherty who wrote *Shame the Devil* and rising above that to some new
view?

Famine is different from any of O'Flaherty's previous works, that
is certain, but the difference is not the difference in time or the difference in characters. Although *Famine* is a historical novel set almost
one hundred years in the past, except for a detail here and there—the
potato famine, the landlord problem, the Fenians, the Young Irelanders
—the scene is unchanged from O'Flaherty's contemporary provincial
Ireland. The peasants live in backward poverty, the emigration continues, the greedy merchants still prey on the peasants, the parish priest
still plays his dominant role.

The gallery of characters is almost a grand finale from his previous
works. John Hynes the merchant is motivated by the same avarice that
dominated Ramon Mor, both of whom rose from poverty by peddling
around the countryside until through the utmost frugality they saved
enough to establish a shop in town. Mr. Coburn, the Protestant minis-
ter, is like the vicar in *Thy Neighbour's Wife* or Mr. Willis the Protestant parson in *Skerrett*—good-hearted, liberal, but ineffectual men
with no real spiritual convictions. Dr. Hynes is like all of O'Flaherty's
country doctors (except Dr. Cassidy from *Thy Neighbour's Wife*
who is an aged eccentric)—young men uncomfortable in their social
roles, of the lower classes but determined to rise above them. Sally
O'Hanlon, the good neighbor woman who goes berserk when her
husband dies, is like Katie Higgins, the poor widow from "Two
Lovely Beasts." In their widowhood and most dire poverty both
spend what little money they get on sweets and gimcracks for their
children. Michael Kilmartin, the tubercular son, is a direct descendant
of Thomas in "Going Into Exile" whose "lungs made a singing sound
every time he breathed." Old Brian Kilmartin the wiry peasant father
is like Francis O'Neill's old father, still full of fire despite his years, and
in the same pattern as the old man in "Galway Bay," probably all
stemming from O'Flaherty's recollections of his own father. These are
only a few of the parallels. O'Flaherty built the world of *Famine* out
of familiar materials.

The main difference is in O'Flaherty's approach to the subject; and
this approach is determined for the most part by his acceptance, for
the first time, of a social structure, of a pattern of norms and values.
The famine, a common enemy, is the determining factor. Society can
be judged by its reaction to it. In the previous novels O'Flaherty was

above good and evil. Ramon Mor was not presented as an evil avaricious merchant and, as such, an enemy to the common good. Avarice is part of his character. What O'Flaherty is most concerned with is the grandeur Ramon Mor achieves through his power and his passion. But John Hynes is an evil man because he uses the famine and the desperation of the peasants as a means for his own gain. In *Famine* the choices a man makes are clear and clearly judged. Chadwick is an evil force because his own sensuality drives him to enforce the letter of the law on the peasants for his own satisfaction. Dr. Hynes must choose between middle-class security and serving the needs of humanity. Thomsy achieves the nobility that so excites Benedict Kiely by taking a stand, by being inspired by the message of hope from the Young Irelanders. A ne'er-do-well, a social drone, he achieves dignity by his courageous search for Martin. Everything is in black and white. The problem to be solved, though tremendous, is clear, and men define themselves by their reaction to it.

O'Flaherty sets himself firmly on the side of humanity and goodness. He sympathizes with the peasants. Their cause is his cause. The injustice they face is real to him. No longer does he view the human scene with Olympian detachment but comes down to earth with human sympathy. Man's struggles and sorrows are weighed in the scale of human feelings, not set against a cosmic background which for O'Flaherty makes those struggles and sorrows objects of beauty and not of pity. When Padraic Colum reviewed *The Black Soul* in the *Saturday Review of Literature* (May 30, 1925), he thought that for all O'Flaherty's talents he had much to learn, most importantly "to be humane." Although Colum recognized that to write about the Irish peasants with the light of Tir-nan-og ever over them was unreal, O'Flaherty's picturing them without spiritual history, "as of being what the elements and their own appetites make them," was equally unreal. He thought that when O'Flaherty could give his peasants a "manifold existence . . . with affections as well as passions" he would be able to write a fine Irish novel. This is what O'Flaherty did do in *Famine*, and the Irish critics who had deplored his lack of humanity responded with applause.

In his other novels of provincial life O'Flaherty's peasants exist as background—local color—for the main action and play no significant part in it. This is as true of *The Black Soul* as of *Skerrett*. In each a man is central, and the drama he enacts. His acts have no immediate social meaning nor can they be judged by social standards. In the short stories the peasants are not social beings but elemental men, contending not with the artificial structure of society but with nature itself. In either case O'Flaherty is not sympathetic. It is not his aim. His aim is beauty, which for him is contained in the passionate acts of men and the awe and wonder of existence. In *Famine* the peasants are social beings whose fortunes are the central concern. In a scene like the one in which Chadwick has his thugs smash down Halloran's hut, with the women wailing in the yard and then signaling to the men in the hills, it is injustice and indignation that is the center of interest, not the potential beauty, though this is what the artist in "The Child of God" would have seen. In the same way it is the pity of the scene that O'Flaherty draws and not the beauty in its horror when Mary comes in to see Sally O'Hanlon's children "quiet as lambs," their crying stopped at last in death, stretched out on the bed, killed by their mother after she appeased their hunger with the meat of a dead dog she has found. This intensifies the social injustice. The scene is presented as an awful, glaring example, to move the reader's sympathies to the utmost.

Famine is a warm novel because it is a humane novel and full of hope. Human feelings and aspirations have a value in their own right and are not the raw materials from which the artist extracts beauty. Human life is not presented as a drama played against the universe with tragedy the inevitable lot, but is presented with sympathy. Suffering is not beautiful; it is sad, heart-rending. Horror is not esthetic, it is sensational. Because *Famine* plays upon sympathy, the ending is happy, satisfying to the feelings. This is the only novel (except *Land*, which is generally acknowledged as a commercial venture) that has a hopeful ending. O'Flaherty's preferred ending for *The Black Soul* had a tragic emphasis, with Fergus O'Connor strangled in a death grip with Red John and Little Mary throwing herself over a cliff, though for apparently commercial reasons he followed Garnett's suggestions and struck an optimistic note in the published version.

Famine is full of sorrow, not tragedy, which is above sorrow. *Famine* is also full of hope, though suffering and death are everywhere. Thomsy returns inspired with a message of hope from the man with the golden hair who preaches the doctrine of the Young Irelanders. And Mary Kilmartin and the new baby are reunited with Brian Kilmartin on their hopeful escape to America. The central movement builds to this ending. The last scene has a sweet-sadness, the drawing of a melancholy curtain after the young Kilmartin's departure. In a passage reminiscent of James Joyce's ending of "The Dead" the last scene begins: "Hoar frost had fallen in the night. It shone in the morning light upon the mountainsides and all along the Valley's bed. It lay in a whitish crust upon the sagging thatch of the empty houses and on the blighted fields that were already falling back into the wilderness. The stone walls, the granite boulders, and the gorse bushes were white with it. It had formed a thin crust of ice on the surface of the Black Lake. The river was the only thing that moved here beneath the grey sky" (p. 465). In this atmosphere old Brian Kilmartin dies, vainly striving to open the ground for a grave for his dead wife. And his old dog utters a loud howl and then nestles against the dead man's shoulders. This wistful close is in sharp contrast to those fierce dark endings of *Mr. Gilhooley* ("Whither? Whence?"). *The House of Gold* (Ramon Mor's unblinking eye), *Skerrett* ("I defy them all"), or the other novels which set man against the universe in an unequal contest that destroys him. Old Brian Kilmartin sadly fades away, but before he goes his seed has sailed into a new life of hope.

Only in Dr. Hynes is there a familiar O'Flaherty crisis in which a character is driven to make a choice, the import of which is tremendous but the direction not clear. Dr. Hynes is described as being "sensitive and kindly, even ambitious to be of service to his community," but incapable of a total commitment: "He belonged to that large class of timid and mediocre people who lack the moral courage to obey by their own dynamic force the urge towards the idea. They feel that urge, owing to their sensitiveness and a suspicion that they are missing something in life. A consciousness of being frustrated by a mysterious force beyond their control drives them to sporadic extremes of conviction; at one moment to action, at the next to cynicism. They crave to belong to an army marching toward a distant goal. Alone, or against opposition, they are helpless and prone to despair" (p. 407).

This is the familiar black soul pattern, and the poles between which Dr. Hynes vacillates are like those O'Flaherty describes for himself in *Shame the Devil.* It is significant that the two courses Hynes pondered and tentatively adopted were "the doctrine of loving Ireland as a mother," the "vague mysticism" of which failed to hold him, and the doctrine of revolution, which he was too timid to hold when he sees the revolutionary efforts of others aborted by the bayonet charge of the police. These parallel O'Flaherty's own two directions for commitment when O'Flaherty the man governs, when his creative fire is out and he is caught up in social contentions.

But Dr. Hynes is not the major character, and *Famine* is not his individual drama as in the pattern of the black soul novels, nor does O'Flaherty attempt to transcend himself through this character as he does with Dr. Jim Fitzpatrick of *The House of Gold*, another provincial doctor with vague idealistic yearnings which he is powerless to effect. Dr. Hynes is just another character in a panoramic picture composed of familiar O'Flaherty materials. *Famine* is an entirely conventional historical novel composed of familiar O'Flaherty ingredients. His subject is humanity for the sake of sympathy, not passion for the sake of beauty. The subject is almost nostalgic, as if by setting back the time one hundred years one could escape to a time when the issues were clearer, when a courageous man could take a stand—as Dr. Hynes could not—and expend himself in a cause that he could accept without question. O'Flaherty presents clearly and sympathetically the world that he knows, but a world stripped of cosmic uncertainty, and there is all the difference.

When O'Flaherty wrote *Joseph Conrad: An Appreciation* (1930) he set out a higher aim than humanism for his own art. He found Conrad amusing enough, "the songster to amuse the tired warriors" when a halt is called in man's great voyage to storm the heights, but lacking in true greatness because he has accepted the God of the British Empire, the conventional God, a symbol of fixed laws and decent standards, who is "a good honest trader, a man brave in adversity, a homelover, a man who keeps his word." Within this limitation Conrad achieved his excellence, but his excellence is based upon the pleasure he gives; and "the saying of Turgenev that books are written to amuse becomes the only just scales of judgment" (p. 6).

O'Flaherty thought "some sort of brutal denial" was necessary to this kind of art "or the human intellect reverts to the state of mind of the servant maid, who feeds her romantic desires on the wildest and most uncouth drivel in order to stupefy her instincts for revolt against the unhappiness of her daily life" (p. 7). Conrad's work is a "sweet fountain," but drinking there is dangerous on the heavy march up the "steep road of death with all its horrors." Yet there is undeniable pleasure at that fountain "to believe that Christ was indeed God and that all that is now ordained, as to honour and justice, was always so and is and is to be" (p. 10). But O'Flaherty holds a higher view of art and beauty: "What is beautiful in man is that he is unhappy as a man and wishes to be a god, to be free from death and the restraint of the earth's balance; that he wants to fly into space and loot the universe; that he is always hankering after the true of knowledge; that he creates gods only in order to break them; that he is a being constantly in revolt and in his highest form, finding beauty only in wild tragedy" (p. 7).

In *Famine* O'Flaherty has abandoned this higher path of stark tragedy and descended to the plane of acceptance and pleasure giving. As he said, there is pleasure in such art, but it is a dangerous pleasure of a lower order, and it represented for him a turning aside from his own artistic challenge and his own highest aims. Whether he did this out of deepest personal feelings or to show the Irish critics that he could or as an experiment in the historical form or for frank commercialism, it was a performance that he did not repeat.

Nine years after *Famine* O'Flaherty turned once more to Irish history for the setting of his next novel, *Land*.[14] He turned to the period of Michael Davitt and the formation of the Land League in 1879, when the Fenian Society organized the peasants into a disciplined movement against the landlords who found it more profitable to have cattle than peasants occupying their land. The difference between *Land* and *Famine* is more in the focus than in the historical setting, however. *Famine* places the peasants in the foreground; *Land* uses the peasants for a background in developing its theme. But the Ireland of O'Flaherty's historical novels is almost indistinguishable because of its historical period and even indistinguishable from his contemporary settings. In one way this reflects Ireland's unchanging nature. The same basic forces contend in the past as in the present. On one side are the leaders of social revolt—sometimes Fenians, sometimes members of the Irish Revolutionary Brotherhood sometimes Young Irelanders. Opposing them are the forces of the established order—the Royal Irish Constabulary, Black and Tans, or Free Staters, depending upon the period of history. The peasants and the parish priest are in the middle. The parish priest plays his own game, sometimes leading, sometimes following. Father Reilly in *Thy Neighbour's Wife*, Father Moclair in *Skerrett*, Canon McElroy in *The Martyr*, and Father Cornelius Costigan in *Land* are all examples of the clever parish priest who bends one way and another between social reform and established power, intent above all on maintaining his own position, regardless of right or wrong. The peasants are a mob, one moment inflamed to passionate and idealistic action against social oppression, the next cowed by fear, both of civil authority and of the parish priest who uses his religious authority to quell the absolute revolt which might displace him.

In *Land* the forces opposed are Fenians and landlords, the latter with their supporting force, the Royal Irish Constabulary. Father

Costigan is the subtle priest, and the peasants are O'Flaherty's usual peasants. The action involves chiefly the vengeance of Michael O'Dwyer, an idealistic young Fenian, against Captain Neville Butcher, a particularly obnoxious and determined landlord who was responsible for the hanging of O'Dwyer's father in a previous land conflict.

In the course of the action the tactic of isolation is introduced as a social weapon against the landlords and those that support them, a tactic which later came to be known as "Boycott" from an occasion of its subsequent use. Raoul St. George, the inventor of this social pressure, is shocked at the name given to his policy of isolation: "And as a final insult, they baptize it in their own image, by giving it the name of some common lout" (p. 352).

Aside from these few details the historical aspects of the novel are superficial. O'Flaherty's intention is not to develop the distinctive atmosphere of the period but to use the conflict brought to a focus as the occasion to cause men to reveal themselves in fullest expression. In this case the Fenian uprising is no different from the skirmish between the Free Staters and the Volunteers in *The Martyr*, or the Easter Rebellion of 1916 in O'Flaherty's next novel, *Insurrection*. Historical significance is subordinate to human significance. The events of certain periods have caused men to act passionately. The particular period is immaterial as long as it evokes the passionate response.

When Francis Hackett reviewed *Land* in the New York *Times* (May 12, 1946), he saw that it was no accident in O'Flaherty's evolution as a novelist. He pointed out the similarity between Kate and Tracy from *The Martyr* to Lettice and O'Dwyer from *Land* to show how O'Flaherty transposed characters from one novel to another. The relationship between *The Martyr* and *Land* is much stronger than that indicated by single details, for *Land* develops more completely a theory of character that had its beginnings in *The Martyr* and was to be developed still further in *Insurrection*. Prior to *The Martyr* O'Flaherty's characters were brought to an individual crisis, and they dissociated themselves from any cause. They faced the meaning of their own existence alone, without reference to any social commitment. With *The Martyr* O'Flaherty began to see his characters in crisis as souls not naked but clothed in ideals. And three fundamental types of man began to emerge in O'Flaherty's theory, representing three distinctive responses to the absolute challenge that an occasion in history presented. In *The Martyr*, the types are there, but the classification is not explicit. In *Land* the theory is developed more completely. Raoul St. George, the intellectual force in *Land*, describes the three sublime human possibilities: "The soldier, the poet, and the monk represent what is finest in man. They represent man's will to power, to beauty and to immortality. They alone among men are capable of complete love, because they love the unattainable" (pp. 75–76). "The soldier, the poet, and the monk . . . must be ruthless with their own emotions and indifferent to those of others when in pursuit of their ideal" (p. 166).

Jack Tracy in *The Martyr* clearly represents the type of the soldier. Tyson describes him (contrasting him with Crosbie) as a "brave undisciplined soldier." Before the battle Tracy exhorts his men: "A soldier's death is a glorious thing that living slaves'll envy if we fail to capture the enemy" (p. 79). After Tracy is wounded, O'Flaherty describes him: "His pale-blue eyes . . . had lost none of their strange inhumanity, that passionless stare of the adventurer, in whom burns a devouring fire that only death can smother" (p. 209). He shares with Crackers Sheehan, his enemy in this conflict, the common bond of a soldier: "Danger of death, which makes most men afraid, was a tonic to his peculiar temperament" (p. 244). For O'Flaherty, the soldier is not a hot-blooded killer but a type of man who through a combination of temperament and will can achieve his full expression only in those situations that force him to face death. Then only does he feel the exaltation of being genuinely alive, genuinely himself.

Michael O'Dwyer is the soldier in *Land;* and through the interpretation of Raoul St. George, the type is further defined: "Danger is to him what tragedy is to a poet, the ultimate beauty" (p. 82). O'Dwyer has a compulsion to face death. He takes his bride out into a storm with his small sailing boat and for six hours they battle the sea. Lettice, his bride, describes it: "During every moment of that time we treaded the brink of death. . . . He had opened the innermost door and allowed me to enter. . . . I understood why beauty could be found in danger and why rapture could be dark as well as bright" (p. 306).

O'Dwyer is a man of destiny for whom the common pleasures of life are forbidden. He must leave Lettice almost immediately to fulfill his higher mission. His faith drives him. "It makes me do cruel things, to myself and to others," he tells an old peasant woman he meets on the road. And she blesses him seeing the mark of destiny upon him: "We must be gentle with that man and show him great respect. He's on his way to meet the dark stranger" (p. 326). When O'Dwyer meets his destined end in a battle with Captain Butcher, Elizabeth, Raoul's sister, describes him as "one of those on whose foreheads tragedy is written for even the least intelligent to read." His end is not mourned with usual sorrow—"one cannot feel sorrow in the ordinary way for one so strong and so certain of his purpose." On the contrary, "the people feel proud and triumphant" (p. 345). When Raoul St. George learns of O'Dwyer's death he cries out: "Oh! How I envy him the way he died!" (p. 347).

The soldier represents one kind of dedication in which a man commits himself absolutely to an ideal. The monk is another, but this type goes through a process of evolution from *The Martyr* through *Insurrection*. Brian Crosbie is the monk in *The Martyr*, the man dedicated to immortality, for whom the challenge of history is the challenge to be true to his own soul's destiny. According to Crosbie, God endows different men with different talents. Crosbie's talent is "prayer and contemplation and suffering." He plans to leave the fighting to those who are suited for it and "to give up everything and become a hermit, to try and gain from God by self-denial and by prayer" what he does not believe can be gained by fighting (p. 66). But there is something weak and selfish about this compulsion to martyrdom. Tyson chides Crosbie for becoming a monk and exposes Crosbie as one more concerned for his own soul than for the cause for which he is pledged (p. 195).

In *Land* Father Francis Kelly is the monk. He is a priest who because of his fighting with the insurgents against the English has been forbidden the rights of priesthood. Raoul describes him as one who "has remained fixed ever since in that single act of revolt. He can neither advance beyond it, nor regain the state of mind that preceded it" (p. 85). Father Francis retired to a stone hut to be a hermit in protest against Raoul's harsh program of isolation that caused a man's suicide; and when Raoul seeks him out for assistance, he protests that he has his own soul to save. But when Raoul explains that for a conquered nation such a ruthless policy is necessary (and the discussion between them parallels the discussion between Crosbie and Tyson, in which Tyson maintains that "an enslaved person or race struggling toward freedom can only achieve a feeling of dominance through triumphant action") Father Francis understands the selfishness of his position. He realizes that he is "a terrible sinner for having deserted the people" and vows to do his share, shoulder to shoulder with O'Dwyer and Raoul (p. 244). Father Francis is given a nobility denied to Crosbie because he recognizes that the quest for personal immortality is a selfish and sinful act if it means neglecting one's duty to humanity. But with Father Francis this character type, though defined, is not clear. He represents a certain kind of religious dedication distinct from Crosbie's, but no further explanation is given. It was not until *Insurrection* that

O'Flaherty completed his theory on this character type and changed the designation from monk to saint, no doubt to distinguish the kind of commitment it involved.

The third type, which O'Flaherty calls the poet, first appears in *The Martyr* in the character of Tyson. But Tyson as a poet can be understood only as Raoul St. George is a poet. The term, as O'Flaherty uses it, describes a man's relationship to life and has nothing to do with his creating verse. Tyson, like Raoul, is distinguished by a superior intellect which grasps the essential truth and is relentless in its dedication to that truth. Tyson fulfills Raoul's description of the type in that he is ruthless with his own emotions and indifferent to those of others when in pursuit of his ideal—"welding this new state into something that coheres" (p. 197). Similarly, Raoul's plan of isolation, which he defends because "an enslaved nation is forced to find means other than the traditional ones . . . for imposing its will upon defaulters" (p. 242) is based upon "the whole people . . . disciplined and acting in obedience to a single will" (p. 76). Tyson and Raoul share the same definition of religion. Tyson says that religion "is the poetical expression of the people at large; their impulse towards immortality and the conquest of the universe" (p. 191). Raoul says that in a free society "religion is the poetry of the people. It is the dark ecstasy by means of which even the most lowly confront suffering and death with dignity" (p. 235). What characterizes both is a kind of creative ruthlessness, so that Tyson is like the weasel in O'Flaherty's often-recurring image, somehow a facet of O'Flaherty's own creative genius, a demon, inhuman in not being humane. Father Francis describes a similar quality in Raoul: "You'd destroy the whole of humanity for the sake of proving a theory correct. . . . In other words, you are completely inhuman" (p. 241). They are both like Shelley's poet, with the greatest emphasis on their legislative function. That Raoul is the poet in this three-part scheme, even though he writes no poetry, is supported by his daughter's witness. Discouraged because he has spent more than twenty years of his life "trying," only to have his ideas debased, he is consoled by his daughter, who reminds him that he once said "that it is a very fortunate poet who is able to realize even one-millionth part of his dream" (pp. 352–53).

Land is more interesting as an illustration of the development of O'Flaherty's thought than for its merits as a novel. Critical opinion is almost unanimous with Benedict Kiely who called *Land* "indubitably one of the worst things that O'Flaherty has written." [15] But there is good reason to believe that O'Flaherty speaks directly through Raoul

St. George, who dominates the book. Raoul is fifty-one, just O'Flaherty's age. Lettice, Raoul's daughter, is about the same age as O'Flaherty's daughter, born in 1927. Much more significant than this slim
biographical evidence, however, is the fact that the pattern of character
types that Raoul expounds is the pattern of *The Martyr, Land,* and
Insurrection. It is a direct O'Flaherty theory. Raoul describes himself as
a freethinker: "That means that I adopt a purely personal attitude
toward ideas and the phenomena of life" (p. 36). He is a writer who
has not been writing, at an age "at which the intelligent man eschews
the external world as much as possible" (p. 82). Returning to Ireland
causes him to commit himself in the struggle against the landlords, not
for any reason of nobility but somehow to reunite himself to the land,
and in a speech that is more likely for a twentieth-century intellectual
like O'Flaherty than for a nineteenth-century returned exile he
expresses his position:

> It is terrible to have lost faith. It is really terrible to be an
> educated man in our age of transition. For thousands of years, the
> human intellect had remained at the same level, insofar as knowl-
> edge of the universe was concerned. Then suddenly, in this
> astounding century of ours, fantastic discoveries are made. The
> steam engine, the internal combustion machine, the telegraph, the
> telephone and other startling innovations radically change our
> relation to the earth and to universal space. Tomorrow, even more
> fantastic inventions will appear. The whole structure of our mor-
> tality has come toppling down about our ears as a result of this
> new knowledge. Our gods, who seemed omnipotent yesterday, are
> today no better than abandoned scarecrows. . . . We are at a
> loss, all of us who are capable of abstract thought, overwhelmed by
> the avalanche of scientific discoveries. While we hysterically re-
> examine the idea of God, with the object of making it conform to
> our changed conception of the universe, our moral conscience
> flounders about in the vacuum created by our genius. We cry out
> desperately for authority, even while we smash all authority. Poor
> suffering humanity can endure just so much iconoclasm and
> anarchy. Then reason cracks. Or else, one returns to the womb for
> protection. What womb? The earth is the common womb of all
> humanity. I have returned to the womb of my ancestors. It is the
> land I seek and not the people. I am afraid and I seek refuge in the
> earth, just as a sick man climbs into his bed and draws the blankets
> up about his ears. (p. 84)

The intellect of Raoul St. George dominates *Land*. His theory interprets the characters of the soldier, the monk, and the poet. His plan of isolation is the most significant social development. All the other characters ultimately yield to his superior vision, even those, like his sister, who were initially opposed. He is Prospero-like in his control of the course of events. He refuses to let his sister attribute what happens to God's will: "I planned the whole thing down to the most minute detail . . . and I don't believe in God. So it could not possibly have been God's will" (p. 227).

But for all his intellectual power he is afraid. The sea is a relentless reminder of his mortality: "I detest the sound of the sea. . . . It's like the ticking of a clock, reminding me that I'm getting old, that I'll soon lose consciousness and dissolve into unrelated particles of matter" (p. 347). He envies Michael O'Dwyer the manner of his death. He envies Father Francis' "fixity of thought" (p. 85). When he learns of O'Dwyer's death, he is "overcome by an almost unbearable loneliness" (p. 347). But when he is discouraged, he looks at his daughter in "her ecstasy of motherhood," and he looks upon the land "that had again renewed its beauty in the fire of spring," and "a passionate love of his native earth" surges through his blood. Then "he felt humbled and exalted before the unending march of life" (p. 353).

This is Fergus O'Connor of *The Black Soul* twenty-two years later. The problem is the same. The intellect has destroyed the old notion of God, and it is terrible to have lost faith. O'Connor cries out for an authority to which he can yield absolutely as Catholics can to the Pope, but his intellect forbids it. The sea for him is the ultimate symbol of motion without purpose and it gives him visions of utter annihilation. When he finds his peace, it is with nature, with its ongoing life before which he feels wonder and awe. Although the treatment is different between *The Black Soul* and *Land*, the essential theme is the same in the relationship between intellect and annihilation.

Insurrection (1950),[16] which like *Land* is a historical novel concerned only incidentally with the meaning of history, continues the development of the character types which began in *The Martyr*. The novel is set against the background of the Easter Uprising of 1916, but this event made no real impact upon O'Flaherty when it happened. In *Two Years* he says it failed to make an impression "because the issue there had been confused by the local racial antagonism between the English and the Irish" (pp. 70–71). Despite the stereotype which led so many critics to consider O'Flaherty as somehow the official historian of the Irish Civil War and to judge his work by his effectiveness in depicting it, to praise *Insurrection* because it is illuminating to history, to regret, as Anthony West does in his review in *The New Yorker* (May 26, 1951), that so gifted an artist as O'Flaherty can "after twenty-five years, make full use of his powers only within the narrow field of the Irish Civil War," the historical meaning of the Easter Uprising is far from the central issue. It serves as the occasion for men to test themselves. That is its main artistic function. It cuts men off from the regular social routines—the buying and selling, farming and marrying—and demands from them a total expression of what it means for them to live by setting them bolt upright against annihilation. The action of that day depicted in O'Flaherty's last novel serves the same purpose as Hugh McMahon's setting himself out to sea in the first, over twenty-five years before. It is another expression of O'Flaherty's main theme: what it means to be a man.

Insurrection, which is much more an idea book than *Thy Neighbour's Wife* or the succession of novels that dealt with men's passionate expressions, has a clearly worked-out theory, an extension of the poet, soldier, and monk theory of *Land,* by which the fundamental expressions of passionate men can be classified. *Insurrection* is mainly concerned with explaining and dramatizing the various possibilities for men who have the courage to face the fact of life and death. Bartly Madden, Michael Kinsella, and George Stapleton are not as much characters as representatives of O'Flaherty ideas.

Madden, in the tradition of Gypo Nolan, Ramon Mor, Bill Gunn, and Skerrett, is the strong passionate man without intellect. But he is developed more clearly than any of these. His meaning, not the grandeur of his passionate actions, is O'Flaherty's concern. A Connemara man, he is on his way back home to use his English earnings to purchase a farm and the wife that goes with it when he is entangled, unwillingly, in the events of that Easter Monday. His only interest is peace and domestic security. But within him is the idea, a vague inexpressible something associated with the flight of wild geese, that is stirred by the events around him, by the words of the poet Pearse that "were beyond his comprehension" but which "rent his soul with longing for a beauty that he could not comprehend" (p. 31). Symbolically, a line of priests marches down the street to clear the crowd listening to Pearse, and Madden, driven "from the contamination of revolt by the silent black-robed shepherds of the Lord" (p. 33), temporarily forgets the idea and concerns himself with his own safety and fortunes. When he sees Michael Kinsella, a Captain in the Irish Volunteers, the idea finds a leader: "The vague mystical longings inspired in him by the poet's words had taken flesh, in this lean man with the ascetic face and the mysterious eyes of a monk" (p. 80). He is possessed of "strange raptures" which become "constant and unchangeable by his act of faith" in Kinsella, and he is "liberated from his torments by a complete surrender of himself to the authority of a leader" (p. 93). In the "dark ecstasy" that arises in him as he engages in battle gradually he becomes aware of the "stark beauty that makes men fight and die in pursuit of a love they cannot possess or comprehend" (p. 138).

When Kinsella is killed, Madden is momentarily in panic: "The wings of the wild geese no longer whirred through the silent vastness of the starry firmament," and "order and the certainty of faith were both destroyed." He becomes what he was before he joined the action "a penniless vagabond . . . not knowing where to go or what to do, without a heroic purpose to glorify his life" (p. 227). But he is saved "from the trembling indecision of a slave" by looking at Kinsella's dead features which "still bore witness to the gentle lordliness and discipline of the intellect that had ruled them" (p. 240). With this for inspiration he rises superior to even Pearse and Connolly, whom he sees surrender. "Images of stark beauty, from his native earth and sea" pass through his memory, "and he is possessed by a force beyond his will." In this ecstasy he attacks three Imperial soldiers, killing them and falling himself in a storm of bullets. In the end he had done what Stapleton had predicted and envied, met his destiny "doing what he was born to do" (p. 202).

Madden is the soldier in O'Flaherty's design, with the nobility of the soldier that O'Flaherty had come to admire from his own army experience, but needing a leader, something to embody the vague idea which inspires the courage and dark ecstasy. Kinsella, the saint in O'Flaherty's scheme, is that embodiment. He is more significant for what he inspires than for what he is. He is dedicated and disciplined, unmoved and courageous in battle, having in his manner and the gaze of his monk's eyes the power to inspire courage in others.

Only two chinks reveal what is behind that gaze. He tells young Tommy Dolgan, the youth terrified in battle, of his own fears which he had to conquer by an act of will. And he reveals himself in a nightmare in dreams which Stapleton interprets. In this dream, from which he awakens in horror "like a hermit monk grappling with a violent temptation of the flesh" (p. 194), he stands in an immense valley in front of a river. Behind him lie the barren ruins of cities devoid of life, and before him, across the river, a Celestial City of great beauty with people godly in appearance and radiant with happiness. Before the city a marvelous flower grows in a never-ending cycle, rising to great height, dropping its petals in a shower of perfume, then disappearing only to grow up again immediately. Kinsella wants desperately to reach the city but is prevented by a reptile that twines around his legs. Stapleton explains the dream: the reptile is Kinsella's tragedy that kept him from "the glorious voyage of discovery towards the ever-lengthening horizon of human knowledge" (p. 198). A promising young chemist, Kinsella had been forced when his mother died to give up his studies to support his brother's education for the priesthood. The brother died in an accident before he could be ordained. At first bitter, Kinsella came to believe that sacrifice is its own reward and that "the only thing in life is to do one's duty. Everything else is vanity and foolishness" (p. 199). Stapleton says that Kinsella tried to kill the poet in himself in an attempt to become a saint but that the poet remained, still wanting to continue the glorious journey to the Celestial City. To Kinsella, however, his supreme moment was when he overcame his fear by an act of will and accepted his duty on that Easter Monday.

If Kinsella is the saint who achieves his sainthood by turning from the glorious vision and dedicating himself to self-sacrifice by an act of will, Stapleton is the poet for whom beauty is everything. He comes to the battle with no idealistic social aims, all of which are repugnant to him, but for the beauty of it, war being "a supreme expression of human passion" (p. 120). While Madden fights in his dark ecstasy and Kinsella fights with grim dedication, Stapleton fights and admires. The battle, the nurses dragging away the wounded, the grotesque dance of death of the stricken invoke in him an emotion beyond words, "as if something wonderful had just been made manifest to him; something that enlarged his consciousness of the infinite universe by which he was encompassed and which he was unable to comprehend in its entirety, because he formed part of it and could only realize its existence through the tumult of his senses" (p. 128).

He explains to Kinsella that he came to the battle not because of duty, which he despises, but because he is a poet and a pantheist like Shelley, "in revolt against the whole concept of good and evil" current in his age, against all forms of government, because they are all "based on the same false concept of morality," and, above all, against the idea "that man is the center of the universe and that he is made in God's image." That for him is "the root of all evil" (p. 204). He believes that the whole universe is God and that "He is equally present in all creatures and in all things, whose existence has absolutely no purpose, other than to serve as an expression of His will to love" (p. 204). The most desperate moment of the battle is for him *"la hora de la verdad,"* the supreme moment of passion when the whole of life is expressed in a single gesture; when the soul is stripped naked and its real nature is exposed" (p. 195). He is desperately afraid of that moment, afraid of his own reaction; but when it comes his spirit rises to meet it, although his frail body collapses in uncontrollable anxiety. At his death, which he endures bravely, he begs Kinsella to tell him again about the dream of the flowers.

In contrast to the previous novels which were concerned with presenting experience and not discussing the meaning of experience, *Land* and *Insurrection* have a highly theoretical quality. Action and emotion are subordinate to the meaning of action and emotion. The emphasis is not on how men behave heroically but why they behave heroically. Thus Michael O'Dwyer's honeymoon battle against the storm is not told directly but recounted by Lettie to Raoul. The importance of the battle is not the excitement or the drama but the meaning, which is Lettie's new understanding of the beauty of danger gained through O'Dwyer. Similarly, while the shells burst in the buildings around them, Stapleton and Kinsella hold a philosophical discussion about their own ideals and motives; and since Madden's lack of intellect bars him from this discussion, they talk about him too. Previously O'Flaherty's characters sought the meaning of life directly, in the flesh, not as a theory. No theory could reconcile them to the fact of their own mortality; intellect destroyed all theories about the meaning of life, because the ultimate conclusion of intellect was that life was motion without purpose. There was no objective value to which men could relate themselves.

In *Insurrection* the question of values is settled once Madden passes through his short period of indecision to dedicate himself to the vague idea the words of Pearse stir within him. Then he becomes the soldier as Kinsella and Stapleton are already the saint and poet—all committed to a course which will cause them to choose death in the same act by which they affirm all that is most valuable to them in life. But the value of the cause for which they will give their lives is not at issue. Madden is not convinced of the value of Irish nationalism or Irish freedom but responds to inchoate yearnings within himself. The dedication of the English soldiers is equally valuable. The value is the dedication. This certainty of value is far different from the "Whither? Whence?" of *Mr. Gilhooley,* which puts all in doubt. At

what Stapleton calls "the supreme moment" he, Madden, and Kinsella
are not naked souls as Ramon Mor, Skerrett, or the tortured souls of
the black soul novels are naked. The poet, the soldier, and the saint
have their roles to sustain them. There is an ideal which, though vague
and unattainable, is supremely worthy of man's pursuit. *Insurrection*,
by illustrating Raoul St. George's thesis, attempts to affirm this. If
O'Flaherty's earlier novels raise the question of ultimate value, *Insurrection* attempts the answer.

Land and *Insurrection* explore another recurrent theme in O'Flaherty's work—the relation of the artist-poet to society. Raoul is the
acknowledged leader in *Land*, and both Michael O'Dwyer and Father
Francis submit themselves to his intellectual leadership. But Raoul,
as poet, has no specifically esthetic role. He controls by force and
clarity of mind. Stapleton, on the other hand, is not a direct leader.
His role as a poet is primarily esthetic. He experiences directly what
the soldier experiences dimly and what the saint turns from by force
of discipline and will but still is affected by. The soldier chooses his
role (and gives up the prosaic security of ordinary life) when he is
moved by the words of the poet, which open up for him a dimly per-
ceived vision of something marvelous and distant, like wild geese
flying. But Madden, the soldier, is not capable of sustaining this vision
within himself. Only the dedication and resolve embodied in Kinsella,
the saint, keep him firm in his purpose. The look in Kinsella's eyes dis-
pels for Madden all inclination to return to his own people to marry
and cultivate his own land and life. Kinsella's dedication, however, is
more negative than positive, as Stapleton points out. Kinsella has a
noble resolve to duty; but for him duty is the antithesis of dream, and
the strength of his resolve is a measure of the force of his dream. A
saint (or monk) is a kind of inverted poet who accepts absolutely the
very limitations the poet rejects absolutely. Ultimately all depends
upon the dream which is the essence of the good, the beautiful, and
the true. Only the poet dedicates himself to a direct apprehension of
this dream. Stapleton, the poet, is a pantheist, and he maintains that "all
poets are pantheists like Shelley" (p. 203). He seeks the ultimate good
which is God who is equally present in all creatures and things which
have no purpose other than their expression of His will to love. The
poet perceives God directly and so is the "insurgent *par excellence*," as
Stapleton describes himself, because this ultimate perception supersedes
all the lesser perceptions, all moral and political formulations of those
with a lesser vision.

As O'Flaherty, through analysis and theory, attempted to put into intellectual perspective the roles that could sustain men, acting in accordance with their highest potentials, through the moment of truth, and as he attempted to show the relationship between those roles, so also he attempted to explain a recurrent problem in his thought and work—mystical experience.

In one way or another he continually deals with this special kind of experience. Fergus O'Connor in *The Black Soul* fled to Inverara in despair, sick in mind and body, torn between the futility of life and the fear of death. Brought to an overwhelming awareness of his own mortality, to the point that "he felt sorry he couldn't pray to God without losing his self-respect," he made a profound discovery which he called "the turning-point" in his life. Before the power and vastness of nature that appeared to him as motion without purpose, he had come to say: "I am a part of nature," when previously he had considered himself superior to nature. Sitting in solitude, contemplating the rockbirds and the rolling sea, he became aware that nature was alive, and he felt he was a part of that complex life, in peace, "free from care and danger and sorrow" and that "even death could not touch him" (p. 212). But when he tried to put his understanding into words, into poetry, he found he could say nothing. As will be shown later in connection with his short stories, this is the same kind of experience that O'Flaherty describes for himself in *Two Years* and *Shame the Devil.* Yet his intellect was unwilling to acknowledge the validity of that experience, or at least to acknowledge that the experience was mystical.

In *A Tourist's Guide to Ireland* he rails against this characteristic Irish affliction which he believes is brought about by the mist and fog of the Irish climate (p. 16). And Tyson, who represents the clear-seeing and ruthless intellect, dedicates himself to destroying this kind of mysticism, embodied in Crosbie, because it is mawkish and feminine, a trait of slaves and not free men. In *Land* Raoul St. George specifically denies being a mystic, although he does confess believing in destiny because "a vice of some sort is necessary to maintain sanity" (p. 77). But Raoul fled to Ireland, to the womb of his ancestors, because he was afraid and sought refuge in the earth and, at the end, it is the "passionate love of his native earth" which "surged through his blood" that made him feel "humbled and exalted before the unending march of life" (p. 353). Raoul, like Fergus O'Connor terrified by the sea which symbolizes the relentless, purposeless force that mocks man's mortality and all human endeavor, like O'Connor finds peace in his awareness of the unending march of life.

Fergus O'Connor's experience of the oneness of nature in *The Black Soul* is duplicated by Stapleton in *Insurrection* twenty-six years later. In the midst of battle, before the beauty of its horror, Stapleton's face becomes solemn and reverent "as if something wonderful had just been made manifest to him; something that enlarged his consciousness of the infinite universe by which he was encompassed and which he was unable to comprehend in its entirety, because he formed a part of it and could only realize its existence through the tumult of his senses." The experience is almost more than he can bear, but he cannot explain it: "One can't describe things that are purely sensual. They are beyond words. Passion is silent" (p. 128). In *The Black Soul* the experience is everything, but in *Insurrection* the concern is to put this kind of experience into intellectual perspective, to achieve a philosophical view that can explain this experience. Stapleton's pantheism is an attempt to do this.

The poet is one who is sublimely aware of God in everything, and that man is not the center of the universe but a part of the universe, which is God. That experience, which Fergus O'Connor achieves and which Stapleton makes articulate, is an overwhelming awareness of the oneness of God and himself as a part of that oneness. Life is not motion without purpose, then, but an expression of God's will to love. *Purpose* is a man-centered term, and to seek purpose in man's existence is to attribute to him an unwarranted specialness. Only in his feeling a part of the unity of God can man be reconciled. In their experience of that unity Fergus O'Connor, Stapleton, and, in a measure, Raoul St. George find their peace. Through Stapleton's philosophy, O'Flaherty attempts to make rational the mystical sense of oneness that continually appears in his works.

$$\text{V}$$

The Short Stories: A New Vision

To TURN FROM O'Flaherty's novels to his short stories seems to be a move into another world. The violence of the novels "suggests the scream of a safety valve," as O'Faolain says in "Don Quixote O'Flaherty." The characters are hounded and tortured. Some mysterious relentless force drives them, torments them, sometimes even taking on a vague intense physical form like Gilhooley's man with a club and the brutes that pursue Private Gunn in *The Return of the Brute*. There seems to be no peace for these characters in the world, no resting place. The workings of their tortured minds convulse their bodies, like Red John in *The Black Soul* who "tore his jaws wide open to the utmost with his two hands, as if trying to vomit his fear in the intensity of the yell" (p. 225). They drown their despair in a river, like Mr. Gilhooley or, like the puritan, in babbling idiocy. Or their bullet-riddled bodies mark the end of their torments in death which is not peace, but the end. It is no wonder that those writing about O'Flaherty the novelist see him as does L. Paul-Dubois, "agressif et fougueux, mercuriel, tempêtueux," [1] that O'Faolain can say that O'Flaherty's work "pulses with genuine hatred." This is the vocabulary of those writing about the novels: *violence, passion, fury, rage.*

But the short stories are another world, and to move from one to the other is to pass through the looking glass. Some marvelous transformation has taken place. It is not just that the setting has changed, although indeed it has. The novels tend to be set in town, in the cities, or, more important, among people who aspire and interact. The short stories turn to the country, to animals, and to nature. The society that appears is a part of nature. The characters are rough-hewn from Aran rock. The whole tone has changed. The same vocabulary does not seem to apply. The novels can be described by a vocabulary of heat. The short stories can be described by light. Their surface is cold and shimmering. If the novels are marked by violence and melodrama and fury, O'Flaherty's short stories are best marked by their qualities of calmness, simplicity, and detachment. Or that is the impression so strong that it takes an effort of mind in retrospect to see that the violence is still there. A cow plunges over a cliff. A man crushes a fish to a pulp to relieve his blood lust. A water hen awaits the outcome of a furious struggle to see who will be her mate. Everywhere there is the conflict of nature and the anguish of those who are a part of nature. Yet all *is* changed. And this change must be explored.

H. E. Bates describes his first impression of O'Flaherty: "O'Flaherty had arrived in London with a firebrand swagger, a fine talent and a headful of rebellious fury about the English and had sat down to write pieces of episodic violence about London which he hardly knew at all. Garnett promptly and rightly sent him back to Ireland to write about seagulls and congers, a peasant's cow and the flight of a blackbird, and he at once produced sketches of the most delicate feeling and visual brilliance that few, even among the Irish, have equalled." [2] It is on these stories about cows and cormorants, peasants going into exile and wild goats defending their kids, rockfish and rustic courtship that O'Flaherty's reputation as a short-story writer is based. When O'Flaherty rediscovered Aran in himself, whether that awakening was due to Garnett's prompting or to some relentless impulse in his nature that sent him as a "godless hermit" to begin his "communion with the cliffs, the birds, the wild animals, and the sea of his native land," he found there the source and means for the expression of his turbulent genius.

Although it is evident that a change has taken place, the stories themselves would seem to offer little clue to what this change has been. There is an air of inevitability, an austerity and simplicity that seem to defy analysis. The stories do not appear to be constructions, that is, arrangements of details to achieve an esthetic effect. Nor is there any meaning in the sense that the details are the garb of any systematic intellectual arrangement. The stories cannot be called symbolic as the term has come to be used in criticism, with a *this* representing *that* relationship of details and events. Indeed, the contemporary scholar who has become accustomed to approaching short stories as an intellectual challenge or problem in need of scholarly interpretation or explication will find no rich mine in O'Flaherty.

Simplicity is the keynote. The short stories do not *mean;* they *are.* And the essence of this simplicity is that O'Flaherty brings no outside furniture—theories, philosophies, or other impedimenta—to bear upon his material to cause that interrelationship of subject and author which results in complexity. That which is most usually the material for analysis is not there. What is left can be described as a quality of vision focused on a pattern of simple events tremendously significant but only half-understood.

The change that has taken place is not a change of mind or of ideas that can be discerned by analysis and explained in intellectual terms. And the change is one that cannot be explained as merely a change in technique. Something more profound takes place, the explanation of which lies beyond the bounds of conventional literary analysis. William James's *Varieties of Religious Experience* [3] describes many such changes, and his account of the phenomenon of conversion and mystical experience describes O'Flaherty's change. In studying the phenomenon of religious experience James sees a classic pattern. Some healthy-minded "once born" individuals can shrug off the evil in life as an unhealthy aberration. But for the sick souls this evil is too deeply ingrained in the essence of things to be so easily dismissed. The precariousness of human existence weighs too heavily upon them. Regardless of life's pleasures "the spectre of death always sits at the banquet." Sometimes the effect is numbing, but for those individuals inclined to melancholy in its more acute forms, there is a profound disaffection. Life loses all meaning and this loss is the cause of positive anguish. For the melancholiac "the world now looks remote, strange, sinister, uncanny" (p. 151). As James recounts in the case of Tolstoy, the question of Why? and Wherefore? became obsessive. And like Tolstoy, these sick souls become convinced that "the meaningless absurdity of life is the only incontestable knowledge accessible to man" (p. 153). The whole range of habitual values comes to appear "a ghastly mockery" (p. 156).

One common characteristic of these disenchanted souls who must be "twice-born" to come into any sense of harmony is a divided self, what James calls "a certain discordancy or heterogeneity in the native temperament of the subject, an incompletely unified moral and intellectual constitution." As an example, he cites Alphonse Daudet who is appalled at his own reaction to his father's cry at his brother's death: "While my first self wept, my second self thought, 'How truly given was that cry, how fine it would be at the theatre.' " "Oh, this terrible second me, always seated whilst the other is on foot, acting, living, suffering, bestirring itself" (p. 167). This discordancy in self may have many manifestations, and a strong degree of it "may make havoc of a subject's life" (p. 169).

Conversion is the process, gradual or sudden, by which this discordancy is reconciled. Sometimes conversion is achieved by an effort of will, but more often by a process of self-surrender. For one whose spiritual turmoil is greatest, no deliberate process seems possible. The evil and absurdity that appear to be the warp and woof of the very nature of things cause a disenchantment so profound that no effort is possible that could make a soul so afflicted believe that any other view could exist. "So long as the egoistic worry of the sick soul guards the door, the expansive confidence of the soul of faith gains no presence" (p. 212). The only cause is exhaustion and despair; for as James goes on to explain, as long as one "center of consciousness" holds the fore, there is room for no other, but let this lapse, even for an instant, and that dramatic process of conversion may take place. It is the yielding and giving up, the surrender of self and will, that is at the center of the case histories of conversion that he then gives. James's explanation is psychological, but it is not important whether these experiences be explained in psychological or religious terms. What is important is that there has been a change, "the man *is* born anew" (p. 241).

James gives three main characteristics of this new "state of assurance" as he calls it: "*A willingness to be,* even though outer conditions should remain the same." "A sense of perceiving truths not known before." And "an objective change which the world often seems to undergo." "An appearance of newness beautifies every object" (p. 248). The second of these characteristics is that which underlies mysticism, that phenomenon of consciousness which harmonizes best with twice-bornness. For one of the essential marks of a mystical state is its "noetic" quality, a sense of perceiving truths "unplumbed by the discursive intellect," an "illumination . . . full of significance and importance" (p. 380); this, along with its ineffability—a directness of experience that eludes communication—its transiency, and its passivity —a sense that the will is in abeyance (p. 381).

James gives many case histories of those telling about these mystical states, among them Charles Kingsley, who tells his experience as follows: "When I walk the fields, I am oppressed now and then with an innate feeling that everything I see has a meaning, if I could but understand it. And this feeling of being surrounded with truths which I cannot grasp amounts to indescribable awe sometimes" (p. 385). He notes that "certain aspects of nature seem to have a peculiar power of awakening such mystical moods." James quotes from Amiel's *Journal Intime:* "Moments divine, ecstatic hours; in which our thought flies from world to world, pierces the great enigma, breathes with a respiration broad, tranquil, and deep as the respiration of the ocean, serene and limitless as the blue firmament; . . . instants of irresistible intuition in which one feels one's self great as the universe, and calm as a god" (p. 395). And Malroida von Meysenbug, who kneels "before the illimitable ocean, symbol of the Infinite" and feels that he knows prayer is "to return from solitude of individuation into the consciousness of unity with all that is" (p. 395). There is no need for further examples. Descriptions of this kind of experience are common in literature. The point that James makes is that this kind of experience, something of this impact, has the power to restore a sick soul and that this experience, carrying with it continuing authority, becomes a lasting part of the field of consciousness.

Whether or not the pattern of experiences that James discusses is indeed religious is of no concern here. Nor is there any concern as to how or why this phenomenon takes place or to what its value might be. It is the *fact* of this experience and not its meaning that relates to O'Flaherty, because it lends perspective to and points the direction through which his work can be understood.

It is the change of character that O'Flaherty seems to undergo between the novels and the short stories that this excursion into the psychology of religion is to illuminate. Changes of centers of consciousness do occur and with them profound transformations. That is evident from James's case histories. And these changes present the world in an entirely different perspective to those who have undergone the change. Although conversion may, it need not be a distinct event in time, before which a man is one thing and ever after another. The nature of the conversion is dependent upon the complexity of the psychological makeup of the individual. Infinite variations are possible. The fundamental mechanism is the shift from one center of consciousness to another. Everything about O'Flaherty indicates he would be most susceptible to this kind of experience: his discharge from the army with *melancholia acuta*, his acute consciousness of being a divided self (discussed previously in connection with his role as an artist), and the record of spiritual turmoil that permeates his autobiographical works. But probably *The Black Soul* presents this pattern of crisis and resolution most vividly, and it will be remembered from the previous discussion how deeply personal this novel is.

The Black Soul presents a classic account of the sick soul, the divided self, conversion, and mystical experience. Life has lost all meaning for Fergus O'Connor, the black soul, when he flees to Inverara after a futile effort to find answers "burrowing in the bowels of philosophy, trying to find consolation one day in religion, next day in anarchism, next day in Communism, and rejecting everything as empty, false and valueless . . . at last, despairing of life, flying from it as from an ogre that was torturing him" (p. 33). Fantastic visions crowd into his mind, "cries of the wounded, shrieks of the damned, corpses piled mountain-high, races wandering across deserts, chasms opening everywhere, devils grinning, wild animals with gory jaws rushing hither and thither in dark forests, myriads of men talking in strange languages . . . the wails of women, the bodies of children transfixed on spears" (p. 61). The vision of death haunts him: "He could see his own corpse lying stiff and naked" (p. 70). The cormorants croak from the rocks that all ends "in ashes and oblivion" (p. 90). He is aware of distinct contending forces within him: "Two personalities grew within him side by side. One embraced Little Mary and loved her bodily with the love of nature. The other hated her and kept hidden behind a gloomy silence" (p. 133). "The thought of suicide came to him now seriously, as a result of the hopelessness of thought" (p. 183).

Then, after numerous struggles, he experiences conversion. When he is poised at the edge of the sea, ready to plunge, something in him clutches onto life. The sea takes on new meaning: " 'Ah, beautiful fierce sea, he cried aloud, as if he were speaking to a mistress, 'you are immortal. You have real life, unchanging life.' And just as one morning in Canada when he had seen the reflection of a vast pine forest at dawn in the eastern sky, he had stood in awe, his imagination staggered, thinking that a new world had suddenly been born before his eyes, so now, looking at the sea, the meaning of life suddenly flickered across his mind. It flashed and vanished, leaving wonder and awe behind it." (p. 185). Although his black soul still grows on him, it loses its grip. Nature now can transport him into ecstasies of contemplation. He sits in the solitude of nature "for hours at a time thinking, without moving a muscle" (p. 210). He feels possessed of great and inexpressible knowledge: "He felt he knew something nobody else knew," but when he tries to say it "there was a pain in his heart as if something moved within him trying to come out and yet nothing came out. It was impossible to write anything about the sea. It was too immense" (p. 211).

The pattern here is unmistakable. There has been a profound change, and call it religious, spiritual, or psychological, it is the same kind of change that marks the difference between O'Flaherty's novels and short stories. The importance of this change is that the novels and short stories are not merely different in form and technique. They emanate from entirely different viewpoints. The shift is not just from the city to the country, from society to nature, but from one center of consciousness to another. When O'Flaherty writes about nature in his short stories something entirely new is involved.

Some readers might think it an anomaly that an excellent short story like "The Caress" should be buried within the autobiographical *Shame the Devil*, as if it were an intrusion, or an accident. But that is only if *Shame the Devil* is read as an autobiography concerned primarily with the external details of O'Flaherty's life. And though this book is concerned with the events of his life, it is not mainly that. It is mainly an attempt on his part to learn about himself, and especially that most valuable part of himself—that which makes him an artist.

In essence, *Shame the Devil* is the record of a quest. Something has been lost. As the book begins, O'Flaherty is depressed. Without money, without creative fire, on the edge of despair, he flees London in a desperate attempt to recover his gift of creativity. In the course of this quest he must rediscover who he is. As a part of this he explores his past. Present events evoke memories, and he turns from the present to his childhood, to his mother, to his native Aran. He recalls his education, his army experience, his early literary ventures. Present events—conversations and arguments about communism and Ireland—further this self-definition. Family scenes recall to him his own personal problems. He has hallucinations, as the two sides of him alternately take on tangible form and chide him. The issues become clearer. He sees himself as possessed by the terrible spirit of creativity. His genius drives him from life, cuts him off from normal pleasures and normal solaces. And this genius has provided no rewards. He sees himself as a failure and contemplates suicide. Impetuously, desperately, he sets out with some Breton fishermen to their island. In their company, on the sea, flickering life and spirit begin to revive. The fishermen are Communists, and vestiges of hope appear, but this is a false hope, a hope for mankind, a hope for betterment and progress. As an artist it is none of his concern. He must reject it. But where, then, is hope?

He recalls an incident from a Donegal beach where he watched a sand insect build its lair. In order to annoy it, O'Flaherty put a pebble across the entrance it had made. With great effort the insect struggled to remove it. O'Flaherty replaced the pebble, and again the struggle. With frequent repetitions of this, eventually the insect was unable to remove the pebble properly. But O'Flaherty was moved by the courage and perseverance and relented, and would have provided a supply of food for the winter if he had known what the insect ate.

It is within this ongoing spirit of life that he must find his harmony. Gradually, the island does its work as O'Flaherty begins to see himself in the larger perspective of nature. His creativity begins to flow. A story which he had been unable to write at Concarneau now "rushed out of its own accord." "The rhythm flowed without interruption, finds its own balance without needing my direction." He sees that this story has nothing to do with truth, "if truth lies hidden in the social shibboleths" about which he had been raving. In a "triumphant lust" he writes until his paper is exhausted and then in a rush of joy and humility he bursts into tears (pp. 242–43). He recognizes that the evil in his nature lay in his shame at being humble and innocent. He sees that even his confessions were conceived in arrogance. And to make his humiliation complete, he tears up his manuscript. But he recognizes that even that humility is denied him, because he must write for a living.

More despondent than ever, he probes deeper into his own nature. He recalls an incident in which pride seemed to keep him from begging, even though he was cold and hungry, but he sees that not pride but malice on his part was responsible. He had blamed society for the wrongs inflicted on him. Now, as an artist, he sees that criteria of right and wrong are not possible. A malign eye, a snake's eye proud and arrogant, appears to him. He recognizes it as his own. He sees he cannot flee from it. It is his; it is what he is. He can only put it into harness. The ongoing life of the fishermen, in harmony with nature, rejoicing in good fortune and accepting evil, shames and inspires him. He sees his role, his job. Theirs is fishing. His is accepting his role and writing. And he set to work again and rewrote "The Caress."

Shame the Devil culminates in "The Caress." The story is not adventitious. It is the central issue. It is the whole reason for the book —not this particular story, though it is representative of O'Flaherty's finest achievement, but a story as representing the result of the creative process. And the creative process is the result of a spiritual exercise in which O'Flaherty rediscovers that part of himself which is his gift and his curse, accepts it, and sets (though this word makes the process far too deliberate) himself into a relationship with nature that enables the rhythm of creativity to flow.

In a sense *Shame the Devil* is the direct, personal, autobiographical rendering of the kind of spiritual experience indirectly, in some degree or other, represented in many of his novels. *The Black Soul* is certainly the clearest example of this. Fergus O'Connor, who is essentially O'Flaherty, suffers from the same malaise that O'Flaherty does in

Shame the Devil. Although he is not represented as being a writer, he is possessed by a black soul, which is in essence that quality which makes artistic creativity possible. It is that special kind of intellectuality which cuts him off from society, which sets him apart even from nature. It is a detachment which brings with it the gift and curse of second sight. It is the malign eye of the snake—cold, proud, arrogant, and terrible. It is the vision that sees life, the wonder and the terror of existence, but prevents living life. It is the state of absolute detachment. This is the root of Fergus O'Connor's spiritual turmoil. Possessed by this spirit, he is afflicted with sickness almost unto death. He verges on despair and suicide. But gradually the restorative powers of nature, of the life of Inverara close to nature, bring healing to his sick soul. Life begins to well up in him. He accidentally kicks a starfish over on its back, and a piece of periwinkle shell falls on the myriad legs. Gradually the legs move the shell along and over the edge. For him it is motion without purpose, but it is life, and as such it is real and important and valuable.

This is the antidote to the black soul—life itself, ongoing life that does not question. It is the black soul that questions: "Not content with enjoying the surface of nature or the beauty of a woman, it must look down into the depths beneath the fair surface, probing the depths with futile shafts of thought, discovering nothing, blinded by the chaos it causes and which it cannot control" (p. 178). But when the black soul is quiet, absorbed into the wonders of nature's ceaseless flow, the surging of the never-quiet sea, the unquestioning movement of life itself, Fergus O'Connor, left with the residuum of delicious sorrow that stamps all the black soul touches, is possessed by a "creative frenzy": "He wanted to write a great poem about the cliffs and the sea. He felt that he knew something that nobody else knew, that he was scratching at the door behind which the secret of life lay hidden. His poem would be about that, not about the secret, but about the scratching. Nobody had ever even scratched before. He was assured of that when he recalled all that had ever been written about the sea or nature or life. It appeared superficial to him. 'They never felt what I feel. I understand' " (p. 211). And though he cannot explain what he understands, and even casts aside as impossible the idea of writing the poem, he still clings to nature, humbly, as if appealing to it for protection: "He became intimate with every ledge and slit and boss and weatherstain on the cliffs, with every wave on the bay, with every rock that jutted from the water, with its red wet mane of seaweed floating around it. He even felt kinship with the fishes prowling in the depths. . . . The tide coming in and going out was a living thing to him. He felt that he was a component part of this complex life, that he could rest in peace, that he was free from care and danger and sorrow, that even death could not touch him" (p. 212).

The connection between *Shame the Devil* and *The Black Soul* is apparent. In both cases sensitive men are driven to despair by a probing, destroying spirit that possesses them. Life is rendered meaningless. All appears equally chaotic and futile. Then, at the blackest moment, life, the unquestioning life of nature, asserts itself. What the black soul, the dark destructive spirit of intellect, saw as motion without purpose, prompting detachment and despair, now is the only sure ground of value. For it is life itself, and with this O'Flaherty and his self-representation in O'Connor feel themselves caught up and absorbed. Though nothing essentially has changed, all is transformed. Where the black soul found no meaning, now the whole man, in a new vision, finds the greatest meaning. And both feel impelled to express this newfound meaning and vision in poetry and story.

There is no more significant pattern in O'Flaherty's work, and there is no better commentary on the germinal spirit of his short stories than these records of spiritual experience. It has been shown that the theme of spiritual quest pervades his novels. Whether the central character is an O'Flaherty alter-ego, as in *The Black Soul*, or a grosser spirit like Gypo Nolan, or Mr. Gilhooley, or Skerrett, that which drives him is a profound need for meaning and belonging, not on a social but a cosmic scale. The novels tend to take, in some form, the central pattern of *Shame the Devil*. More often than not the outcome of the struggle is despair and death, but that is because O'Flaherty is interested in the struggle and has created characters incapable of resolving their experience. But even these characters instinctively turn toward nature when all else seems to fail, as a flower turns to the light. In *The Informer* Gypo Nolan, frantic in his escape, notices "the wind, the lifting clouds, and the far-away sky. He smelt the wind as he breathed in great gasps through his nostrils, to ease the pressure on his heart and lungs. Then suddenly, he longed for the mountains and the wide undulating plains and the rocky passes and the swift flowing rivers, away to the south in his own country" (p. 162). In *Thy Neighbour's Wife* Father Hugh McMahan abandons himself to the wild sea in his spiritual crisis. Skerrett achieves his nobility as he turns more and more to nature. For O'Flaherty it is nature, not society, that holds the significance.

When O'Flaherty is drifting and confused in New York City, as he recounts in *Two Years,* searching for his role, it is the memory of the sand insect that gives him new impetus. And he notes the same scene that he tells of in *Shame the Devil.* In a letter to Edward Garnett (July 23, 1923) he says that towns demoralize him. Only when he can feel "the vastness of the empty firmament" above him and "the clean smell of unvarnished nature" about him can he think. His conceit vanishes. He softens. He says he has no necessity "to put on armour in the country in the face of nature." "One lays bare the breast, the heart, the soul to drink in God which is beauty." For O'Flaherty nature, creativity, and spiritual experience are all wound almost inextricably together. He sees his genius as something within him that separates him from his fellows, that makes him a spectator and not a participant in life. But this genius is also his black soul which cuts him off from everything in terrible aloneness, which shows him the world as terrifying, fantastic, and absurd. In nature this sense of self-division reaches a crisis. The awesome motion without purpose of nature drives his black soul to exhaustion and despair, and in this bleak moment, when all seems hopeless and lost, the black soul ceases to struggle. Then, as if by miracle, a new consciousness floods his being. All seems one and harmonious and marvelous. Nature is both the cause and cure of his anguish. But this new awareness cries out for expression, and as an artist O'Flaherty must heed this cry. In the harmony of the new vision all is one, but now the artist must detach himself from the scene not to participate but to observe. Again the divided self and the apartness, and the cycle begins anew.

What is it that O'Flaherty sees when he emerges from his spiritual chaos and desolation into his new vision, the expression of which is both his gift and his curse? But that question assumes that he has seen some new truth which his stories are an attempt to communicate. What he sees is just what he has seen before; what is changed is the relationship. Before the vision the I, the black soul, the Dark Daniel side of O'Flaherty is wrenched into the most extreme separation from life and nature. And then the arrogance, pride, and selfhood which have been brought to an unbearable intensity scream out a No! of despair. From this storm there is a moment of emptiness. And then life flows back, simply, symbolized, and embodied in a sand insect that persistently, without reflection, removes the barrier placed before it. It is unquestioning life in nature, and O'Flaherty feels as one with this ongoing life. The world becomes new again in him.

To express this, the I or the creator does not stand off aloof and apart, shaping, manipulating, or analyzing. The I has almost ceased to exist. The vision, then, is nature expressed, *in its own voice*. It is not what O'Flaherty sees, for this subject-object relationship has ceased to exist. The writer is not standing apart, describing. Yet the detachment is greater because the writer is not selecting from nature and shaping nature to satisfy his own esthetic ends. He has become a part of nature. He feels within himself the rhythm of creation, as O'Flaherty said about writing "The Caress." He becomes the speaking part of nature. As a part of the oneness of nature he is detached from every part, severally, including himself. All is one, and the one is the vision.

For O'Flaherty the artist the sense of harmony and oneness with nature—the new sense of significance which suffuses the natural scene —is not the end of the experience. It is his role not merely to experience, but to express. And if Fergus O'Connor finds the new and wondrous vision wrung from the agony of his despair ineffable, O'Flaherty the artist must find a means to express that which is almost beyond expression, yet containing all of real significance. The nature of the vision and the new relationship of author to subject which gives rise to this vision make certain demands upon the artist. First, and mainly, O'Flaherty is overwhelmed with a sense of the momentous significance of his experience. He has discovered a secret. He is "scratching at a door behind which the secret of life lay hidden." To capture and recreate this experience is the reason for the story. But the relationship from which the new vision arises is not one of an author— an I—who observes or creates a pattern of significance in nature. Ego is merged and obliterated. This is an essential demand on the form that must express the vision. There must be no evidence of an artist choosing and arranging. He is a medium, a clear glass. We do not hear the author's voice. We see no evidence of his presence, only the scene, the wondrous vision, not told but imposed directly upon us.

Now, as might be expected, this has significant consequences in artistic form and explains the characteristic form of an O'Flaherty short story. Take "The Rockfish," [4] for instance, a sketch in the higher mood that, O'Flaherty tells Garnett (May 2, 1924), is far superior to "Selling Pigs," which is a conventional peasant story. "The Rockfish" is a story that springs directly from the kind of vision described above. The subject is "the fishes prowling in the depths" with which Fergus O'Connor has felt a special kinship. The story is short—not 1,500 words. And it is simple—a fish is almost caught. That is really all there is to it. Someone is fishing. The bait drops into a group of smaller fish who nibble and snatch the bait away. The hook is rebaited and a large rockfish emerges from his lair and gulps the hook. He is hauled nearly to the fisherman's hand when the hook tears out of his mouth and he escapes. It is almost easier to describe what the story is not than what it is. There are no characters in any common sense in which the term is used. The fisherman is merely there. Except that he is large, there is no special quality about the fish. The story is not a vehicle for the author's descriptions of nature. What little happens is not important as far as any sense of plot is concerned. Nothing is symbolic of anything. There are no hidden meanings, no allegory. The author makes no observations about the meaning of the experience. If any conventional expectations about what stories should be or contain are used as a criterion, the reader would find himself among those persons of inferior taste who would prefer "Selling Pigs."

What is expressed is the vision, the kinship and oneness of the author with the natural scene in the most direct expression possible. The order of events is natural, inevitable. "Flop. The cone-shaped bar of lead tied to the end of the fishing-line dropped into the sea without causing a ripple." For some reason the equilibrium has been disturbed. There is an action, and a set of events follows. The fisherman never emerges as a person. His function is to fish as it is the function of stars to fall or clouds to rain. The bait stirs up other action. The little rockfish churn around and draw the attention of the large fish. He acts, struggles against the line and the fisherman, and tears himself loose. "He was free." The story ends, as the original equilibrium is restored. Apparently, the author does not arrange the parts. Each event occurs after every other. The connective is *then*, not *while* or *meanwhile*. Each sentence either depicts a static scene or advances the action. Nothing is described as being contemporaneous, for this would require the presence of an author holding one set of actions in abeyance while another took place. There is no backward or simultaneous flow. From the moment the lead hits the water until the fish is free all motion is forward and relentless, like the ticking of a clock.

As the special relationship of the author to his material must eliminate the complexities of time (and with it those words used to denote these complexities) so the careful elimination of author intervention in any form must eliminate intellectual and logical complexities. No relationships are stated through the use of logical words like *though* or *because*. No such words appear, for these are intellectual "author" words not a part of the natural scene which contains no intellect probing beneath the surface. That depicted is pure vision. No author is there explaining relationships, standing outside the material and seeing the parts relate to each other temporally or causally.

The intellect, the black soul, fixed outside the scene would see motion without purpose. But the author, driven to despair and to vision by his black soul, is not outside the scene. He is submerged, absorbed in it. A word like *purpose* has no meaning from this view. This is what man attempts to impose upon or extract from nature with his intellect. But it cannot be understood in these terms. There is a significance far beyond purpose, a significance in the very being of the scene, the import of which envelops but which cannot be understood. No part is more important than any other, no relationship need be pointed out or explained. All is important. All is wondrous. All is holy. So the details emerge, not significant because of some complex arrangement that the author is building, but because they are a part of the whole. They are not understood but are important because they are there. Their importance is felt as the import of the whole story is felt. All is significant. Nothing must be overlooked. The significance may be the number: the weight sinks *twenty-five* feet, *three* short plaits of horsehair extend along the line, *three* baited hooks swing from the line, the little rockfish nibbles timorously *three* times, the fish jumps *twice*, the bar of lead bobs up and down *twice*. Why these numbers? From the point of view of the story, the question cannot be asked. The details are important as the details of any overwhelmingly significant experience are important, more important even, as they cannot be understood.

The scene, the story, embodies the secret of life, which the author must express as felt, not understood, for the secret of life is not accessible to the understanding. Each detail is a part of this secret: The baited hooks show white against the broad strands of red seaweed. The man rests the fishing-rod in the crutch of his right arm. Excited, the man breathes through his nose. The large rockfish's belly is dun color. The man braces himself with his right foot. The top hook catches in the seaweed. The function of these specific details is not description, in the sense of an author describing. The vividness of the scene is incidental. The author apparently is not there observing, selecting, constructing this or that segment to be in harmony with his total design. The details appear not to have been chosen but to exist, and to exist as some significant manifestation of the marvelous incomprehensible vision which constitutes the whole of the story.

There is no reason to believe that O'Flaherty's spiritual experiences were not real, that from his spiritual turmoil did not arise a new sense of wonder and awe and significance. We can accept as true his sense of oneness, of peace, of marvelous insight. But to express the ineffable he had to create an illusion, and that is his art. For if O'Flaherty the man escapes from his black soul's torments by obliterating himself and merging into the life force of nature, O'Flaherty the artist must deliberately try to recreate this experience. Of course he is not one with what he represents. Of course he must choose and arrange. What appears in "The Rockfish" is a most deliberate arrangement according to a most rigid plan, and the most deliberate part of the arrangement is that it not appear as an arrangement at all.

Up to this point the story has been described from very much inside the story, as if indeed the story did happen. But the laws which govern the story's structure should be clear. The characteristic form is primarily the result of the author, because of the nature of that which he is attempting to express, deliberately removing all sense of himself from the story. And this is carried to a degree much further than mere technical objectivity. Not only is the *I* removed, but all sense of narrator is removed. The objectivity goes further even than the dramatic, for in a dramatic presentation there is still the sense of a deliberate arrangement of speeches for preconceived purposes. In "The Rockfish" there appear to be no preconceived purposes. The intellect is removed by eliminating the characteristic intellectual sense of causality and complex time relationships. With this go all complex plot relationships and character analyses and relationships. The simple sentences laid end to end, clearly and separately, while perhaps the most obvious characteristic of the style, are not the cause of the simplicity but the result of this other process. The spiritual insight, experienced so intensely and personally as to be ineffable, is expressed so objectively that the author goes to unusual means to eliminate every possible trace of his presence. And through this artifice, in a full circle, is expressed just that which is most significant in the spiritual insight: the fusion of the black soul-intellect-divisive force into the whole man who loses all sense of self in a union and harmony with the ongoing, unquesting life force and process of nature.

Not all O'Flaherty short stories are as rigorously patterned as "The Rockfish," but those demands imposed by the peculiar nature of his vision which controlled form in "The Rockfish" continue to operate in the majority of his other stories. His fundamental concern is *seeing*, not *making*. And always it is the quality of the seeing which is his concern. In *Shame the Devil* O'Flaherty tells of looking into a goat's eyes "watching with the haughty calm of understanding." That is the writer's position. "That is the way a writer should look at life, with the calmness born of understanding, instead of wasting his frenzy on the destruction of ideas and in teaching false philosophies to fools" (p. 154). But the goat's eye is also the snake's eye—malign, cold, arrogant and hateful—a part of himself that O'Flaherty must learn to accept and harness. Sometimes it is a vision of horror. When he recalls seeing a lost, terrified rabbit pursued by a carrion crow hurtling down a cliff into the sea, he falls moping on "the horrible phenomenon of death." All life seems meaningless in reference to millions of years before and after the fact of existence. He becomes convinced that "the life of the individual was too momentary in relation to the universe to allow one event more importance than another" (p. 85). What O'Flaherty must express is the difference between this kind of seeing, with the seer detached and despairing, and the seeing that understands, is awed, accepts, and celebrates.

The problem is enormous, because as profound as is the difference between these two kinds of seeing, this difference is intensely personal and subjective. To an external observer, nothing would appear to be changed. And not only this, but the latter kind of seeing which accepts is entirely dependent upon the former seeing which rejects and despairs. All must be rejected before all can be accepted. The solution lies in the paradox shown in the construction of "The Rockfish." The essential difference is in the relationship of the *I* to the scene. The most intense separation of the *I* leads to the complete merging of the *I*. But because the nature of this merging obliterates the perceiving *I* (what is seen is not a personal experience in the sense of a subject perceiving an object), it is only through the most extreme detachment that the essence of the new seeing can possibly be expressed. Only the greatest objectivity can represent the experience so intensely subjective that the subject experiencing melts into the total experience. Thus O'Flaherty sees the writer as possessing a goat's eye, or a snake's eye, or a weasel's eye, as one who is condemned to observe but not participate in the richness of life. In a letter to Garnett (July 16, 1915) about style he tells of striving for "a feeling of coldness." This is the coldness of extreme detachment, pure artistry, where the artist's warm human qualities represent a blot or an imperfection if they are allowed to intrude. For as these qualities intrude, the subject-object relationship is reestablished, and the essential quality of the oneness of the vision is imperiled or destroyed.

One way of classifying O'Flaherty's short stories is through the diversity and complexity of materials to which he is able to bring this coldness of vision, remembering that the coldness represents the detachment which his expression of intense personal experience requires.

It is as if O'Flaherty tests how much experience the artist can encompass before the man breaks through and shatters the illusion. Those stories without human participants are at the simplest level; the most extreme of these is "The Wave" in which no living character, animal or human appears. Here at its bleakest and grandest is a natural process—motion without purpose in its barest essentials. It is the "poem about the cliffs and the sea" that Fergus O'Connor, the black soul, wanted to write to express the marvelous understanding wrought from his despair. If the material is the simplest, it also represents the greatest leap, for the impersonal inexorable sea *is* the motion without purpose that the intellect–black soul sees as intolerable, that renders all human life and activity meaningless, that motion of the waves from "Dover Beach" which

> Begin, and cease; and then again begin,
> With tremulous cadence slow; and bring
> The eternal note of sadness in.

They move Matthew Arnold to observe that the world "Hath really neither joy, nor love, nor light,/ Nor certitude, nor peace, nor help for pain."

But "The Wave" contains no melancholy brooding which represents someone observing and moralizing about nature. The black soul has observed and brooded and moralized and despaired, utterly. And from the void emerges the new vision with the brooding *I* nowhere apparent. Now it is nature, appalling and wonderful, expressed not described, incomprehensible, exulting in its own voice. A cliff towers two-hundred feet high. Waves pulse and lash about its base. Red seaweed throbs with the sea's beat and is pulled taut with each receding wave. A giant wave, dwarfing all the others, gathers in the distance, charges forward, and smashes against the cliff, and the cliff with a crash and a rumble and cloud of gray dust disappears into the sea. The wave has disappeared, but already another gathers in the cove.

Although "The Wave" lacks the extreme patterning of "The Rockfish," the same fundamental principles apply: the natural order, the simplicity and brevity, the details which seem to carry a significance far beyond their descriptive force—most of all is the detachment and objectivity which results from the observer being so merged into the scene that he ceases to be. That is the marvel of the illusion: in a story that is pure description there is no effect of description. As the subject-object relationship has disappeared in the experience that prompts the vision, so the artist creates the illusion that this does not exist in the expression of the vision.

Although "The Wave" represents the ultimate leap, it is also the simplest because it is the least human and least likely to involve the man rather than the artist. The leap into a oneness with that which is most unhuman is the ultimate spiritual step, but it poses the fewest artistic problems for O'Flaherty because the detachment requisite for expression is most easily achieved. But as materials more nearly human are brought into the vision, the vision and the illusion of the vision are more difficult to maintain. Human sympathy, anger, impatience, vexation, and amusement have no place in the vision in any aspect that involves the man viewing or participating in the scene, for this establishes a subject-object relationship incompatible with the vision. Because the expression demands the greatest detachment and objectivity for the artist, these same human concerns are forbidden to him if he is to sustain the illusion.

What must be expressed is always nature, in the relationship that has been explained, and as life enters, it must enter as a manifestation of this nature. Always the law of detachment, objectivity, and nonparticipation governs the artist. He is not interested in how the animals are like people or how the people are like animals, but how both are manifestations of life and nature. Nor is he interested in the complexity of human relationships for the sake of the complexity or for the sake of the human relationship, but for the relationship of the complexity to the simplicity of the vision. The problem is to sustain the vision through greater and greater complexity, through more human concern, always keeping the human concern in such a perspective as to be primarily a fact of nature.

Stories like "The Wild Goat's Kid," "The Blackbird," "The Wounded Cormorant," "The Water Hen," and "The Wild Swan" contain animals only. The patterns are the inevitable patterns of nature like "The Wave" and "The Rockfish": something disturbs the equilibrium and a new equilibrium emerges. The wild goat gives birth to a kid, defends the kid in a fierce encounter with a dog, flees from the dog's gored body to other pastures. A cormorant, its leg broken by a falling rock, is pecked to death by the flock. A cat patiently stalks a blackbird which flies safely off at the cat's last leap. The water hen mates with the victor of a savage battle. The wild swan leaves its dead mate to migrate south and return the next season with a new one. The author does not intrude to judge or moralize. The stories have no

meaning other than what they are. The subject is nature expressed.
Fierce battles rage, intense dramas are enacted, great cruelty is per-
petrated, but all is one to the artist's impassive eye.

But in "The Wild Goat's Kid" there is a break in the technique, a
flaw, and this is most revealing in relation to the artist's problem. The
wild goat emerges too much as a character, engaging sympathies, becoming a heroine. As a result, detachment and nonparticipation are lost;
and though the story may be more personally gripping, it is artistically
less successful. It tends to be just another animal story. O'Flaherty's
magic is not there.

Up the scale of complexity are stories like "The Rockfish," "The
Hawk," "The Hook," and "The Conger Eel" in which human beings
enter, but as agents or forces, not as characters. They retain the imper-
sonality of the rock that fell to break the cormorant's leg. In "The
Conger Eel" it is of no moment whether the eel escapes the men and
regains its freedom or whether the men kill the eel that has destroyed
their nets. As in "The Rockfish" the fish escapes, but this has no
special significance. To have either of them caught would tend to
shift the emphasis from the fish to the men and introduce an unneces-
sary complexity to restoring the equilibrium. The hawk is killed in an
unsuccessful attempt to save its mate from human capture. The
problem is not with the human characters but with the human characteristics of the animals that they engage sympathies. In "The Hook"
a seagull falls into a trap laid by some boys and snatches a piece of
liver in which a hook tied to a string is hidden. The string breaks, but
the hook imbeds itself in the seagull's beak. The seagull flies back to
his nest where his mate snips the string and tears the hook loose. In
many respects this is like the other nature stories—the simplicity, the
natural order, the restored equilibrium. But the detachment and
objectivity are lacking. The author intrudes, interpreting. The seagull
would swoop down and get the liver "but he wanted to bring a share
to his mate that was sitting on the eggs." The other seagulls make a
tremendous noise "blinking their eyes in amazement at the hook
sticking from the trapped one's bill." His mate on seeing the string
cackles shrilly "like a virago of a woman reviling a neighbour." When
the hook is removed, his mate "smoothed her feathers with a shrug and
closed her eyes in a bored fashion." Successful expression of his vision
demands that the objects or creatures of nature behave according to
their own laws, speak in their own voices. Here the animals behave like
human beings, are described in human terms. The author observes and
imposes his humanity upon the scene. A subject-object relationship is

established, the coldness is lost, and with it the wonder and awe of the vision.

As human characters are introduced into these story patterns they are not set against nature in any kind of separation. In "Birth" the peasants, the sea, the sounding birds, the chomping sheep all join in the natural ceremony of birth. The old man hears in the running sea the change in the tide that he knows will set the birth throes in motion. He knows as the heifer knows, as the sheep know. O'Flaherty's characters do not struggle against nature. They are nature.

H. E. Bates tells how Edward Garnett sent O'Flaherty back to Ireland to write a story about a cow.[5] The story that resulted was "The Cow's Death," which O'Flaherty came to regard as a touchstone for stories of this type. His letters to Edward Garnett discuss short-story technique. He calls "The Cow's Death" Garnett's sketch: "You taught me how to write that one" (June 4, 1923). He thanks Garnett for pointing out that "damn cleverness of expression" is no good "without the bones" (May 5, 1923). Looking back, O'Flaherty sees "The Cow's Death" style is ideal. At that time it seemed to him he could not duplicate it. The style had that "feeling of coldness" for which he was striving (July 16, 1925). "The Cow's Death" follows the same basic pattern that has been described—objectivity and simplicity in style and structure. A cow has given birth to a stillborn calf. The peasants shake their heads in silence, then drive the cow away and drag the dead calf through a series of fences and throw it over a cliff into the sea. They force a hot oatmeal drink down the cow's throat and leave. The agonized cow in a growing frenzy searches for the calf. She follows the trail through the fences, pushing down a fence and cutting herself on the stones. At the cliff's edge she pauses, confused, then strains out to see the calf's body below. There is no way down. Waves wash against the body. A large wave sweeps the body from the rocks. "And the cow, uttering a low bellow, jumped headlong down."

The achievement here is the "feeling of coldness," for the essence of the story is not pity and sympathy, but wonder and awe. Only one sentence, or part of a sentence, breaks, momentarily, this spell, and it is worth noting because in a negative way it points up by contrast O'Flaherty's achievement in the rest of the story. The peasant woman rubs the cow's forehead, with a tear in her eye "for she too was a mother." O'Flaherty has brought his special vision to a scene full of occasion for participation and sympathy. This scene he must encompass in detachment and coldness, for just in the proportion that he can bring this coldness to a scene making the most intense demands for personal involvement lies his artistic success. When he writes "for she too was a mother" he has reached the breaking point. What he says may be true, but it is not appropriate, because the author too obviously is saying it. This points up the close relationship of the vision to the expression of the vision. Sympathy has intruded, or appears to intrude. The author's presence is felt, in interpreting and feeling, and detachment and coldness are lost. Whether through a momentary failure of the man or the artist, for an instant the illusion is broken.

In any collection of O'Flaherty stories, whether by chance or design, one cannot help noticing the mixture of stories about animals with stories about people. The effect is to show the similarities, of course, but not primarily in an intellectual sense or in any sense that judges animals or people. The main effect is to put them into the same perspective. They are all manifestations of life and nature as the stories are expressions of life and nature. A common coldness covers all. In man and animal nature behaves according to her own laws.

O'Flaherty's vision turned to the human scene is shown at its simplest in stories like "Blood Lust," "The Struggle," and "The Fight." The participants are all human beings, but their expressions of passion are viewed not as they are characteristically human but as they are a part of nature. The most elemental forces operate. Two brothers are out fishing. The idea, the compulsion, bubbles into the mind of one to kill the other. It possesses him and he struggles. At the moment he is about to plunge a knife into his brother's back, the fishing line pulls tight and he hauls in a fish. He crushes it into a pulp with his bare hands. "His blood lust was satisfied." In "The Struggle" two young men are out in a boat. They have been drinking. One snatches the bottle from the other and they fight. In the furious melee the boat overturns. Both are drowned. "The Fight" is about Black Tom, a peasant who in his periodic drunks tries to fight Sweeney, who for some unknown reason has become his sworn enemy. After bragging speeches on both sides Tom reels drunkenly to the attack and crashes helplessly against a wall. Sweeney strikes one blow and the fight is over. Embarrassed, Tom leaves, muttering on the way home against his enemy. At home he breaks all the delph. Next morning he has a sick head. "He did that twice every year." And so the story ends. In each of these stories the interest is not in the characters, in who they are, or what character traits they illustrate. Nor is the interest in what, in particular, they do. Their relationship is not with society. They are manifestations of nature, in some of the elemental ways that nature is manifest through human beings. And O'Flaherty brings to this aspect of nature the same cold view that he brought to the inanimate and animal aspects of nature.

Complexity increases as the subject becomes not man as passion flames and dies in him in the restoration of natural equilibrium, but people in fundamental, elemental relationships. This too is a manifestation of nature. Stories of this kind include "Spring Sowing," "The Landing," "Life," "Going Into Exile," and "Galway Bay." In "Spring Sowing" a young couple together sow their first potato crop and become a part of the land that will claim them. In "Landing" peasant women on the shore are exhilarated in the wild terror that accompanies the landing of their men's frail boat in the raging waves. Infancy and old age are depicted in "Life," in which an old man withers as an infant develops. Their lives cross when the infant is weaned and the mash made for one is also the food of the other. As the lusty infant takes hold in the world the old man fades from it. "Going into Exile" is about the separation of a family as two young people leave their poor home for America. The unquenchable fires in doughty old age are the subject in "Galway Bay," as an irascible old man takes his old cow to the market in Galway. He will have sport in Galway and then return with enough money for his funeral and for a mass to be said over his grave. But a loneliness unto death seizes him as he and the old cow walk slowly down the pier.

It is only when the spell has been broken that one can be aware that a spell has been cast in these stories. Frank O'Connor notes about "Going Into Exile" that O'Flaherty "with his own natural innocence . . . could ignore everything except the nature of exile itself—a state of things like love and death that we must all endure." [6] But if the subject is exile itself—and surely it is this: there is no concern for the why of the exile or for individual psychological reactions to it—it is exile viewed under the aspect of eternity, in the cold view of O'Flaherty's vision. It is exile as a manifestation of nature somehow beyond individual human concern. That is the spell that O'Flaherty casts as his art controls and enforces this view. When a human relationship or a human reference point intrudes, the spell breaks, just as other violations of the stories' strict disciplines break the spell in "The Hook" and "The Cow's Death." In "Going Into Exile" this kind of break occurs in the portrayal of Mary, one of the young people going into exile:

> And as she sat on the edge of the bed crushing her little handkerchief between her palms, she kept thinking feverishly of the

United States, at one moment with fear and loathing, at the next with desire and longing. Unlike her brother she did not think of the work she was going to do or the money she was going to earn. Other things troubled her, things of which she was half ashamed, half afraid, thoughts of love and of foreign men and of clothes and of houses where there were more than three rooms and where people ate meat every day. She was fond of life, and several young men among the local gentry had admired her in Inverara. But . . .

Mary begins to emerge as a character, a personality, for her own sake. A reference point is established beyond the bounds of the story. A human dimension is established, interesting because it is related to other human concerns. The author's cold view, essential to his spell-casting, becomes a personal view as he probes beneath the surface. But it is essential that the story be all surface, for any break in this surface is a break in the author's illusion of objectivity and detachment. A break in the surface brings an awareness of an author telling, speculating, looking at, and interpreting the scene. But the same principles apply that governed "The Rockfish." The essence of the vision is that in the experience the experiencer becomes so at one with nature that he ceases to be a self experiencing. And to create this illusion, the artist must feign the most absolute coldness and detachment, must remove all evidence that an *I* is perceiving or creating the scene. What is told must appear to *be*, a fact in itself, nature revealing herself in her own voice. The story exists—cold, self-contained, absolute. O'Flaherty's stories at their best appear so inevitable that only when the spell is broken is the reader made aware that through the special coldness and objectivity a spell has been cast.

The most complex relationships that O'Flaherty attempts in his stories are the relationships between man and society. If in the stories involving elemental human relationships and emotions the artist must avoid sympathetic participation to keep his cold view, in these stories he must avoid intellectual participation. The opportuny for polemic is great, for man's social institutions are involved. But these too must be seen as a manifestation of nature, under the aspect of eternity. There is no better or worse. As the wave crashes against the cliff, so man attempts economic success, or the religious spirit is expressed, or the artist is estranged from his society. In "Two Lovely Beasts," "The Fairy Goose," and "The Child of God" the subjects are these three aspects of human life.

Against the wishes of his wife and family, against the traditions of his society, Colm Derrane takes the risk and attempts to raise a second calf on his barren twenty acres. This act and its consequences are the materials of "Two Lovely Beasts." What he did was unheard of. It violated every principle of the community tradition. It appeared to be against the will of God. But with this initial leap made, Colm's resolve to rise up in the world was not to be daunted. He beats his wife into submission, and the whole family undergoes extreme privation as Colm makes every effort to gather capital. He is a shunned outcast from society. He now risks holding the two calves a second winter and uses his money to begin trade and open a shop. Success is almost immediate. His neighbors now accept him and consider him a wise man. Now his family has everything and more that it had been denied. Colm's ambition presses on. He decides to hire help and open a shop in town. Now his neighbors turn against him again. He is indifferent to their jeers. As the story ends, "His pale blue eyes stared fixedly straight ahead, cold and resolute and ruthless."

The objectivity seems complete. There is no judgment of Colm or of society. This is what happens. There is no commentary, no interpretation. But this is not a perfect example of cold vision, because the story seems to mean something. It appears to have a significance beyond that of its surface. Interpretation seems necessary. This is because O'Flaherty's technique here is primarily dramatic. He achieves objectivity by refraining from comment and using dialogue to advance and explain the action. Drama has depth because what the characters say requires interpretation. Their words relate to them. The sequence of speeches seems to be an arrangement. A whole series of cross-currents of meaning and consequence is set up, and in the resulting complexity the wonder and awe of O'Flaherty's vision is lost. The vision is expressed by a cold surface. The eye, not the ear governs. "Two Lovely Beasts" achieves a technical objectivity through dramatic technique, but this is not the absolute detachment and coldness achieved by the artist expressing an intense subjective relationship. The materials of nature are merely handled at a distance. They have not been put through the intense process which relates them to the oneness of O'Flaherty's vision.

"The Fairy Goose," says Frank O'Connor, in *The Lonely Voice*, is in essence "the whole history of religion." It is not, however, O'Flaherty's commentary on religion. It is the expression of religion as a manifestation of nature. As O'Connor says, "O'Flaherty never permits the shadow of a sneer to disturb the gravity of the theme" (p. 38). He attributes this to O'Flaherty's feeling rather than thinking, but this is a superficial explanation. In that which O'Flaherty expresses in the truest conformity to the demands of his vision, his coldness and detachment are so complete that no author who *can* sneer is evident. Sneering is social commentary. Sneering is a reflection of author personality. These are completely unrelated to the essential spirit of O'Flaherty's short stories, especially this one.

"The Fairy Goose" is about a scraggy little gosling hatched in Mary Wiggins' kitchen behind the stove. Although it was runted and deformed, she and her husband believe it would be wrong to kill it. It grows slowly into a most ungooselike goose. It ignores other geese, is afraid of water, cleans itself by rolling in the grass, makes tweeky ungooselike noises. The woman begins to think it is a fairy and adorns it with ribbons and blesses it with holy water. She begins to believe that the goose has given her supernatural powers. She gains some reputation for her powers and this report reaches the priest. He gallops out to end this pagan practice. He routs out the pampered delicate goose, strips it of ribbons, scatters its strange nest, and strikes Mary Wiggins a sharp blow as she attempts to stop him. Warning the village about the evil of this, he leaves. Now Mary Wiggins and her goose are no longer considered sacred. Boys stone the goose to death. Mary curses the village, and though the curse has no immediate effect, it is believed that the village has been quarrelsome ever since. O'Flaherty brings his cold vision to that which would be most likely to stir O'Flaherty the man to polemic—peasant superstition and priestcraft. In "The Fairy Goose" there is no trace of polemic. All is accepted and inevitable. The priest cannot be other than he is, nor can the peasants. All behave according to their own laws, and the law governing all is the inexplicable law of nature. "The Fairy Goose" is not the expression of social criticism and satire, but of the wonder and awe of human beings as manifestations of nature.

"The Child of God" depicts the relationship of the artist to society, in this case closely paralleling O'Flaherty's own relationship to the peasant community of his native Aran Islands. In *Shame the Devil* O'Flaherty refers continually to this estrangement. When he returned to the Aran Islands after his disappointment with the reception of *The Black Soul*, all the people on the boat "looked askance" at him, for he had "already become a damned soul in their eyes." The people on the pier spoke to him and shook his hand, but there was fear in their eyes, a fear that was "deeper than hatred and unapproachable." O'Flaherty looks at the familiar scenes "glancing shyly, with a timid lover's eyes," but he is aware of the antipathy of those watching him. Somehow he has become contaminated. "With what?" he asks: "The madness of prophecy, no less. This is the greatest sin in the eyes of the herd. And when one of the herd becomes gifted with this madness, he at once becomes an object of fear for the rest." In a weak and poor herd this fear often leads to the expulsion or even death of the artist, he says. But "to sing of beauty should be such a lovely thing" (pp. 58–59).

Peter O'Toole, the Child of God, like O'Flaherty is a bright boy who tells his mother marvelous stories. At ten he decides he wants to be a priest, and the proud family gathers all its resources to finance his education. But after some time a letter comes from the seminary telling that Peter has been expelled. A year later Peter returns home. He had been expelled because he had ceased to believe in God. Now he is an artist. Like O'Flaherty he had worked a year in London as a laborer, waiter, and porter—in Peter's case to finance his art education. Their son's remoteness somehow terrifies his parents. "It is impossible to explain the instinct of peasants, their aversion for anything unlike themselves." And Peter too feels a strangeness and hostility in the land and the people. But this alienation melts for Peter as the beauty of the land and people is impressed upon him. The peasants gather one day in their kitchen, and Peter is moved by the "strange, beautiful faces, all sombre and dignified; mysterious faces of people who live by the sea away from civilization; age-old people, inarticulate, pitiless, yet as gentle as children." He shows them his pictures, "sketches of fierce, terrible men, everything done with a tremendous, almost uncouth power, the work of a raw, turbulent, half-developed genius." They are horrified. His family is shocked and disappointed. After that Peter is left alone and reverts to peasant dress. He takes up with the wild young people of the island; and between bouts of frenzied creative energy he carouses. An old man dies and the wild gang to which Peter belongs perpetrate a fantastic drunken wake. At the height of the debauch Peter hurries to get his paints and canvas and to everyone's horror begins to sketch the appalling scene: "the corpse, the carpenter lying drunk in the coffin, the stupefied men lying on the floor in gruesome attitudes, the dark kitchen, with sagging, black earthen roof and the silence of death." This is the final atrocity. Peter's house is stoned. The priest is called and Peter is banished from the parish.

This story is worth looking at in some detail, not as an example of O'Flaherty's most characteristic achievement but because it shows him as he sees himself in the role of an artist. It is noteworthy that Peter is a painter, for it is the visual with which O'Flaherty's art is most concerned. The artist is attracted by the natural beauty of the land and people but also alienated from it by the fact of his being an artist. When this "unexplainable gulf" which separates him even from his mother is bridged by "the force of their natural love," Peter feels reconciled and gay and delights freely in the joys of the natural life. But regardless of his personal feelings as a man, the absolute separation of the artist from society is revealed by that to which he brings his artistic vision. As an artist he is cold and detached, and to that scene which in the normal man would evoke terror and horror he feels impelled to bring his vision. The others are either drunk or appalled, but Peter is sober and detached. He has been a part of the scene as a man, a leading participant in all the debauchery. But always the second self—the artist—is watching, and when the scene reaches the stage when no normal man can watch unaffected, the artist detaches himself and makes the scene the material for his art. He wishes to express not the horror of a shocked observer—a subject-object relationship in which the artist's real subject is his personal feelings—but the absolute quality of the scene, the wonder and awe that lie beyond personal expression.

An artist must bring his vision to scenes profoundly moving to the man, but as an artist he must transcend mere human personal affection. The scene may be an inexorable wave destroying a cliff, a frenzied cow crashing to destruction after her calf, a wounded cormorant pecked to death by its flock, a young couple taking on the yoke that will bind them to the earth, or a horrible scene of debauchery and death. All that moves a man the artist must transcend and translate by his cold vision. The artist must express the wonder and awe of nature, alien to all that man is and yet all that man is, that as a man he accepts in despair in a mystical leap.

The pattern of alienation in these last three stories is apparent. In each the central figure is set apart from society—Colm by his decision to raise two calves and improve his lot, the fairy goose by its strangeness, the Child of God by his art. After partial reconciliations in which society attempts to come to terms with and even to admire the central figure, the ultimate fact of strangeness and difference is the determining factor. In the end his neighbors jeer Colm's success, but he is unaware of their jeers, "cold and resolute and ruthless." The fairy goose, once pampered and admired, in the end is interdicted by the priest and stoned to death by the mob. So too the Child of God is showered with stones and banished by the priest.

Each of these stories bears the unmistakable imprint of O'Flaherty's personality in an archetypal pattern. In each he recreates the relationship to society which his genius forces upon him. This is the ultimate in the increasing scale of complexity by which his stories have been classed, for in these stories O'Flaherty must bring his cold goat's eye or snake's eye or weasel's eye to view that which is most himself, as the wave was most not himself. This is the limit of his art, and his success depends upon the extent to which he can scrutinize himself under the aspect of eternity, transcend all that most deeply concerns him, see himself as a manifestation of nature, and express through his cold vision the wonder and awe of the fact of his own existence.

This scheme of classification does not include one whole group of stories tangentially related to it, those stories involving a prank or trick where intellect is used for deception. Stories typical of this group are "Colic," "The Shilling," "The Pot of Gold," and "The Red Petticoat." In a letter to Garnett dated May 23, 1924, O'Flaherty says that he is vexed that Garnett has rejected "Colic" from a collection. O'Flaherty insists that it be included because he considers it "an excellent humorous story." He accuses Garnett of having a prejudice against humorous stories. And the story was included in the *Spring Sowing* collection. "Colic" is representative of this group. Two village ne'er-do-wells are without money and in need of a drink. The sharper one concocts a scheme. He has his partner feign an acute attack of colic at the door of Mrs. Curran's public-house. Only brandy will help. Reluctantly Mrs. Curran gets a noggin of brandy, the sick man revives, snatches it from his partner's hand, gulps it down, and runs. Everyone laughs except Mrs. Curran and the schemer until an old farmer settles the bill and treats him to a drink for the laugh he has had. In "Pot of Gold" a man tells his cronies that he has had a dream about finding a pot of gold. Amply supplied with whiskey (the cronies' whiskey) the group sets out to follow up the clues in his dream. He leads them up into the hills to a rock. While they dig, he drinks and then disappears, leaving them to discover the trick. In "The Shilling" a group of bums have the problem of getting a shilling they spy lying on the deck of a boat anchored at the pier. All sorts of plans are presented until the cleverest of them asks a man on the boat to hand him back the shilling he has dropped. Mary Deignan tricks the shopkeeper in "The Red Petticoat" in a similar kind of story.

As has been said, these stories are tangentially related to those stories in the main current where O'Flaherty brings his cold vision to bear on scenes of great emotional impact. In the "trick" stories he employs the same objective technique. Only now the subject is the intellect in its elemental form in the lives of simple people. This too is nature, or ought to be. But for O'Flaherty this nature exists as an intellectual concept. It is not nature as felt—awesome and wonderful— to be expressed, where the art is in the tension between the subject and the telling. In the "trick" stories there is no tension. Nature speaking in her own voice does not evoke laughter. O'Flaherty brings the wrong formula to the subject, for the essence of his art is based in feeling. "When O'Flaherty thinks, he's a goose, when he feels, he's a genius," O'Connor quotes George Russell as saying.[7] But feeling is the tragic quality—tragedy for those who feel, comedy for those who think. Comedy plays intellect over the subject. In the "trick" stories nothing plays over the subject nor is any deep feeling transcended. Nothing happens. Garnett's excellent judgment saw much more clearly the essential quality of O'Flaherty's art than did O'Flaherty, and Garnett was rightly prejudiced against the humorous stories.

It is noteworthy that this is the only way that intellect appears in O'Flaherty's short stories, this intellect in its simplest problem-solving, tricking sense. All other aspects appear to have been rigidly excluded. Much of this is due, of course, to the subject matter. In the simple lives he depicts, cerebration is not very likely to be an important feature. And much of this is due to O'Flaherty's essentially visual technique. The eye cannot see the complexities of intellect. But all goes back basically to the black soul, the very principle of probing, agonizing, tortured intellect, which is reduced to nothing by inscrutable nature, leaving only accepting unquestioning life. Life in its simplicity is reality for O'Flaherty in his short stories. There is no place for characters who brood, who are tortured by self doubts, who agonize in cosmic uncertainty, or for characters who plan or theorize or are burdened with social concerns. For all complexity is reduced to simplicity in the vision, and from the ashes of the black soul rises life itself.

His correspondence with Garnett would seem to indicate that O'Flaherty did not attach much importance to his short stories. He writes that his stories will be popular, but for himself "these two novels *Thy Neighbour's Wife* and *The Black Soul* will stand out as far greater and of more spiritual importance than anything I may do" (May 23, 1924). He is irked by the obtuseness of Irish taste which does not appreciate his novels. "They go into rhapsodies here about my short stories but they refuse to discuss *Thy Neighbour's Wife*" (May 2, 1924). When he first meets the Dublin literati he is unimpressed. He cites as an example of their taste one young poet who liked the short stories and hoped O'Flaherty would collect them and give up novel writing (March 10, 1924). But O'Flaherty's concern then was almost entirely with his novels. It was with *The Black Soul* that he hoped to storm the literary heights. The short stories did not pay well. He complains to Garnett that "nobody in Ireland has enough money to pay more than a pound for a story of two thousand words" (May 2, 1924). The short stories begin to bore him. "I get no pleasure from writing these short sketches now," he writes to Garnett. "They seem to advance according to a formula." Plans for his novels absorb him. "Big ideas devour little ones," and the short stories have lost all interest (March 30, 1924). Yet he knows that the stories are popular and may be useful to him. He launches on an intensive short-story-writing campaign to call attention to *The Informer*. He tells Garnett of writing ten short stories in three weeks for this purpose, with thirteen more to go (July 16, 1925). But if the stories for their own sake are not important in his career, he will not abandon them. He tells Garnett in a letter that they fill an "instinct for love of writing" (July, 1925). These letters were written during O'Flaherty's most prolific short-story period, when the stories were being eagerly published and acclaimed. He does not disparage them. In a period of physical decline it cheers him to tell Garnett that he has a few supporters from a literary point of view: "*The Conger Eel* was loudly acclaimed here, which to me is more comforting than all the medicines that doctors can pour into my belly with a bull's horn" (January 20, 1925). It is just that they do not seem as important to him as the novels.

It is not just that he is not the best judge of his own work. It is natural that the novels fill his mind. Not only do they offer the greatest opportunity for fame and wealth, but they are more interesting intellectually. He may announce enthusiastically to Garnett the completion of one story or another, but there is little more to talk about, because by their very nature the stories are not intellectually interesting. After the process of creation they *exist*. They do not contain ideas. They are not controversial. They contain no complex problems of plot and character development that fill his letters to Garnett concerning *The Informer* and *The Black Soul*. But O'Flaherty's more unerring "instinct," which O'Connor sets above his judgment, keeps the perspective aright. Out of the spiritual crisis described in *Shame the Devil*, where O'Flaherty discovers what and who he is, emerges not a novel, but "The Caress." This is what he writes when he accepts in understanding and humility his lot as a writer. *Shame the Devil* explores and exhausts openly and directly the spiritual quest that lay at the basis of the novels preceding it. When the vanity and arrogance and rhetoric are burned away, he writes a short story.

Critical opinion is almost unanimous in its conclusion that O'Flaherty's short stories contain his most enduring achievement. And few would disagree with Vivian Mercier's final judgment in his Introduction to the 1956 edition of O'Flaherty's stories: "If Liam O'Flaherty's work survives, posterity will not regard him as the novelist historian of a turbulent era but as the celebrant of timeless mysteries—mysteries rooted in Nature and in that portion of Nature embodied in the life of Man" (p. viii). The effect of the stories is direct and immediate. Rhys Davies in his Introduction to *The Wild Swan and Other Stories*, notes that these "exhibitions of life's primal forces, though they may lack the development of sophisticated passion become memorable in their simple directness." Francis Hackett believes that it was O'Flaherty's "deep folk quality" akin to the Russian that made Garnett take hold of him and that the short stories suited O'Flaherty's gift admirably. The stories are "charged with nervous force and the life of his people. . . . Aran is alive in them." [8] Benedict Kiely parallels Mercier in believing that the most important aspect of O'Flaherty's work is not found in novels like *The Informer* or *The Assassin*, nor in connection with Irish-Ireland ideals or the revolution. "It is the understanding of the earth, of animals worthy and human beings not always worthy of the earth, that makes O'Flaherty's work important." [9] O'Flaherty as a novelist, H. E. Bates observes in *The Modern Short Story*, is "scrappy, sensational, and often cheap." But in his stories about nature "O'Flaherty extracted a wild, tender, and sometimes violently nervous beauty" (p. 158). Sean O'Faolain in the course of his discussion of the violence of O'Flaherty's novels also concludes that the short stories are best.

Most critics stop here, yet always the question remains: What is the cause of the visual quality of the short stories, which have the "freshness of new paint," as Bates says. What does it hide? What does it represent? The reader of the short stories is aware of the turbulence of the novelist. L. Paul Dubois cannot but see the ferocity of the novels as a mask: "Nous trompons-nous en pensant qu'en ce sens son réalisme lui tient plus au moins lieu de masque, et que sa <<férocité>> n'est là que pour recouvrir sa sensibilité?" And this is the view that Benedict Kiely takes in *Modern Irish Fiction*. He believes that O'Flaherty's effort to protect himself from the softness of genuine love produces the Dark Daniel side of his genius. The simple life of nature in the short stories is a contrast and a retreat. The birds and beasts of the early short stories are "perfect children of the earth" existing in "absolute and undisturbed harmony." They are a safe haven and an ideal, the "ecstatic acceptance" of which produces the animal stories (p. 34). Kiely believes that O'Flaherty creates his human characters in contrast to this natural harmony, but occasionally "*raises* them to the level of animals, making them worthy of the earth" (p. 37). It is to this earth that O'Flaherty flees in his short stories.

Mercier stresses in his Preface that O'Flaherty's true subject, and this is found almost entirely in his short stories, is "the relationship between Man and Nature." But Mercier makes this an intellectual relationship. He has O'Flaherty looking at Nature and its relationship to man, judging it, moralizing upon it. From this view "Spring Sowing" excellently symbolizes O'Flaherty's conception of the relationship between man and nature. Man can only triumph over nature by cooperating with her; in the end he becomes her victim. "Life," that story of the crossing of young life with old, becomes "a wild cry of protest against 'the human condition.'" Mercier believes O'Flaherty's nature stories are full of lessons: "Over and over again . . . the point is made that Nature is both friend and enemy. She destroys us, but our greatest happiness . . . comes from yielding to her." "Red Barbara" is given as an example to show that "the thwarting of Nature by Man entails its own punishment." And though O'Flaherty sometimes mars the objectivity, "he always makes the reader see before urging him to judge" (pp. vi–viii).

In *The Lonely Voice*, Frank O'Connor points out two important hallmarks that he believes characterize and govern this strict form. The short story does not have a hero. Instead it has a "submerged population group." And the mood is akin to Pascal's saying: "The eternal silence of those infinite spaces terrifies me." These are his touchstones, and from one comes the other. O'Flaherty's short stories are marked clearly as conforming to this standard. O'Connor points to "The Fairy Goose" as one of the great Irish short stories because the author does not intrude. What O'Connor says surely lies near the heart of the matter. O'Flaherty is aware of giving voice to a "submerged population group." In a letter to Garnett he writes: "I don't think I exert any judgment whatsoever in my writing at the moment of writing but seem to be impelled by the Aran Islanders themselves who cry out dumbly to me to give expression to them" (July 31, 1925). And this expression could be extended to the cliffs, the birds, the wild animals, and the sea of his native land with which he began his communion at the end of *Two Years*. Moreover the effect of this expression is not a comfortable intimacy, but wonder and awe. It is not familiarity but coldness that O'Flaherty strives for in his art.

Must analysis stop at what O'Connor has said as truth enough or must the critic go further? Sartre, writing on Faulkner, tells us that the novelist's esthetic always sends us back to his metaphysic and that the critic's task is to bring out the author's metaphysic before evaluating his technique. In less technical terms this is what O'Flaherty asks Garnett to do in reading *The Informer* because he admires Garnett's criticism of *Fathers and Sons:* "I was greatly struck by the clarity with which you probed the very initial dreams of the author and their subsequent materialization in the finished creation" (September 18, 1924). At the very basis of the art is what O'Faolain calls a *manière de voir,* the essential of all fiction that is not merely entertainment.[10] It is to O'Flaherty's *manière de voir* that the critic must bring his attention, the special vision which grows out of profound spiritual crisis and puts O'Flaherty into a relationship with nature that can be explained in no other way.

In his discussion of the Irish school in the short-story tradition Bates was aware of some such influence coloring the greater part of Irish writing: "The consequent struggle between the artist and religion, between religion and experience . . . is a heritage that infuses a greater part of the best Irish writing with a quality of poetic mysticism" (p. 150). (Bates attributes this to the effect of the Catholic Church.) Though O'Flaherty is among those so affected, Bates, except for this general observation, makes no further use of this insight in discussing O'Flaherty's stories in particular.

Bates's impressionistic description of the surface of O'Flaherty's stories is true. The stories are primarily visual, and "in a strong light," displaying "sensuous poetic energy." And Kiely is right in recognizing that "ecstatic acceptance" produces the animal stories and that O'Flaherty's importance lies in his understanding of the earth. Mercier rightly describes O'Flaherty as "the celebrant of timeless mysteries— mysteries rooted in Nature and that portion of Nature embodied in the life of Man." O'Flaherty's stories may be rightly appreciated, but they cannot be rightly explained without taking into account the experience described in *The Black Soul* and *Shame the Devil* that lies at the root of their creation. The intense visual qualities that Bates describes, that impress him with their sensuous poetic energy, are a part of the art. This is the *effect* of the story. But this effect is not produced as directly as the description might imply. The description calls to mind a sensuous, hot-blooded, sensitive writer projecting directly his vivid impressions and experiences. This is not the case at all.

As an artist O'Flaherty stresses his coldness and detachment. Sometimes it is the goat's calm eye he strives for or the snake's cold eye he regards as his curse. In either case he is talking about the detachment he needs as an artist to express his absolute, self-obliterating experience as a man. "The meaning of life suddenly flickered across his mind. It flashed and then vanished leaving wonder and awe behind it." This is the essence of O'Flaherty's short-story art.

In a sense this described what Kiely called "ecstatic acceptance," but it is in no way a retreat. O'Flaherty does not view nature as a warm, understanding mother. In *I Went to Russia* he describes taking a trip up into the mountains when the ship docks at a Norwegian port: "Here brutal nature, by her sinister silence, brought vividly to my mind the realization that human life is governed by the same ruthless competition and brazen anarchy which governs the growth of nature. Plant wars with plant. . . . All is in continual movement, ever changing, blindly moving, being born, flowering, dying, from a miraculous beginning to an unexplainable end, beautiful only in movement, incomprehensible in purpose" (p. 82). This is O'Flaherty's nature, viewed with his reason, his black soul which makes all appear equally futile. His "ecstatic acceptance" does indeed accept this nature but only after profound spiritual agonies in the classical pattern of religious-mystical experience. Nature is not ideal, or comfortable; it is awesome and wonderful in a way that transcends all that man is. Expressing this is the aim of his art.

"All things appear equally futile when examined by reason," O'Flaherty concludes (p. 83). And this is especially true of nature whose whole lesson, viewed intellectually, is futility. If O'Flaherty's true subject is the relationship between man and nature, as Mercier says, it is not a reasonable relationship. Reason has no place in nature, because nature has no reasons. Stories about man's relationship to nature can have no lessons to teach because nature is incomprehensible. If man brings reason to nature, or to O'Flaherty's stories about nature, his only lesson will be futility. O'Flaherty does not urge us to judge, as Mercier suggests, because judging is a process of reason, and no judgment is possible. O'Flaherty celebrates nature's timeless mysteries, but he does not in any way moralize on nature. His subject is not the relationship between man and nature as if these are separate and in conflict, but man *as* nature, as a manifestation of nature that cannot be thought about except in despair but whose wonder and awe can be celebrated in O'Flaherty's art.

It is in the light of the kinds of experiences that William James describes that O'Flaherty's art is best understood. At its root is a profound conflict. And whether this conflict and its resolution are explained in naturalistic or theological terms, it is an experience that is significant, because it causes change and transformation—the sort of radically altered points of view that exist between O'Flaherty's novels and his short stories. When O'Flaherty shifts to nature in his short stories, it is this new point of view that is most important and not the change in subject. For though in one sense nature could be said to be the cause of the new point of view, it is not a simple relationship.

Nature represents not a solace, but essentials. Nature is that which must be faced. Nature and O'Flaherty's relationship to it are the source of the conflict on the most elemental level. When O'Flaherty turns to nature, it is the apartness that he feels, nature's indifference. The extreme of separation is at the heart of his experience, for the intensity of this separation causes the exhaustion and emptiness from which a new consciousness can emerge. The new consciousness is a sense of oneness with nature commensurate with the sense of apartness that had previously existed. This is O'Flaherty's subject—not the oneness, which is an intellectual concept, but the *sense* of oneness, which is wonder and awe. Because O'Flaherty has chosen perfection of the work and not the life, his spiritual experience results not in saintliness, but art. This is what *Shame the Devil* shows. His anguish drives him to acceptance and creativity, and the short story "The Caress" is the result.

For O'Flaherty the short story is not the development of an idea but the expression of an experience. The story is not an arrangement of details, events, or symbols to produce an epiphany. The epiphany has already taken place before the story begins. For O'Flaherty the story is *all* epiphany. Stories that are developments are in the realm of *becoming;* O'Flaherty's short stories are an attempt to express pure *being.* This is why they elude conventional analysis which, bringing mind to the scene, attempts to extract meaning. O'Flaherty's stories mean as nature means, and the meaning of nature is so inaccessible to man that all attempts to plumb its depths must be futile.

No better parallel exists to O'Flaherty's experiences with nature than the Book of Job. Here too is a representation of a profound spiritual experience. In Job's torment his reason cries out for answers, and the comforters' moralizing is no comfort at all. When the comforters fail and Job's reason still persists, the Voice out of the Whirlwind quenches his reason in the wonders of nature:

> Doth the hawk fly by the wisdom,
> and stretch her wings toward the south?
> Doth the eagle mount up at thy command?
> and make her nest on high?
> She dwelleth and abideth on the rock,
> upon the crag of the rock and the strong place.
> From whence she seeketh the prey,
> and her eyes behold afar off.
> Her young ones also suck up blood;
> and where the slain are, there is she.

This is the very world and spirit of O'Flaherty's nature. His short stories are made from the same materials that make the Book of Job. As William James has shown, the spiritual experiences of the sick soul exist as an archetypal pattern. When the desolate spirit of man can find no rational comfort, nor any comfort, comes the Voice out of the Whirlwind that silences rationality with the wonder and the awe of nature. This is what O'Flaherty sees in his vision and what his art is to express: "I have heard of thee by the hearing of the ear: but now mine eye seeth thee."

∝ VI ∝

Conclusion

MORE THAN ANYTHING else, John Millington Synge saw in the Aran Islands the heightened contrast between life and death, represented most vividly in the same chant for the dead that often rises in O'Flaherty's stories:

> This grief of the keen is of no personal complaint for the death of one woman over eighty years, but seems to contain the whole passionate rage that lurks somewhere in every native of the island. In this cry of pain the inner consciousness of the people seems to lay itself bare for an instant, and to reveal the mood of beings who feel their isolation in the face of a universe that wars on them with winds and seas. They are usually silent, but in the presence of death all outward show of indifference or patience is forgotten, and they shriek with pitiable despair before the horror of the fate to which they all are doomed.[1]

This is the mark with which O'Flaherty was stamped and on which his distinctive manner of seeing depends. Reality was life and death in awesome contrast. No philosophy could explain nor could culture weave an intricate tapestry to obscure these elemental facts. To focus on life called up inevitably a vision of death. To focus on death called up a vision of life. The intensity of the one increased the intensity of the other. O'Flaherty's art is an expression of the tension between these two poles. The novels focus on life; as the reality of life comes to heightened awareness, death, equally real, rises in proportionate measure to consume it. The short stories emerge from the vision of death in the novels, and focusing on that death calls up a vision of life.

From the beginning, O'Flaherty's true subject was the meaning of life—the fact of existence—in the face of the awful reality of death. This is the central drama in all the black soul novels and the central issue in O'Flaherty's own life. His autobiographies ultimately dwell on

182

this issue. It becomes the central feature of his account of his visit to Russia. In relation to the awesome reality of life and death the petty social intrigues of man in society, accepting society's norms, are so inconsequential as not to warrant the artist's concern except perhaps as a background where the intensity of the central drama emphasizes the pettiness. In the black soul novels O'Flaherty reenacts in his characters his own spiritual crisis, projecting himself into them, giving them life and consciousness from his own consciousness. They are defined as they face their heightened awareness of their own existence. The violence of their actions is commensurate with the intensity of their spiritual turmoil. As they are weak, like McDara, Gilhooley, and Ferriter, they end in despair, suicide, and insanity. If they are gifted, like Fergus O'Connor, they rise to a new spiritual vision. Only if they are strong can they smash themselves against life in a grand tragic gesture, like Ramon Mor and Skerrett. Regardless of their end, their passionate intensity is everything; for above them is O'Flaherty the artist watching, describing, like Stapleton the poet or the artist in "The Child of God," absorbed in the beauty of passion, feeding on the horrors that would make weaker men cry out in terror or be overcome with sympathy. This is the role of the poet, the artist, who, as O'Flaherty says in *Land*, must be ruthless in the pursuit of his ideal, which is beauty.

Only *Famine* among the novels does not have for its real subject man's plight in a universe of frightening immensity which appears totally indifferent to his dreams or fears or aspirations. Regardless of the horror of famine and plague, these afflictions are within the scope of man's measure. They may inspire fear, but the fear is definite and the relief from fear is definite. The problem in *Famine* can be solved by food, medicine, and better government. Men can band together against this kind of fear. They have common aims against a common enemy. But there is no relief from the dread that sends a strong man like Gypo Nolan into spasms of terror. Compared with the terror of existence, the terror of famine is almost comforting in its definiteness. *Famine* is an anomaly among O'Flaherty's novels because it is not about individual men, isolated within their own consciousnesses, but social men measurable by social norms. Because *Famine* is about man in opposition to nature, some critics see in its peasants and natural scenery part of the same spirit as in O'Flaherty's short stories, but these critics mistake the subject matter for the real subject. The difference between *Famine* and the short stories is profound. *Famine* is a warm novel, full of human sympathy. It is a humanitarian novel containing common human values. But the short stories spring from no such sympathy. They achieve their effects through the coldness, not the warmth, of their vision. They express the beauty of the awesomeness of nature. The vision of the short stories brought to *Famine* would dwell on the beauty of the horror, as Peter O'Toole, the Child of God, drew his inspiration from the grotesque wake. Human sympathy is entirely alien to the true nature of O'Flaherty's creative genius. As Stapleton expressed it, the poet's love showers its bounty on all, without exception, the oppressor and the oppressed. All is holy. The poet is allowed no special human partiality.

Set in a world which allows human values and human sympathies, *Famine* is not the best but the most conventional of O'Flaherty's novels. For the critic who feels as Margery Latimer did when she read O'Flaherty's short stories, "a chilled, locked place in her bones" which only feeling could loosen and his stories did not,[2] *Famine* offers affirmation, sympathy, and hope. As Benedict Kiely said, Dark Daniel is not there, but because Dark Daniel is not there, O'Flaherty's genius is not there. The world of *Famine* is a comfortable old-fashioned world, but it is not O'Flaherty's world. To prefer *Famine* over the earlier novels is to prefer the comfort of affirmation over the chill of absolute negation, although the latter is O'Flaherty's truest expression; and to link *Famine* with the short stories because both are about peasants and nature is to miss the whole informing spirit of O'Flaherty's genius.

In O'Flaherty's last novels, *Land* and *Insurrection*, the subject is the same as in his earlier novels, but the tension is lacking. In *I Went to Russia* O'Flaherty said that "they who effect a harmony between their reason and their actions lose the power to create beauty" (p. 83). This is exactly what has occurred in these last works. Michael O'Dwyer sees the beauty of danger, but it is a theoretical beauty derived from a theoretical danger. O'Flaherty has arrived at a rational position, an understanding, and with the understanding the negative quality of intellect disappears. Previously he could say "All things appear equally futile when examined by reason," but in the last novels reason conquers the futility. When confronted with his moment of truth, Fergus O'Connor, truly a naked soul, was at the nadir of despair. All thought merely increased his awareness of futility and intensified his despair. His new awareness which arose from this despair was not an intellectual awareness or a set of beliefs or ideals which he possessed. His moment of truth occurred in absolute negativity, when all beliefs and all hopes became equally futile and he was left with nothing. Stapleton, Madden, and Kinsella also are brought to a moment of truth, but it is their belief which sustains them. Their ideals, which they possess with their minds, are absolutely positive, and their choice is positive. Each is sustained, even unto death, by his vision of truth, which is an intellectual vision. For Fergus O'Connor, reason leads to despair. For Stapleton, reason leads to truth, for it is reason which grasps the highest truth, which has the ultimate vision of the good, the beautiful, and the true. In the last novels O'Flaherty effects the greatest harmony between the actions and reason of his characters, and in a thoroughly Platonic atmosphere they undergo their deaths like Socrates, without doubts but firm in their resolve.

In his last novels O'Flaherty has arrived at a thoroughly Platonic philosophy. The poet is the "insurgent *par excellence*," as Stapleton says, because he, like Plato's guardians, has seen the ultimate good, while conventional government and morality still live in the shadow world of deception and illusion. The types of poet, soldier, and saint are more real than the persons who fill the types. The theory of beauty and tragedy is more important than the expression of beauty and tragedy. In the last novels the question of values appears settled. The characters make no choices because when they chose their roles (which are as much destiny as choice) they made the ultimate value choice. The earlier novels, in which reason was a negative, destructive force, would have stressed the ironies of these choices, all being equally futile when viewed with reason. In the last novels the reasonable world is accepted as the true world.

But the philosophy which represents the triumph of reason is a construction that answers the need of Fergus O'Connor and Raoul St. George, both of whom cried out desperately for authority to sustain them in a universe of apparent chaos. The earliest and the latest novels are based upon the ultimate question: What is man in the face of death and annihilation? The earlier novels approach the question subjectively, existentially, and record the struggles of men impelled toward truth foredoomed to failure because there is no objective truth. The beauty is in the intensity of the struggle, a tragic beauty, as men extend themselves to their limits in their desperation. The last novels approach the question objectively, theoretically; and reason, asserting its preeminence over life, builds in its own image a universe in which individual man and his struggles illustrate the truth of the theory.

In the earlier novels the men are individuals, stripped of all their theoretical qualities to the essence of what it means to be a man in the horror and wonder of existence. In the last novels the men are types, divested of choice, of passion, of doubt, of terror, of all the qualities of individual life. The earlier novels are suffused with the tension of uncertainty and life. The last novels are enveloped in the philosophic calm of certainty and death. In the last novels O'Flaherty ceased being the artist whose role is to sing the beauty of life's tragedy to become the philosopher for whom life is less important than the constructions of reason. The latter role is more comfortable, but it does not yield art.

The intensely subjective and personal quality that forms the basis of his artistic vision was already fixed before O'Flaherty returned to Dublin to work among those who were the writers in Ireland's literary revival. He was a man before he was an Irishman, just as he was a man before he was a Communist. And being a man—isolated, individual, intensely conscious of his own existence as a person in a universe that his reason showed him as impersonal and indifferent—he could not choose to be an Irishman or a Communist, for he could not choose to be what he was so forcefully aware he was not. To *be* meant to be isolated and individual, faced always with absurdity and annihilation. He might cry out for belief, for authority, for a cause in which to lose himself. He might try to escape from himself by throwing himself into Irish affairs, but always his negative intellect was there, forcing him back upon himself. He could not choose to dream the Irish dream, because the dream was a quality of being, not a conscious choice.

O'Flaherty's relationship to the Irish literary revival is an index to the force that impelled that revival, for his conscious effort to be a part of the revival indicated that the revival had lost its force to absorb consciousness. The literary revival came from the Irish dream, a shared consciousness. The dream was quality of consciousness, not something apart to be accepted or rejected. Within the dream existence was not absurd and man was not isolated and individual. The dream was the meaning of existence, a faith that existence had meaning so pervasive that there could be no questioning. It existed when it could absorb men's consciousness. It ceased to exist when it could not. O'Flaherty could not choose the dream. It either possessed consciousness or it did not. When it possessed consciouness it was reality, not an alternative, not a cultivated faith, not something to be affirmed or denied. It was a reality as O'Flaherty's individual being was a reality with its awareness of absurdity and annihilation. Both realities were undeniable. That O'Flaherty had the one sense of reality and not the other, that his sense of reality was even possible, is an indication of the disintegration of the binding force of the Irish literary revival.

O'Flaherty's style is a direct consequence of the furious intensity of his manner of seeing which made anything but immediate and direct expression seem superficial and irrelevant, a self-indulgent toying with frivolities. He was impatient with Garnett's efforts to have him cultivate a deliberate style, a "mania" as he called it, which had crippled most of the young English writers of talent. He set himself against style: "Damn it man, I have no style. I don't want any style. I refuse to have a style. I have no time for style. I think style is artificial and vulgar," he tells Garnett (April 2, 1924). He thought a writer a fool to sidetrack his creative energy in an attempt to develop a style. He meant, of course, style in the sense of a deliberate effort to write beautifully, as if the words themselves and their patterns were the artist's end. For O'Flaherty did not conceive of words alone as being certain good. He did not think of writing as incantation or symbolism whereby the artist evoked powers and emotions outside of himself. Nor did he think of art as that which is interposed between man and the harshness of reality. What he had to express was the momentous quality of his manner of seeing. For him the poet was not a craftsman but a seer. That which characterized the poet for Stapleton in *Insurrection* was not his way with words (O'Flaherty's poets are not necessarily creators) but his awareness of the true nature of things. When O'Flaherty thought of his own creative activity he could describe it only as a "creative mania" or a "fever in the bowels" which was inexplicable. Art for him was not a subtle refinement of civilization, the delicate weaving of shreds of beauty into harmonious designs. As he said in his study of Conrad, the artist is the "cold-eyed adventurer" who "peers over the brink of chaos in search of truth."

Thus in O'Flaherty's work there is little deliberate artistry where the craftsmanship itself is a part of the artistic experience. Only in *The Black Soul* does O'Flaherty deliberately try to be "poetic" and this was at the insistence of Edward Garnett, who urged him to raise the language to a poetic level. For the most part his writing is characterized by impatience and simplicity. What he has to express is not a subtle perception of the nuances of human experience where intricate shadings or techniques are needed to explore character and society. A stream of consciousness technique would emphasize the converse of what he attempted to portray, for he wished to dwell not on the irrelevancies which make up so much of the flow of experience but on the one relevancy which so overshadowed everything else in its import that it could be the only true matter for artistic expression. Beside his overwhelming awareness of existence and mortality, anything else seemed to be error or escapism.

William York Tindall described O'Flaherty's novels up to *The*

Martyr as "crude," and measured by the usual standards of craftsmanship there can be no other judgment. Frank O'Connor thought that O'Flaherty's novels could be used as evidence to prove that an Irish novel was impossible. Each considers O'Flaherty's novels by the conventional criteria—plot, character, dialogue, description—or by refinements of technique to explore human consciousness. When thought of as representing human beings in society, as describing the delicate interplay between characters, as revealing any humanistic values or insights, O'Flaherty's novels do appear crude and inadequate. The characters generally are not skilfully drawn but sketched in rapidly and roughly and set into motion as soon as they are given sufficient body to support motion. The appearance of Fergus O'Connor or Francis Ferriter is of little consequence compared to O'Flaherty's main concern with these characters. The characters do not develop either within themselves or in their relationship to others. When they talk, it is to convey information about themselves or others necessary to advance the plot or to tell of their own motives. There is no wordplay, no exchange of ideas. The characters do not modify one another. For the most part their actions are described directly by the omniscient author. By every conventional norm (and the appearance of O'Flaherty's novels is entirely conventional) O'Flaherty displays no skill as a novelist.

Yet his best novels have unquestionable power, not because of the refinement of any part but from the movement of the whole. Although the technical point of view is external and omniscient, the best novels move with an inevitability that has no hint of author manipulation. They move like a storm, a cloudburst, over which the author has no control. Typically they begin like *The Assassin* ("At three o'clock in the afternoon, Michael McDara alighted from the tram-car at the corner of Findlater's Church") or *The Puritan* ("Shortly after midnight on Sunday, June 21st, Francis Ferriter left the offices of the Morning Star in O'Connell Street, Dublin, and returned to his lodgings in Lower Gardiner Street"). From some simple beginning they move swiftly and relentlessly to a furious climax, with all the violence of a storm until the storm is spent. That is the end. There is no sunlight or rainbow. The clouds gather swiftly. An occasional lightning flash shows up this or that portion of the scene, a face perhaps, a street or a room. The author describes what he sees.

O'Flaherty's novels are not about man in society but the storm in the human soul as it comes to an intensified awareness of its own existence in a universe where existence has no meaning. He is not a Renaissance artist celebrating the joy of life but more akin to the medieval, following the advice of Fra Lippo Lippi's superiors who counseled him to "Give us no more of body than shows soul." O'Flaherty's true subject is the individual soul, becoming individual as it is separated from its role in society, focused in upon itself. The external world in the novels is not a systematic realistic drawing of society. It is what O'Flaherty sees clearly and harshly in the lightning flashes that occasionally illuminate the soul's storm. The real focus is on the soul's struggle, and to record that struggle O'Flaherty grabs out furiously at the most immediate material at hand to hurl it upon the page.

He does not seek stylistic refinement that focuses upon itself but the immediacy of the horror and the wonder of the storm. The external violence that all critics note mirrors soul states. The enormity of the soul's upheaval can be expressed only in the most violent external action. At the end of *Shame the Devil* O'Flaherty says, "I reach the spirit through the flesh" (pp. 284–85). This is the essential technique of the novels. He is like Dante in that the physical represents the spiritual. But O'Flaherty's is no systematic allegorical construction. It is the immediacy and not the meaning of the storm that absorbs him. To catch that immediacy his work is rapid, impatient, raw, turbulent. The lines are dark, bold, and slashing, unfinished, like nature herself. If his novels take the form of melodrama, it is because the storm he represents is melodramatic, as William Troy defined the term, "the elaboration of human motives on a grand scale, against immense backgrounds, and to the accompaniment of enormous music." O'Flaherty's form, however, is not a courageous choice, as Troy suggested, but the inevitable result of his real subject.

To appraise O'Flaherty's novels by conventional novel standards is to assume that the novelist's subject is man in or opposed to society and to look at the man and the society as being his subject. But except for *Famine* the novels are essentially asocial. Man does not define himself in or against society's norms but against the fact of his own existence. To judge the novels by the skill with which he delineates society—characters in relation to their social roles or one another—is to miss O'Flaherty's real subject which is not concerned with any of these.

If O'Flaherty's novels are the storm, the short stories are the calm that follows the storm or, better, the eye of a hurricane, for the short stories are not happy moments that follow the stress, as if man can ultimately win peace if he can only endure. Like the novels, the subject of the short stories is the awe and wonder of existence. The stories are moments of vision that arise out of the ashes of the struggle. They represent not the frenzy of man struggling against his tragedy but the chill vision that arises when the inevitability of annihilation is accepted. The style of the short stories depends upon the nature of that acceptance, because a man as long as he is a man cannot accept that inevitability. In the short stories the man who can accept has been annihilated, merged into the awe and wonder of the experience. The short stories are suprahuman. Man appears not as man distinct from nature but as manifestation of nature, as a wave or a seabird is a manifestation of nature. The simplicity of the short stories owes to the elimination of human complexity, the tangles of reason constructed to explain what reason is futile to explain. The novels are dashed upon the page, furiously, to catch the violence of the soul's storm. The short stories appear to arise out of nature itself, beyond human control.

Regardless of his protests to Garnett, O'Flaherty does have style; but because it depends so entirely upon experience forcing itself upon the artist rather than the artist arranging experience, he is not a stylist. As an artist he is the instrument and not a creator of life: "I am no philosopher, but vessel into which life pours sweet wine or vinegar, from a hand that is indifferently careless. Wine or vinegar, I must accept it and drink it to the dregs." [3] He does not use his genius to create. He *is used* by his genius to express. And what he expresses is the immediacy of the experience of what it means to be a man. Sometimes it is storm, sometimes calm. The style is frantic or simple in measure. O'Flaherty has not developed a style to order experience. His style is the consequence of the intensity of his manner of seeing.

The change that occurred in O'Flaherty's novels with *Famine* was accompanied by an abrupt decline in the quantity as well as the quality of his literary productivity. From 1937 to the present just three novels have been published in addition to the short-story collection of 1948, *Two Lovely Beasts*. Surveying Irish literature in 1945, Kelleher saw that a decline in quantity was general and that the few Irish works being published scarcely constituted a literary movement. He attributed this to the rapid use of Ireland's literary resources during the height of the revival which had mined out most of the material. He thought the writers of 1945 were looking at a "diminished reality," and by "faithfully drawing a paltry truth" they got, too often and "with much effort, a paltry result." He classed O'Flaherty with O'Connor and O'Faolain who were trying to discover their country's history with their historical novels, but he believed that the heroes of Irish history were too small and too mortal to inspire worthwhile expression. He saw *Famine* as a part of this historical trend.[4]

However, O'Flaherty during the peak of his creativity had not been mining Irish resources but spiritual resources. When he turned to Irish history, it was not because he could not find materials around him. The lack was within him. During the course of all the novels up to *Famine* he had but one theme—man's desperation to find meaning in an inscrutable universe. In the black soul novels he repeated an essential pattern of struggle until it was apparent that mode was exhausted. And with *Skerrett* he achieved the fullest development of the alternate mode, creating the tragic hero not possible within the black soul consciousness. E. M. Forster, of course, is the classic example of the writer who wrote what he had to say and stopped. In a way O'Flaherty was like this, but because he was not the conscious craftsman that Forster was, depending, rather on a distinctive tension for the impetus of his art, his decline in productivity was due more to the decline in tension than to a conscious awareness that his artistic resources had been used up.

Nothing seems more apparent than that spiritual torment is the essential ingredient of O'Flaherty's art. The last novels, lacking the torment, do not illustrate his real power. The struggle is gone. In the midst of battle a philosophic calm prevails. In those novels there is the reconciliation of thought and action that O'Flaherty earlier said destroyed the power to create beauty. If all the earlier novels were expressions of his own spiritual awareness and torment, they were expressions derived from his own tension between his will to believe and his intellect which destroyed all belief. The tension could not be understood and still be tension, because the understanding itself was one pole of the tension. The tension was dependent upon O'Flaherty's divided self, each self asserting its own claim. The earlier novels depended upon his division, not unity of being. He could not understand himself and still be the artist he was, because his unity of being was achieved within and not outside his art, and the unity was the expression of the tension. There was no understanding *I* who could say I am this or that. The earlier novels were Oedipus-like efforts to find identity, and like Oedipus the protagonists found their identity in the horror of the awareness of their own existence. It was as if O'Flaherty were condemned, like Sisyphus, to a continual repetition of a struggle foredoomed to failure, with the clearest awareness of identity possible only at the moment of clearest awareness of the ultimate annihilation of identity.

In 1934 O'Flaherty wrote *Shame the Devil* to tell the truth about himself. But it was also a self-analysis of searching intensity in which he looked directly at those segments of his being previously dramatized in his novels. *Shame the Devil* was a direct and deliberate quest for unity of being in which O'Flaherty explored his past and his present, saw himself as the artist and the man. He achieved a view of himself in which the subjective and objective coalesced; and whether or not this self-analysis brought his subconscious into harmony with his conscious mind, he achieved a whole view and understanding of himself, and the tension between the artist and the man yielded to this understanding. He saw the malign snake's eye, his mocking genius, as a part of himself and knew it was impossible to flee from it: 'I must face it boldly and try to put it into harness" (p. 250). He felt that he had undergone a torment from which he emerged purified: "This is the end of my journey. I have been to hell and now I may rise again" (p. 251). After *Shame the Devil*, and whether because of this or because of the exhaustion of his theme, he wrote no more novels about souls in spiritual torment. If his previous novels had not, *Shame the Devil* exhausted the topic.

Yet his last two novels, though historical in setting, were not historical novels in Kelleher's sense of trying to discover his country's history. Rather, they used the occasion of historical events to draw from men a full expression of their being. In one sense O'Flaherty returned to his familiar topic—what it means to be a man—in that men are put into situations which call for a full expenditure of their spiritual resources. But the test is not the ultimate crisis of the earlier novels. It is based on understanding reason and not passion. Men do not struggle; they endure.

O'Flaherty's art is based on power due not to his careful use of words but to the passion of the artist who in a creative fury hurls the material closest at hand upon the page to catch the immediacy of his impressions. O'Flaherty was aware of this quality of his work. He told Garnett that he was not aware of exerting any judgment whatsoever at the moment of writing: "And of course that has the drawback of all instinctive writing, that it appears to be unfinished, just like a natural landscape" (July 31, 1925). He chose to cultivate the power rather than the skill, preferring the unfinished as a truer representation of his creative expression. But because the power was generated within himself, he consumed himself in his art. In the last novels he could no longer overwhelm because the source of power was gone, and he lacked the skill (or he felt such use of skill was false) to achieve with finesse the effects he had previously achieved with personal fury.

O'Flaherty's essential artistic vision derived from the intensity of his awareness of his own existence in a universe that gives no meaning for existence. His subject is man as he becomes aware of himself in a universe which his reason shows him is absurd. In this sense O'Flaherty can be considered an existentialist. His awareness of the absurdity of existence, however, was not a philosophical position but a condition of his being. It was a condition from which he constantly struggled to escape, not a way of seeing he wished to promulgate. O'Flaherty is an artist, not a thinker. Man's existential plight was the subject of art, not of truth. When O'Flaherty sought truth and became a positive thinker as the last novels indicate, he ceased being an artist.

O'Flaherty's subject is existence because he is a modern writer who sees man not as a manifestation of culture, tradition, or civilization, but as a naked soul alien to the culture, tradition, and civilization that offer only deceptions to obscure from men the true and awful nature of their being. His view of the artist is that which Lionel Trilling considers the characteristically modern belief: "the man who goes down into that hell which is the historical beginning of the human soul, a beginning not outgrown but established in humanity as we know it now, preferring the reality of this hell to the bland lies of the civilization that has overlaid it." [5]

When O'Flaherty moved out from the isolated world of the Aran Islands into the world of Western culture, the image of reality that he bore from those elemental storm-lashed rocks was not shattered, but confirmed. The Aran Islands were reality in microcosm, for the Aran Islands were to earth as earth was to universe; and individual man on the islands, confronted with awesome nature, isolated, constantly aware of life because of his proximity to death, screaming out in horror at his inevitable fate, was true man, not overlaid by a complex culture that deceived. And because O'Flaherty was a modern writer he could not be an Irish writer in the sense of belonging to Ireland, speaking for Ireland, expressing Ireland and Irish dreams. What made Ireland significant for the Irish literary revival was a distinctive culture and tradition to which the Irish writers felt they belonged. It did not deceive them but sustained them.

O'Flaherty could only look at Ireland and envy, but he could not belong; for he had seen, felt to the marrow of his being, the awful truth of his own existence. He could cry out like Kurtz, "The horror! The horror!" but he could not deny that truth when, as an artist, he forced himself again and again to peer over the brink of chaos.

Notes

Introduction

1. Sean O'Faolain, "Don Quixote O'Flaherty," *London Mercury*, XXXVII (1937), 170–75.
2. *Shame the Devil* (London: Grayson and Grayson, 1934), p. 26. Subsequent references to this edition will appear in the text.

I: In Dublin: Patterns of Change

1. *Inishfallen, Fare Thee Well* (New York: Macmillan, 1960), p. 282.
2. All the letters from Liam O'Flaherty to Edward Garnett referred to in this study are in the manuscript collection of The Academic Center Library of The University of Texas at Austin. Quotations from these letters are with the permission of the Committee of The Academic Center Library. O'Flaherty's frequent irregularities in spelling and punctuation are preserved. Not all the letters are dated exactly; sometimes O'Flaherty gives only the month and year.
3. Alexander N. Jeffares, *W. B. Yeats: Man and Poet* (London: Routledge, 1949), p. 223.
4. Liam O'Flaherty, *A Tourist's Guide to Ireland* (London: Mandrake Press, 1930), p. 54.
5. W. B. Yeats, "The Need for Audacity of Thought," *Dial*, LXXX (1926), 115–19.
6. *Inishfallen*, p. 169.
7. Quoted in *W. B. Yeats: Man and Poet*, p. 241.
8. *Inishfallen*, p. 371.
9. John V. Kelleher, "Irish Literature Today," *Atlantic Monthly*, CLXXV (1945), 70–76.
10. *The Irish Writers, 1880–1940: Literature Under Parnell's Star* (London: Rockliff, 1958).

11. "Literary Ideals in Ireland: A Comparison," *The Irish Statesman,* V (1925), 399–400.
12. *The Living Torch* (New York, Macmillan, 1938), p. 183.
13. Gibbon, "Literary Ideals," pp. 399–400.
14. *Anglo-Irish Literature* (Dublin: Talbot Press, 1926), p. 296.
15. *The Irish: A Character Study* (New York: Devin-Adair, 1949), p. 165.
16. *The Modern Irish Writers* (Lawrence: University of Kansas Press, 1954), p. 39.
17. *The Road Round Ireland* (New York: Macmillan, 1926), p. 284.
18. *Inishfallen*, p. 393.
19. Sean O'Faolain, quoted in David Krause, *Sean O'Casey: The Man and His Work* (New York: Macmillan, 1960), p. 45.
20. *Shame the Devil*, p. 184.

II: The Man and the Artist

1. Liam O'Flaherty, *Two Years* (London: Jonathan Cape, 1930). Subsequent references to this edition will appear in the text.
2. O'Flaherty's letters to Garnett tell about Professor Curtis and about the difficulties with the Church. The marriage is inferred from the March 3, 1932, letter, which mentions divorce.
3. (London: Jonathan Cape, 1931), p. 10. Subsequent references to this edition will appear in the text.
4. *No! In Thunder* (Boston: Beacon Press, 1960), pp. 6, 17.
5. Liam O'Flaherty, *The Black Soul* (London: Jonathan Cape, 1924), p. 182. Subsequent references to this edition will appear in the text.
6. (London: Joiner and Steele, 1931). Subsequent references to this edition will appear in the text.
7. *Joseph Conrad: An Appreciation* (London: Lahr, 1930), pp. 9–10.
8. Fiedler, *No! In Thunder*, p. 18.
9. H. E. Bates, *Edward Garnett* (London: Max Parrish, 1950), p. 37.
10. (London: Mandrake Press, 1930). Subsequent references to this edition will appear in the text.
11. *The Lonely Voice* (New York: World Publishing, 1962), p. 38.

III: Into the Destructive Element

1. *The Informer, Mr. Gilhooley, The Assassin,* and *The Puritan* are classed with *The Black Soul* as forming a black soul group, all illustrating in some way the black soul pattern.
2. (New York: New American Library, 1961). Subsequent references to this edition will appear in the text.
3. Afterword to *The Informer*, p. 184.
4. (London: Jonathan Cape, 1926). Subsequent references to this edition will appear in the text.

5. (New York: Harcourt, Brace, 1928). Subsequent references to this edition will appear in the text.
6. (New York: Harcourt, Brace, 1932). Subsequent references to this edition will appear in the text.
7. (New York: Boni and Liveright, 1924). Subsequent references to this edi- will appear in the text.
8. *Forces in Modern British Literature* (New York: Knopf, 1947), p. 329.

IV: *Toward Objectivity*

1. (New York: Harcourt, Brace, 1929). Subsequent references to this edition will appear in the text.
2. L. Paul-Dubois, "Un Romancier Réaliste en Erin," *Revue des Deux Mondes*, XXI (1934), 884–904.
3. *Forces*, p. 99.
4. (London: Mandrake Press, 1929). Subsequent references to this edition will appear in the text.
5. (New York: Ray Long and Richard R. Smith, 1932). Subsequent references to this edition will appear in the text.
6. *The Stories of Liam O'Flaherty* (New York: Devin-Adair, 1956), p. vi.
7. (London: Victor Gollancz, 1933). Subsequent references to this edition will appear in the text.
8. *The Irish Writers*, p. 157.
9. (New York: Random House, 1937). Subsequent references to this edition will appear in the text.
10. *Stories of Liam O'Flaherty*, p. vi.
11. *Modern Irish Fiction* (Dublin: Golden Eagle Books, 1950), pp. 36, 37, 90.
12. "Irish Literature Today," p. 75.
13. (London: Victor Gollancz, 1935). Subsequent references to this edition will appear in the text.
14. (New York: Random House, 1946). Subsequent references to this edition will appear in the text.
15. *Modern Irish Fiction*, p. 37.
16. (Boston: Little, Brown, 1951). Subsequent references to this edition will appear in the text.

V: *The Short Stories: A New Vision*

1. Paul-Dubois, "Un Romancier," p. 890.
2. *Edward Garnett*, p. 47.
3. (London: Longmans, Green, 1929). Subsequent references to this edition will appear in the text.
4. O'Flaherty's short stories were published in six major collections: *Spring Sowing* (London: Jonathan Cape, 1924), *The Tent* (London: Jonathan Cape, 1926), *The Mountain Tavern* (London: Jonathan Cape, 1929), *The*

Short Stories of Liam O'Flaherty (London: Jonathan Cape, 1937), *Two Lovely Beasts* (New York: Devin-Adair, 1950), and *The Stories of Liam O'Flaherty* (New York: Devin-Adair, 1956). The last is a collection of thirty-six stories selected from all his previous works plus six previously uncollected stories. All the stories discussed in this chapter are contained in the last collection.

5. *The Modern Short Story* (London: Thomas Nelson, 1945), p. 157.
6. *The Lonely Voice*, p. 38.
7. *Ibid.*
8. *On Judging Books* (New York: John Day, 1947), p. 290.
9. *Modern Irish Fiction*, pp. 17–18.
10. Sean O'Faolain, *The Vanishing Hero* (Boston: Little, Brown, 1956), p. 101.

VI: Conclusion

1. J. M. Synge, *The Aran Islands* (Dublin: Maunsel, 1907), p. 40.
2. Review of *The Mountain Tavern*, New York *Herald Tribune*, June 2, 1929, p. 5.
3. *Shame the Devil*, p. 235.
4. Kelleher, "Irish Literature Today," p. 72.
5. *The Partisan Review Anthology*, ed. William Phillips (New York: Holt, Rinehart and Winston, 1962), p. 274.

Bibliography

Works by Liam O'Flaherty

The Assassin. New York: Harcourt, Brace & Co., 1928.
The Black Soul. London: Jonathan Cape, Ltd., 1924.
A Cure for Unemployment. London: E. Lahr, 1931.
Darkness: A Play. London: E. Archer, 1926.
The Ecstasy of Angus. London: Joiner and Steele, 1931.
Famine. New York: Random House, 1937.
Hollywood Cemetery. London: Victor Gollancz Ltd., 1935.
The House of Gold. New York: Harcourt, Brace & Co., 1929.
I Went to Russia. London: Jonathan Cape, Ltd., 1931.
The Informer. New York: The New American Library, 1961.
Insurrection. Boston: Little, Brown and Co., 1951.
Joseph Conrad: An Appreciation. London: E. Lahr, 1930.
Land. New York: Random House, 1946.
The Life of Tim Healy. New York: Harcourt, Brace & Co., 1927.
The Martyr. London: Victor Gollancz Ltd., 1933.
The Mountain Tavern. London: Jonathan Cape, Ltd., 1929.
Mr. Gilhooley. London: Jonathan Cape, Ltd., 1926.
The Puritan. New York: Harcourt, Brace & Co., 1932.
The Return of the Brute. London: The Mandrake Press, 1929.
Shame the Devil. London: Grayson and Grayson, 1934.
The Short Stories of Liam O'Flaherty. London: Jonathan Cape, Ltd., 1937.
Skerrett. New York: Ray Long and Richard R. Smith, Inc., 1932.
Spring Sowing. London: Jonathan Cape, Ltd., 1924.
The Stories of Liam O'Flaherty. New York: Devin-Adair, 1956.
The Tent. London: Jonathan Cape, Ltd., 1926.
The Terrorist. London: E. Archer, 1926.

Thy Neighbour's Wife. New York: Boni and Liveright, 1924.
A Tourist's Guide to Ireland. London: The Mandrake Press, 1930.
Two Lovely Beasts and Other Stories. New York: Devin-Adair, 1950.
Two Years. London: Jonathan Cape, Ltd., 1930.
The Wild Swan and Other Stories. London: Joiner and Steele, 1932.
"Art Criticism," *The Irish Statesman*, IX (1927), 83.
"Fascism or Communism," *The Irish Statesman*, VI (1926), 231.
Foreword to *The Stars, The World, and The Women*, by Rhys Davies. London, 1930, pp. 7–9.
"Introduction," *Six Cartoons by Alfred Lowe* [sketches of Barrie, Bennett, Chesterton, Kipling, Shaw, and Wells]. London, 1930, pp. 7–8.
"The Irish Censorship," *The American Spectator*, November 1932, p. 2.
"Irish Housekeeping," *New Statesman and Nation*, XI (February 8, 1936), 186.
"Kingdom of Kerry," *Fortnightly Review* CXXXVIII (August, 1932), 212–18.
"Literary Criticism in Ireland," *The Irish Statesman*, VI (1926), 711.
"*Mr. Tasker's Gods*," *The Irish Statesman*, III (1925), 828.
"National Energy," *The Irish Statesman*, III (1924), 171.
"The Plough and the Stars," *The Irish Statesman*, V (1926), 739.
"Red Ship," *New Republic*, LXVIII (September 23, 1931), 147–50.
"A View of Irish Culture," *The Irish Statesman*, IV (1925), 460–461.
"Writing in Gaelic," *The Irish Statesman*, IX (1927), 348.
Letters to Edward Garnett, May 5, 1923–March 3, 1932. In the manuscript collection of The Academic Center Library, The University of Texas, Austin.

Secondary Sources

A.E. "Anglo-Irish Literature." *The Irish Statesman*, VII (1927), 477–78.
——. "*The Black Soul*," *The Irish Statesman*, II (1924), 244.
——. "A Drama of Disillusionment," *The Irish Statesman*, II (1924), 399.
——. *The Living Torch*. New York: The Macmillan Co., 1938.
——. *The National Being*. Dublin: Maunsel and Co., Ltd., 1918.
——. "National Self-Consciousness," *The Irish Statesman*, I (1924), 742.
——. "Notes and Comments," *The Irish Statesman*, VI (1926), 89.
Bates, H. E. *Edward Garnett*. London: Max Parrish, 1950.
——. *The Modern Short Story*. London: Thomas Nelson and Sons, Ltd., 1945.
Boyd, Ernest. "Joyce and the New Irish Writers," *Current History*, XXXIX (1934), 699–704.
Canedo, Anthony. "Liam O'Flaherty: Introduction and Analysis." University of Washington, unpublished Ph.D. dissertation, 1966.

Clarke, Austin, and F. R. Higgins, "Art and Energy," *The Irish Statesman,* III (1924), 237–38.

——. "Art and Energy," *The Irish Statesman,* III (1924), 270.

Colum, Padraic. "*The Black Soul,*" *The Saturday Review of Literature,* May 30, 1925, 787.

——. "The Promise of Irish Letters," *Nation,* CXVII (1923), 396–97.

——. *The Road Round Ireland.* New York: The Macmillan Co., 1926.

——. "Ulysses in Its Epoch." *The Saturday Review of Literature,* January 27, 1934, 433, 438.

Doyle, P. A. "A Liam O'Flaherty Checklist," *Twentieth Century Literature,* 13:49–51.

Eglinton, John. *Anglo-Irish Essays.* Dublin: The Talbot Press, Ltd., 1917.

Emery, L. K. "A Primitive," *To-Morrow,* August, 1924, 7.

Fiedler, Leslie A. *No! In Thunder.* Boston: The Beacon Press, 1960.

Fox, R. M. "Realism in Irish Drama," *The Irish Statesman,* X (1928), 310–12.

Frierson, William C. *The English Novel in Transition.* Norman: University of Oklahoma Press, 1942.

Gibbon, Monk. "Literary Ideals in Ireland: A Comparison," *The Irish Statesman,* V (1925), 399–400.

Greene, David H. "New Heights," *Commonweal,* LXIV (June 29, 1956), 328.

Griffin, Gerald. "Liam O'Flaherty," in *The Wild Geese: Pen Portraits of Famous Irish Exiles.* London, 1938, pp. 191–95.

Hackett, Francis. "*Land,*" *The New York Times Magazine,* May 12, 1946, 4, 33.

——. "A Note on Criticism," *The Irish Statesman,* VIII (1927), 568–69.

——. *On Judging Books.* New York: The John Day Co., 1947.

Heilbrun, Carolyn G. *The Garnett Family.* New York: The Macmillan Co., 1961.

Henderson, Philip. *The Novel Today.* London: John Lane, 1936.

Howarth, Herbert. *The Irish Writers, 1880–1940: Literature Under Parnell's Star.* London: Rockliff, 1958.

Hynes, Frank J. "The 'Troubles' in Ireland," *The Saturday Review of Literature,* May 25, 1946, 12.

James, William. *The Varieties of Religious Experience.* London: Longmans, Green and Co., 1929.

Jeffares, Alexander N. *W. B. Yeats: Man and Poet.* London: Routledge, 1949.

"John Ford, the Man Behind *The Informer,*" *The New York Times,* January 5, 1936, IX, 5:3.

Kelleher, John V. "Matthew Arnold and the Celtic Revival," in *Perspectives of Criticism,* ed. Harry Levin. Cambridge.: Harvard University Press, 1950.

——. "Irish Literature Today." *Atlantic Monthly*, CLXXV (1945), 70–76.

Kiely, Benedict, "Liam O'Flaherty: A Story of Discontent," *The Month*, NSII (September, 1949), 183–93.

——. *Modern Irish Fiction*. Dublin: Golden Eagle Books, 1950.

Krause, David. *Sean O'Casey: The Man and His Work*. New York: The Macmillan Co., 1960.

Krutch, Joseph Wood. *The Modern Temper*. New York: Harcourt, Brace & Co., 1929.

Kunitz, Stanley J., and Vineta Colby, eds. *Twentieth Century Authors* (First Supplement). New York: H. W. Wilson Co., 1955.

Kunitz, Stanley J., and Howard Haycroft, ed. *Twentieth-Century Authors*. New York: H. W. Wilson Co., 1942.

Latimer, Margery. *"The Mountain Tavern," The New York Herald Tribune*, June 2, 1929, 5.

Law, H. A. *Anglo-Irish Literature*. Dublin: Talbot Press, Ltd., 1926.

Magill, Frank N., ed. *Cyclopedia of World Authors*. New York: Harper and Brothers, 1958.

Mercier, Vivian. "Man Against Nature: The Novels of Liam O'Flaherty," *Wascana Review*, I, ii (1966), 37–46.

Moody, William Vaughn, and Robert Morss Lovett. *The History of English Literature*, 8th ed. New York: Charles Scribner's Sons, 1964.

Murray, Michael H. "Liam O'Flaherty and the Speaking Voice," *Studies in Short Fiction*, 154–62.

O'Casey, Sean. *Inishfallen, Fare Thee Well*. New York: The Macmillan Co., 1960.

——. "The Innocents at Home," *The Irish Statesman*, III (1925), 560.

——. "Life and Literature," *The Irish Statesman* (1923), 467–68.

O'Connor, Frank. *The Lonely Voice*. New York: The World Publishing Co., 1962.

——. *The Mirror in the Roadway: A Study of the Modern Novel*. New York: Alfred A. Knopf, 1956.

——. "Two Friends—Yeats and A.E.," *Yale Review*, XXIX (September 1939), 60–88.

O'Connor, Norreys Jephson. *Changing Ireland: Literary Backgrounds of the Irish Free State*. Cambridge: Harvard University Press, 1924.

O'Faolain, Sean. "Don Quixote O'Flaherty," *London Mercury*, XXXVII (1937), 170–75.

——. *The Irish: A Character Study*. New York: Devin-Adair, 1949.

——. "Literary Provincialism," *Commonweal*, XVII (1932), 214–15.

——. *The Short Story*. New York: Devin-Adair, 1951.

——. *The Vanishing Hero*. Boston: Little, Brown and Co., 1956.

Paul-Dubois, L. "Un Romancier Réaliste en Erin," *Revue des Deux Mondes*, XXI (1934), 884–904.

Pritchett, V. S. *"Skerrett," New Statesman and Nation*, IV (1932), 103.

"Querist." "Is Literature in a Blind Alley?" *The Irish Statesman*, I (1923), 685.

Reynolds, Horace. "Riot in the Abbey," *The American Spectator*, December 1934, 14–15.

Robinson, Lennox. "Back to the Provinces," *The Irish Statesman*, I (1924), 655.

——. "The Madonna of Slieve Dun." *To-Morrow*, August 1924, 7.

Saul, George Brandon. "A Wild Sowing: The Short Stories of Liam O'Flaherty," *A Review of English Literature*, IV (July, 1963), 108–13.

S. L. M. "*The Informer*," *The Irish Statesman*, V (1925), 148.

Stephens, James. "Growth in Fiction," *The Irish Statesman*, II (1924), 301.

——. "The Novelist and the Final Utterance," *The Irish Statesman*, II (1924), 140–41.

——. "The Outlook for Literature with Special Reference to Ireland," *Century*, CIV (1922), 811–18.

Strong, L. A. G. "James Joyce and the New Fiction," *American Mercury*, XXXV (1935), 433–37.

Synge, J. M. *The Aran Islands*. London: Maunsel and Co., Ltd., 1907.

Taylor, Estella Ruth. *The Modern Irish Writers*. Lawrence: University of Kansas Press, 1954.

Tindall, William York, *Forces in Modern British Literature*. New York: Alfred A. Knopf, 1947.

Trilling, Lionel. "The Modern Element in Modern Literature," in *The Partisan Review Anthology*, ed. William Phillips and Philip Rahv. New York: Holt, Rinehart and Winston, 1962.

Troy, William. "The Position of Liam O'Flaherty," *Bookman*, LXIX (March 1929), 7–11.

——. "Two Years," *Bookman*, LXXII (November, 1930), 322–23.

Warren, C. H. "Liam O'Flaherty," *Bookman*, LXXVII (January 1930), 235–36.

Yeats, W. B. "The Censorship and St. Thomas Aquinas," *The Irish Statesman*, XI (1928), 47–48.

——. *Collected Poems*. New York: The Macmillan Co., 1956.

——. "The Need for Audacity of Thought," *Dial*, LXXX (1926), 115–19.

Y.O. "*The Assassin*," *The Irish Statseman*, X (1928), 295.

——. "Heredity in Literature," *The Irish Statesman*, VIII (1927), 304.

——. "*The House of Gold*," *The Irish Statesman*, XIII (1929), 76.

——. "*Mr. Gilhooley*," *The Irish Statesman*, VII (1926), 279–80.

Index